Suzanne King and Elaine Robertson are freelance journalists, specializing in travel. Both have lived and worked abroad: Elaine in Austria, Germany and the Netherlands; Suzanne in France, Greece and South Africa. In addition, they are seasoned backpackers and between them have travelled on five continents, visiting countries as diverse as Iran and India, Morocco and Mongolia, China and Chile.

'What a wonderful resource for travellers. *The Backpacker's Bible* is like a well-travelled friend passing on invaluable advice.'

Independent Travellers' World

D1425498

THE BACKPACKER'S BIBLE

Suzanne King
and
Elaine Robertson

ROBSON BOOKS

First published in Great Britain in 1999 by Robson Books,
The Chrysalis Building, Bramley Road, London W10 6SP
Fourth printing 2004

An imprint of **Chrysalis** Books Group plc

Copyright © 1999 National Magazine Company

British Library Cataloguing in Publication Data
A catalogue record for this title is available from the British Library

ISBN 1 86105 871 3

Printed & bound in Great Britain by Creative Print & Design,Wales

NB: The authors have taken every care to check and double-
check the prices, addresses, telephone numbers, and other
factual information in the book, and all were up to date at the
time of going to press, but please bear in mind that such details
can change.

And while you're out there, if you have any great travel tips,
wonderful anecdotes or general words of wisdom that we
should include in the next edition of the book, we'd love to
hear from you. Write to us at backpackersbible@hotmail.com

CONTENTS

ACKNOWLEDGEMENTS

With thanks to all the friends we've met and travelled with along the way, who've helped to make our trips so much fun – especially Jerome, Julie, Ralf, Peter, Rod, Emmanuel, Piers and Jonathan (South America); Murray, Gil and Mr He (China); Thuy and Thuy (Vietnam); Caroline and Ken (Trans-Siberian); Colleen (Southern Africa); and Amanda (around the world).

A huge thank you to Daunt Books in London who allowed us to spend days browsing through their shelves, checking travel books and spending far too much money.

Thanks, too, to all who entertained us with their travellers' tales, including Vivienne Ayers, Kathleen Corrigan, Philippa Dickinson, James Edwards, Liz Halsall, Lisa Jackson, Robert King, Julie Leybourne, Emma Marlin, Fay McDermott, Andrew Morrison, Jane Ogden, Emma Payne, Matt Salmon, Denise Stergoulis, Amanda Stone, Sharon Wilcock, Fiona Wright and Peter Wright.

INTRODUCTION

All places, no matter where, no matter what, are worth visiting.

Paul Theroux, *The Pillars of Hercules*

If you've bought this book, you must be dreaming about taking a big trip – leaving your normal life behind and jetting off for some sun, fun and adventure. And the good news is that it's so easy to do! You don't have to be rich to travel the world. Just take a look at the classified ads in newspapers and magazines and you'll see dozens of companies offering tempting tickets for amazingly low prices. You don't even have to be particularly adventurous – there are some travellers' routes that are so well-worn you'll sometimes hardly believe you're so far from home.

Every year, hundreds of thousands of young Brits head off on the backpacker trail. Before they return home, they'll have been to more places, met more people and done more exciting things than most people do in a lifetime. What you do is up to you. You could find yourself sleeping under the stars in the Namibian desert or watching the sun set behind the Taj Mahal. Maybe you see yourself swimming with the dolphins in Florida or diving the Great Barrier Reef. Do you fancy doing a four-wheel drive trip from the Cape to Cairo or tackling the Inca Trail in South America? What about sailing through the islands of Halong Bay in Vietnam or feasting on champagne and strawberries on the Trans-Siberian? The possibilities are endless.

Dreaming about your big trip is exciting – but trying to organize it can be daunting, especially if it's the first time. There's so much to plan, so many decisions to make, so much to think about. That's why we've taken some of the legwork out of it for you. From planning your route to packing your bags, from saving money to staying safe, there's nothing we haven't thought of. And you'll find tips and tales from other backpackers in the travellers' tales dotted throughout the book.

It's true there are some things we can't help you with. In Cairns, it will be tough deciding whether to spend the next day diving, whitewater rafting or lazing on the beach. On a Caribbean island you may have real trouble deciding which two palm trees offer the ultimate spot for your hammock. And when you're faced with a mouth-watering menu in Thailand it's almost impossible to decide what to go for. But, hey, you'll cope.

Once you've made up your mind to go, you'll find everything falls into place with amazing ease. The most important thing is to go with the right attitude. You can't expect things to be the same as they are at home – after all, that's part of the reason why you're going away. If you travel in developing countries, don't expect constant hot water, flush toilets or transport that runs on time – but do expect the lights to go out just as you're settling down to read your book. Unpredictability is the name of the game. You may end up sleeping on a bench when your train doesn't turn up, spending a day helping to dig your bus out of the mud or being trapped somewhere for three days because of bad weather.

Believe us, we know. Between us, we've been bitten to bits by every bug going and over-indulged in the local brew everywhere from Bangkok to Buenos Aires. We've been ripped off occasionally and browned off frequently. We've slept in huts, haylofts and hammocks, on beaches, benches and bunks. We've travelled in boats that are barely afloat, planes that are barely aloft and buses that barely stay on the road – not to mention elephants, camels, rafts and the rest. But it's all part of the experience – in time, even the disasters tend to become something you look back on with nostalgia. And we keep going back for more.

Because there's just nothing we can think of that's more exciting than travelling. It's fun, it's confidence-building, it's fulfilling. It gives you a wealth of rewarding memories, an address book full of new friends around the world, and an improved knowledge of geography that will stand you in good stead in pub quizzes. The feeling of achievement and the thrill of making new discoveries about yourself and the world around you are things that will never leave you. So what are you waiting for? Get out there and do it – and have the time of your life!

Suzanne King and Elaine Robertson

CHAPTER 1

WHERE SHOULD YOU GO?

More than 400 million people travel abroad each year. Once you've decided to join them, the first question to ask yourself is, 'Where am I going?' The classic RTW (round-the-world) route of South East Asia, followed by Australia, New Zealand and home via the States? A circle round South America, then island-hopping across the Pacific? Head to Moscow, take the Trans-Siberian to Beijing, then travel round China? The overland route from the Cape to Cairo? And what about Eastern Europe? The Middle East? India? Antarctica?

Unless you're planning to travel for the rest of your life, you obviously won't be able to visit every country in the world. First, grab a good atlas and start dreaming up routes. Talk to any friends who've been travelling, and read books set in different countries or continents to get a feel for the place (see Chapter 15). If you're on a tight budget, bear in mind that it's cheaper to travel in destinations such as South East Asia than in the USA or Australia, and save ludicrously expensive countries like Japan for when you're rich.

If it's your first trip, avoid landing yourself in a 'difficult' country on your first stop. India, for example, can come as a hell of a shock if you go straight from the UK. Although most RTW travellers tend to start off in Asia, why not consider flying the other way round and beginning your trip in the US, where the language, culture and customs are familiar, then move on to the more exotic countries? Another advantage of this is that Asia is a cheaper place to be if you're nearing the end of the trip and funds are running low.

Once you have a rough idea of where you'd like to go, visit travel agents for advice and a sample of routes and fares. Don't rush it – you can easily spend an hour or more talking through all the possibilities. In Chapter 2, you'll find a list of agencies that specialize in independent travel. Most are staffed by people who have travelled extensively themselves, so they can make recommendations based on personal experience or suggest a route you hadn't thought of or didn't know existed. They should be able to give you up-to-date advice on health matters and the cost of living, and since 1 October 1998, they've been legally obliged to tell you your visa requirements when you book. Some have their own vaccination and visa services on site; they may also have a bookshop or reference library.

If you have time, go to two or three different agents, then take everything home and spend a day or two considering your options and comparing prices before making a booking. You don't have to go literally all round the world – some people choose to spend most of their time exploring a particular area, say Asia or Africa, in depth.

Wherever you're thinking of going, get up-to-date advice from the Foreign & Commonwealth Office Travel Advice Unit on 020 7238 4503/4; on BBC2 Ceefax page 470 onwards; or on the Internet at www.fco.gov.uk/. This provides the latest information on the political situation in most foreign countries, as well as advising on threats to personal safety arising from internal strife, natural disasters and epidemics. If the Foreign & Commonwealth Office say don't go, then don't go – if you decide to travel against their advice, your insurance will automatically be invalid.

WHEN'S THE BEST TIME TO GO?

Assuming that you're fairly flexible about your departure date, there are two main things to bear in mind before you book your ticket: (a) your route and (b) how much money you want to spend on your flights. As far as airlines are concerned, there are generally three seasons to most destinations: low, high and mid-season. For flights within the northern hemisphere, for example, low season is November to March, high season is July and August and mid-season is any other time.

However, if you're travelling to the southern hemisphere, the seasons are different. So for destinations such as South Africa, Australia or New Zealand, December is high season – which means chock-full flights and the highest fares. If you desperately want to be there in December, to spend Christmas with relatives, say, you should book well in advance and accept that there will be no cheap deals on your ticket.

The cheapest flights are from Monday to Wednesday and it's always best to avoid peak times such as Easter and Christmas. If you're planning to fly at peak period, you will need to book at least three or four months ahead.

Sometimes you can save money by altering your travel plans by just one day. For example, a BA/Qantas One World Explorer ticket from London to Singapore on 1 July 2000 would have cost £1,080 but on 30 June the same ticket cost just £860.

Local events also play a part in determining air fares and availability. For example, if you want to go to Hong Kong in February, you'll be arriving just in time for Chinese New Year. Not only do air fares go up, but there will be very little accommodation available. And the same will apply to neighbouring countries such as China and Vietnam. So while fares remain roughly the same year-round to a destination such as Bangkok, they could increase (and flights will probably be full) at this time of year, because of Thailand's proximity to these countries.

It can be fun timing your visit to coincide with local festivals – but it can also be inconvenient. As well as higher fares and little or no available accommodation, you may find that shops, banks and restaurants are closed. Or if you're in a Muslim country for Ramadan you might find it hard to get food and drink during the day, when everyone's fasting.

If you're travelling in or via Europe, July and August are good months to avoid. This is school holiday time, meaning jam-packed flights, no cheap deals and hordes of tourists wherever you go.

Does your itinerary take in cold climates as well as hot ones? If so, you'll need to carry heavy clothing, so you might prefer to plan an itinerary that – as far as possible – follows summer round the globe. Find out what the weather will be like when you're at each of your destinations. It's not the be-all-and-end-all of a trip, but if you're planning special activities such as trekking, you should obviously avoid the rainy season. Anyone planning an African safari should aim to be there when there's the greatest chance of animal-spotting (in Kenya and Tanzania, for example, it's July and August). But if you're doing an overland truck trip, you should avoid the rainy season or you'll spend days trying to dig the vehicle out of the mud. And, obviously, if you're planning to head up into any mountains, you should remember that some passes will be impassable in winter.

However, on a RTW trip, it's practically impossible to ensure you arrive everywhere at the best time, so don't worry too much about it. Also, some places are cheaper off-season and you're more likely to get discounts in hotels and restaurants when they're competing for your custom.

If you have second cousins in Vancouver, or your sister's best friend is living in Australia, your trip is the perfect opportunity to look them up. Most people are pleased to get visitors, but drop them a postcard or letter first to ask if it's OK to turn up when you're in their part of the world. After being on the road for a while, it's a great treat to stay in a proper house with a proper bed, and get your clothes washed and ironed. You may miss out on the travellers' grapevine, but having a local person show you round their home town or city adds an extra dimension to the place. Be considerate – don't turn up on someone's doorstep penniless, don't bring extra guests without your host's permission and don't outstay your welcome. Bear in mind that staying with friends and relatives won't necessarily save you money. It's true that you'll be saving on accommodation and food but these things are often really cheap anyway – and you'll probably end up buying bottles of wine and thank-you presents instead.

BOOKING IN ADVANCE VS BUYING AS YOU GO

Should you buy all your tickets in advance, or just book as far as your first destination and play it by ear from then on? There are advantages and disadvantages to both methods: we've listed some of the main ones below. You can also discuss the pros and cons of both options with your travel agent.

BUYING IN ADVANCE

Advantages The big advantage of having a return air ticket is security. You don't have to carry extra money around to pay for flights and, if you start running short of money, at least you know you can get home. It can often (though not always) work out cheaper than buying individual flights as you go along. Pre-booking also means you avoid the hassle of trying to buy a plane ticket without speaking a word of Mandarin/Urdu/ Swahili. Finding the airline office in a strange city, queuing up, explaining what you want, being told to come back the next day or finding it closed can eat into your precious time and send your blood pressure soaring.

Most airlines allow you to change the dates of your flights (though some will charge for this) so you can still be flexible to some extent. Knowing roughly where you're going to be and when means you can leave an itinerary behind so that friends and family can write to you – parents will probably be happier with this kind of arrangement.

Disadvantages The major drawback of booking your ticket in advance is the lack of flexibility and ability to be spontaneous. Before you leave the UK, you might think that a month in Thailand or Malaysia will be more than enough. But what if you fall in love with the country and want to stay for longer? What if your next scheduled stop is Harare but you make friends with a great crowd of travellers who are heading to Cape Town and ask you to go with them? If you fly with an airline that charges you for date changes, it could become expensive if you alter your plans a lot.

BUYING TICKETS AS YOU GO

Advantages This is the most flexible option, allowing you to just go with the flow. If you arrive in a city you don't like, you can leave the next day. If you're captivated by Saigon, you can stay an extra week. If you meet someone you really like and want to continue travelling with them a bit longer you can adapt your travel plans to fit. It turns your trip into more of an adventure. However, some countries don't like letting you in unless you have proof (in the form of a ticket) that you'll be leaving again. This can be especially so if you're flying in. Credit cards help (as evidence of funds), as does being as smartly dressed as possible when you arrive at passport control.

Disadvantages It may be a more expensive way to travel and you will need to carry around more money (and avoid the temptation to spend it on other things) or a credit card to buy tickets as you go along. You might not always be able to get tickets when you want them and might have to hang around waiting for days or find alternative forms of transport. If your first-choice airlines are fully booked, you may have to fly on more obscure (and less safe) domestic carriers. People at home may worry because they don't know where you are at any given time, and it's harder for them to contact you if they have to.

TRAVEL EVENTS

An ever-increasing interest in travelling has led to the introduction of travel fairs and exhibitions. These are terrific places to get more ideas of where to go. You can hear experienced travellers talk about their trips, pick up tons of information on all aspects of travelling, enter competitions to win RTW tickets and meet like-minded people. Best of the bunch for backpackers is Independent Travellers' World, held in London and two other UK cities between January and March each year. Further details available on 020 7373 7788 or visit www.tntmag.co.uk. Look out, also, for: Destinations (held at Olympia, London in February); The Holiday Show (G-Mex Centre, Manchester in January); and Female Eye, a women and travel seminar (Commonwealth Institute, London in June).

TRAVEL TALKS

Travellers' clubs (see Chapter 3) organize regular evenings where members can hear about other people's adventures. Look out, too, for the following chances to meet and hear from other travellers:

- **Cotswold** hold regular lectures at their shops around the country; call 01285 643434 for details of your nearest branch or visit www.cotswold-outdoor.co.uk. Most are free; some carry a small charge.

- Many overland travel companies (e.g. **Encounter Overland, Exodus, Guerba**) give video presentations of their destinations. Contact them (addresses in Chapter 3) and ask to be put on their mailing list.

- Bookshops such as **Waterstone's, Dillons** and **Stanfords** host evenings where writers, including travel writers, read extracts from their books and answer questions afterwards. Ring your local branch for details.

- **The Royal Geographical Society** invites speakers to lecture on various aspects of travelling. Ring 020 7591 3000 for details or visit www.rgs.org. For the **Royal Scottish Geographical Society** call 0141 552 3330 or visit www.geo.ed.ac.uk/~rsgs/

'I did a ten-month trip that took in South East Asia, Australia, Canada and the States. I don't know how I managed it but, with uncanny ability, I seemed to end up having rain almost everywhere, even when it wasn't the rainy season. Some of my most vivid memories are weather-related – wading knee-deep through the flooded streets of Kuta in Bali; getting drenched in the Daintree rainforest in Queensland; sitting out a typhoon in Hue in Vietnam; paddling around the pavements of Beijing; getting so wet in Hong Kong that the dye from my T-shirt ran into my sweatshirt and ruined it (that's those cheap traveller's clothes for you); and causing great hilarity in Indonesia when I slipped on a muddy path Laurel and Hardy style and ended up covered in mud from head to toe. The strange thing is, I loved every minute of it and laughed all the way. The weather was always warm, so it's not like miserable British rain – and somehow it seems more of an experience than having good weather all the way.'

'I took eight months off a couple of years ago and intended to go to New Zealand via Hong Kong, China, Vietnam, Thailand, Malaysia, Indonesia and Australia. I didn't make it to New Zealand in the end – mainly because we hadn't thought through what the weather would be like in each country. We went to China in winter, which was fine as we'd taken warm clothing. After leaving China, though, we sent it all back home and then had to buy more when we landed in Australia, where it was also winter. By the time we were ready to go to New Zealand it was July, which would have been their winter, too, so we decided to head for home. I have to admit, I was tired after eight months' travelling, but that trip was the best thing I've ever done in my life. I had a brilliant time and adored the sense of freedom it gave me. I'd love to do it again.'

'The memories you will bring back are worth a thousand times the price of your ticket. During my year-long travels, I visited an orang-utan rehabilitation centre in a rainforest in Indonesia; ate fish straight from the sea on the beach in Sri Lanka on Christmas Day (and saw a seven-foot snake in the jungle); sang Irish songs on a beach in Thailand; was spellbound by the Taj Mahal and saddened by the bridge over the River Kwai; got caught in a monsoon; was invited to dinner at the home of a Vietnamese cyclo driver; shopped in a Bangkok market; was sung to by Vietnamese schoolchildren; travelled on ancient buses, boats and trains as well as on elephants and camels; swam, snorkelled, climbed and cycled – and I still have six months to go! I'll remember my trip for the rest of my life and envy anyone who still has theirs ahead of them...'

'I've spent some time travelling in Australia, South East Asia and South America, and I was struck by the different types of travellers I met there. In Australia, for example, the majority of travellers were young, free and single 18- to 25-year-olds, away from home for the first time. In South America, the age group was older; there were more of the seasoned, bearded travellers and more couples. The age span in India seemed much wider, encompassing the year-off-before-university traveller, the five-temples-before-breakfast traveller and the elderly hippy who has never quite got it together enough to leave. While these are huge generalizations, I think they can be important factors to bear in mind: I recently had a friend cut short her year's travel to Australia and South East Asia because the people and the travel culture there were so young she felt like a grandmother.'

'My boyfriend and I went overland from London to India two years ago, travelling by train and bus (I don't like flying). We spent six weeks going through Europe to Turkey, then across Turkey, through Iran to Pakistan and spent a while travelling around India. I had to buy a chador at the Turkey/Iran border and wear it all the time I was there. Travelling in Iran wasn't as difficult as I thought it would be. We found places to stay by following our Lonely Planet guide and we also got recommendations from the locals, who were very friendly. After travelling around India, we went round South East Asia and Vietnam, which I loved.

We saved up for two years until we each had £4,000. I gave up my job in sales, but had no problem finding another job when we returned. I don't regret it at all. We had a fantastic time and I'd do it again tomorrow if I could.'

TEN TRAVELLERS' HANG-OUTS

Dali, China	Koh Pha Ngan, Thailand
Anjuna and Arambol, Goa	Salvador, Brazil
Hoi An, Vietnam	Byron Bay, Australia
Cuzco, Peru	Lamu, Kenya
Kathmandu, Nepal	Yogyakarta, Indonesia

CHAPTER 2

GETTING THERE AND GETTING AROUND

HOW DO I GET THERE?

Air fares are currently at an all-time low – and there are particularly good bargains on RTW tickets. No one airline can fly you right around the globe but two or three airlines (or more, depending on your itinerary) band together to offer RTW tickets that combine their route networks. To get the cheapest deal, you usually have to travel in one direction only (west to east or vice versa). You'll find dozens of sample itineraries advertised in the newspapers – we give some examples later in this chapter – but basically just about any combination of routes and stopovers is possible. The more stopovers you have, though, the more expensive the ticket will be.

The price of your ticket will also be affected by your departure date and the direction you're flying – some months it's cheaper to go east to west, other months you get a better deal flying west to east (see When's the Best Time to Go, in Chapter 1).

Remember to build in overland (or surface) sections. Few travellers would want a ticket that included flights from Bangkok to Singapore, for example, because it makes more sense and is more fun to do the trip overland. Better to book a flight into Bangkok and out of Singapore. Obviously, the cost of surface travel is not included in your air ticket, so you need to budget for train/bus fares accordingly.

RTW tickets are usually valid for one year and most allow you to change your flight dates as you go along if you decide you want to spend more (or less) time in a particular country once you get there. Check with the travel agent or airline whether or not there will be a fee charged for any changes made.

Always look out for any restrictions – what appears to be the best deal may turn out to cost more if, for example, you have to pay each time you change a flight date. Does your ticket entitle you to free or discounted domestic flights within certain countries? Will you be charged extra for making more than a certain number of stopovers? How long is your ticket valid for? Does it entitle you to discount rates on accommodation and activities once you're away? Is the price particularly cheap because the airline has a reputation for bad service, poor safety standards, lack of reliability or roundabout routings?

Don't always be guided purely by cost. Remember that domestic airlines in some countries, particularly China, Vietnam and parts of Russia, have an appalling safety record. For personal security and peace of mind, it's probably worth shelling out a bit more for a better airline.

Some travel agents specialize in RTW itineraries (see below) and can advise you on the best route and the cheapest fares. There are standard RTW tickets (London–Delhi–Sydney–Los Angeles–London, for example) or you can tailor-make your own. Any itinerary that incorporates African or South American destinations will bump up the cost. If you want a flight with no stops, you have to specify a 'non-stop' flight, rather than a 'direct' flight. Direct simply means you won't have to change planes en route, but there could be any number of stops.

One of the latest developments in the RTW field is the new fares introduced by some airlines, where the price you pay is based on the mileage you cover, rather than which route you choose. For example, Air New Zealand's Great Escapade fare (with Singapore Airlines, Ansett and South African Airways) costs £933, for up to 29,000 miles travel. A Global Explorer fare from Qantas/BA starts at £949 (rising to £1,240, depending on your departure date) and gives you 29,000 miles and up to six free stopovers; unlimited extra stopovers can be added for £50 each.

Once you've booked your ticket and provisional flight dates, phone the airline to double-check that they have a record of your booking.

When you receive your ticket, make sure that the 'status' box has OK in it – if it says anything else, it means you may not necessarily have a confirmed seat on the flight. Check all the other details are correct, too – destinations, dates, times – and that there's a coupon for each separate flight. Photocopy the ticket twice: leave a copy at home with a friend, and take a copy with you in case the original gets lost. (Keep the copy separate from the original.)

Always reconfirm your onward journey 72 hours (three days) in advance. In some countries, failure to do so will mean your name is taken off the computer and your seat given to someone else. If you don't speak the language, ask hostel staff or a local friend to do it for you.

WHERE'S THE BEST PLACE TO BUY MY TICKET?

There are dozens of travel agents offering RTW tickets – look for them in the travel section of the Sunday newspapers or in the back of magazines such as *Time Out*. Remember that the cheapest travel agent isn't necessarily the best. Good service and experienced consultants who know about where they're sending you are just as important. Always check that the agent is bonded with ABTA (Association of British Travel Agents – 020 7637 2444) or ATOL (Air Travel Organizer's Licence – 020 7379 7311). There should be a sticker on the window or door.

Here are some of the more well-established firms. Prices were correct at the time of going to press.

Austravel
50 Conduit Street, London W1R 9FB
020 7734 7755
and 152 Brompton Rd, London SW3 1HX
020 7838 1011
Also in Birmingham (0121 200 1116), Bournemouth (01202 311488), Bristol (0117 927 7425), Edinburgh (0131 226 1000), Leeds (0113 244 8880) and Manchester (0161 832 2445).
www.austravel.net
Sample route: Manchester – Hong Kong – Kuala Lumpur – Bangkok – Singapore – Bali – Sydney – Auckland – Fiji – Los Angeles – London. From £933.

Bridge the World Travel Centre
47 Chalk Farm Road, London NW1 8AN
020 7911 0900 (worldwide); 020 7916 0990 (transatlantic)
www.bridgetheworld.net
E-mail: sales@bridge-the-world.co.uk
Sample route: London – Dubai – Calcutta – Singapore surface Bangkok – Brunei – Darwin – Brisbane – Abu Dhabi – London. From £682.

usit CAMPUS
52 Grosvenor Gardens, London SW1W 0AG
0870 240 1010 (National Call Centre)

Has 49 branches around the country, including Edinburgh (0131 668 3303), Bristol (0117 929 2494) and Manchester (0161 273 1721).
www.usitcampus.co.uk
Specializes in travel for students and young people.
Sample route: London – New York – Los Angeles – Auckland – Melbourne surface Darwin – Bali – Bangkok – London. From £730.

Flightbookers
177–178 Tottenham Court Road, London W1P 0LX
020 7757 2444 (worldwide); 020 7757 2000 (Americas and Europe); 020 7757 2468 (Australia and New Zealand)
www.flightbookers.co.uk
E-mail: sales@flightbookers.co.uk
Sample route: London – Beijing surface Shanghai – Sydney – Christchurch surface Auckland – Tahiti – Santiago – Buenos Aires surface Rio de Janeiro – London. From £855.

Journey Latin America
12+13 Heathfield Terrace, Chiswick, London W4 4JE
020 8747 3108
Also at Suites 28-30, Barton Arcade (2nd floor), 58–63 Deansgate, Manchester M3 2BH.
0161 832 1441
www.journeylatinamerica.co.uk
As the name suggests, specializes in flights and tours to and around Central and South America.
Sample route: Manchester – Buenos Aires – La Paz – Santiago – Manchester. From £854.

Quest Worldwide
4–10 Richmond Road, Kingston upon Thames, Surrey KT2 5HL
0870 758 5100 (worldwide); 0870 758 5300 (USA and Canada)
www.questtravel.co.uk
Sample route: London – Bali – Australia/New Zealand – Bangkok – London. From £457.

STA Travel
Priory House, 6 Wrights Lane, London W8 6TA
020 7361 6262 (worldwide); 020 7361 6148 (Europe)
Has about 200 offices across Europe, Asia, America and Australasia. In the UK, these include: Bristol (0117 929 4399), Cambridge (01223 366966), Manchester (0161 834 0668), and Oxford (01865 792800).
www.statravel.co.uk

Specialists in young independent travel. STA Travel run a unique International Help Desk (you get the number when you buy your ticket). Wherever you are in the world, you can call them (reversing the charges if necessary) to ask for advice on any problems that arise, from lost tickets to lost companions.

Sample route: London – Bangkok surface Bali – Cairns surface Sydney – Cook Islands – London. From £699.

Trailfinders

42–50 Earls Court Road, London W8 6FT
020 7938 3366 (long haul)
194 Kensington High Street, London W8 7RG
020 7938 3939 (long haul)
215 Kensington High Street, London W8 6BD
020 7937 5400 (transatlantic and European)
Also has branches in Birmingham (0121 236 1234), Bristol (0117 929 9000), Glasgow (0141 353 2224), Manchester (0161 839 6969), Dublin (677 7888) and Newcastle (0191 261 2345).
www.trailfinder.com
Trailfinders do gift vouchers (valid indefinitely), which make a nice gift for travelling friends.

Sample route: London – Bangkok – Taipei – Seattle – New York – London. From £819.

Travelbag

373–375 Strand, London WC2R 0JF
020 7497 0515 (Australia and New Zealand); 020 7287 5558 (Far East and Africa); 020 7240 3669 (North America and Canada)
Also at 52 Regent Street, London W1R 6DX
020 7287 5556 (Australia), 020 7287 5558 (Far East); 020 7287 5559 (North America and Canada); 020 7287 5535 (Africa)
And at 3–5 High Street, Alton, Hampshire GU34 1TL
01420 88380 (North America and Canada); 01420 88140 (Africa); 01420 80828 (Far East); 01420 88724 (Australia)
www.travelbag.co.uk
Sample route: London – Hong Kong – Singapore – Perth – Sydney – Auckland – Fiji – London. From £879.

The Travel Bug

125a Gloucester Road, London SW7 4SF
020 7835 2000
Also at 597 Cheetham Hill Road, Manchester M8 5EJ
0161 721 4000
0870 744 0010 (Transatlantic and Europe); 0870 744 0020 (long haul)

Brochure line: 020 7835 2111
www.flynow.com
Sample route: Glasgow – Cape Town surface Johannesburg – Sydney – Auckland – Perth – Singapore – London. From £985.

Travel Mood
214 Edgware Road, London W2 1DS
020 7258 0280
Also at 61 Reform Street, Dundee DD1 1SP
01382 322713
And at 1 Brunswick Court, Bridge Street, Leeds LS2 7QU
0113 209 3900
Brochure hotline: 020 7402 4108
Specialize in Australia and New Zealand.
Sample route: London – Hong Kong – Sydney – New Zealand – Fiji – Honolulu – Los Angeles – London. From £757.

GETTING AROUND WHEN YOU'RE THERE

You'll find there are all sorts of travel passes you can buy, which can be great value, particularly if you have large distances to cover in a short space of time. Some must be bought before you leave; some you can buy on the spot. These are just a few, but keep your eyes out for details of new ones in magazines.

Inter-Rail

Details: Rail Europe, 0990 848 848
Brochure hotline: 0990 024 000
Inter-Rail passes allow unlimited travel on the railways of up to 28 European countries and one African (Morocco). The countries are divided into zones and the price of your pass depends on how many zones you want to travel in. If you're under 26, prices are £159 for one zone (valid 22 days), £209 for two zones (valid one month), £229 for three zones (valid one month), or £259 for all zones (valid one month). For the over-26, the prices are £229, £279, £309, and £349 respectively.

Oz Experience and Kiwi Experience

Details: Bridge the World Travel Centre, 020 7734 7447
www.kiwiexperience.com; www.ozexperience.com
Travel passes lasting up to 12 months and allowing you unlimited travel on the company's coach networks round Australia and New Zealand, getting on and off at any point. Prices depend on how many zones your pass covers: for example, a pass covering from Sydney to Cairns is Aus$295. In

New Zealand, NZ$640 allows you to travel most of the way round both islands. Passes are cheaper if bought before you leave the UK.

The Best of New Zealand Pass

A variety of passes on offer. Buy from your travel agent before you go or on arrival. Up to four weeks travel over six months by coach, train and ferry costs £231, for example.

Greyhound International

Reservations: 01342 317317
www.greyhound.com (USA and Canada)
www.greyhound.com.au (Australia)
Greyhound Ameripasses give unlimited travel within various time limits within America or Canada. For America, sample costs are £229 for 30 days; £315 for 60 days. For Canada, it's £195 for 30 days; £259 for 60 days. There are reductions for holders of YHA, ISIC and Youth Cards.

Greyhound Pioneer offer similar deals in Australia (where the coach experience is much cleaner, more efficient and more enjoyable). There are various Aussie Explorer Passes offering unlimited stops along a fixed itinerary, lasting 2-12 months. The 'Outback and Reef' pass, for example, is valid for 90 days and covers travel from Sydney, up the coast to Cairns and on to Darwin, for Aus$565. Alternatively, there are Aussie Kilometre Passes, where the price you pay depends on how far you go, starting from Aus$215 for 2000kms (roughly the distance from Brisbane to Melbourne).

Holders of YHA, VIP, Euro 26, ISIC and Nomad cards get a 15% discount on passes bought outside Australia and a 10% discount on passes bought within Australia.

'I didn't buy an RTW ticket because I wasn't sure how long I'd want to stay in each place and that turned out to be the right decision for me. I bought a ticket to Bombay and stayed in India for two months, then went to Nepal. I also spent time in Thailand, Malaysia and Indonesia before heading for Australia.

'Friends from home had been writing to tell me that nothing much was happening workwise, so I decided to extend my trip. I had started off with about £4,000, which lasted me until I got to Australia, where I decided to look for work to keep me going. I got a job in a bar in Sydney and loved it. It's still quite easy to find employment in Australia as long as you're willing to work. They pay a decent minimum wage, too, so you can live quite well. As well as the bar work, I waitressed in a Tunisian restaurant and cooked breakfast in a backpackers' hostel.

'Australia was wonderful – it's very easy to get about and the country is really geared up for backpackers. I travelled around on my own a lot and met all sorts of people. Everyone adopts you if you're a solo traveller. Every time I sat down to read a book, someone would invite me for a beer. I gained a lot from my travels – I've got more confidence and feel I can tackle anything. Some of my colleagues say they would like to do it, but they're worried about their careers but taking time out didn't affect my career at all – in fact, one employer said, "At least you've got it out of your system now" and gave me a job!'

'Always make absolutely certain that the dates of your flights are flexible because you never know what might happen while you're away. After four months travelling in South America, we ended up in Ushuaia in Tierra del Fuego, which is where ships leave from to go to Antarctica. We got there just as one of the ships, leaving in a couple of days' time, had a mass cancellation, so they were selling tickets for the week-long trip at a fraction of the normal cost – less than half price. It was a once in a lifetime chance. So even though I had no money left and a flight home booked for a few days later, I reserved my place on the ship, prepared to flex my credit card and went off to the travel agent to rearrange my flight to the UK – only to be told that I couldn't. I knew the ticket wasn't fixed because I'd checked when I bought it. But the guy was unmovable. I phoned the airline's head office in Buenos Aires and tried everything – ranting, pleading, speaking to a dozen different people. But no joy. So I didn't get to go to the South Pole – and it's annoyed me ever since. When I came home, I rang the travel agent to complain and they confirmed that the ticket *was* changeable – but by then it was too late. Next time, I'll make sure I've got it all in writing, on official paper, stamped and sealed!'

'When I went travelling, an RTW ticket seemed the best value. I liked it because you could go overland – you didn't have to fly the whole way – and it gave flexibility of routes – we could go out through Asia and back through Canada and America. We flew into Thailand and went overland through Thailand, Malaysia, Singapore and Indonesia, then took a flight from Bali to Australia. With hindsight, I don't think a RTW ticket is necessarily cheaper. But our ticket was brilliant – we didn't have to pay cancellation charges and it was really easy to change it, which we did several times. Because we wanted to travel in Australia, we flew with an airline that had good deals on internal flights there (Qantas). In fact, we should probably have booked more internal flights – we did most of it by coach but we didn't really need to.

'We intended to work in Australia but didn't in the end – we were having too much fun! I didn't want the trip to end. We went away thinking about six months, and extended it to nine months – but it still wasn't enough. When you're planning it, six months seems a long time, but what impressed me was that once you start a trip like that it's so easy. A year is nothing.'

TEN TRAVELLERS' MUST-DOS

Swimming with dolphins Whale watching
Whitewater rafting   Elephant trekking
Bungee jumping   Boogie boarding
Scuba diving   Camel safari
Dune boarding   Alligator spotting

CHAPTER 3

WHO DO YOU GO WITH?

Now that you know where and when you're going, who will you share your adventure with? There are several options. If you're lucky, you'll have a like-minded friend and you can set off with someone you know well. If you don't know anyone who has the time, money or inclination to travel, there are organizations (see page 23) that will match you up with a travelling companion who's departing at the same time and has roughly the same itinerary. You could join an organized trip, or, if you don't want to travel with strangers, you can be bold and strike out on your own. There's something to be said for all these options.

GOING WITH A FRIEND

Travelling on a budget with a friend means, inevitably, that you have little privacy once you're on the road. It's a 24-hour-a-day commitment; during which time you'll find yourself eating with, sleeping with, travelling on interminable train journeys with, getting ill with, getting ripped off with and getting lost with the same person for months.

You'll have to get used to them being grumpy in the morning; they'll have to get used to you leaping out of bed at 5 a.m. and singing in the shower. You need to know that you can snap their head off when you've missed the last train out of Istanbul or had your bag slashed in Quito and they'll forgive you. And, no matter how good friends you are, there will be times when you each need a bit of space. So if you want to go exploring caves while your friend would rather laze on the beach, just get on with it.

The best part about travelling with someone else is that you'll share some truly unforgettable moments: having a picnic with cold champagne in a Moscow park, watching the sun set behind

Mount Kilimanjaro, strolling through the ruins of Machu Picchu, being adopted by scores of Vietnamese children, playing charades on the Trans-Siberian as it rattles through the darkness of Siberia...And while your friends at home will love hearing your stories and looking at your photos, only the person you were with will understand what it was really like.

A friend will really come into their own if you don't feel well. Who else will bring you a comforting drink or fetch you some food or cheer you up if you feel homesick?

That said, think everything through carefully before you commit yourself to travelling with a friend. Travelling with the right person can be great fun; travelling with the wrong one can be hell. Ask yourself the following questions:

- Do you have similar interests? (You don't have to like the same things all the time, but if one of you wants to go clubbing till 3 a.m. every night and the other wants to get up at 6 a.m. for an all-day hike, you won't get very far.)

- What's their budget? (It's important to have roughly the same amount of money to spend, otherwise you're bound to run into money arguments.)

- Do you have the same amount of time to spend travelling? (If you're prepared to take up to a year, while your friend wants to be back home in six months, you may end up being rushed along faster than you'd like.)

- Are you as tidy (or as messy) as each other? (You'll be sharing rooms/tents/huts, and wildly differing standards of tidiness and cleanliness can cause trouble.)

- Is your friend normally cheerful and optimistic? (There are times on the road when you'll need to buoy each other's spirits up – if you're travelling with someone who's moody or easily depressed, it can ruin the trip for you, too.)

- How flexible are you? (If you like to go wherever the wind blows you, it's no good travelling with a friend who needs the security of a fixed route.)

GOING SOLO

'The man who goes alone can start today; but he who travels with another must wait till that other is ready,' said American writer Henry David Thoreau. If you don't have a friend who can go with you, don't be put off starting out on your own. Travelling alone is less intimidating than it sounds. Budget travellers have a well-worn circuit – favourite bars and restaurants, hotels they use, places they visit – and you'll always meet a crowd you can travel with for part of the time. On a trip round China, we met the same brother and sister in at least eight different cities. They were always a day or two ahead of us and by the time we got to Xian or Shanghai or Beijing, they'd already found the best way to the Bamboo Temple, the cheapest noodle house, the most picturesque (and cheapest) boat trip.

There are advantages and disadvantages to travelling alone. Most people worry about being lonely, but that's unlikely. Single travellers are quickly befriended in hostels and restaurants. All you have to do is join a table of friendly-looking fellow travellers and you could end up hanging out with them for a couple of days or even weeks. Your plans can be more spontaneous and flexible when there's no one else to consider, and you'll probably meet more people. When close friends travel together, they often present a united front that stops other people from approaching them – and stops them making the effort to talk to others.

If you're worried about being lonely, try taking a short trip nearer home first to see how you get on. It also helps to stick to well-trodden backpacker routes (overland through Asia to Australia, for example), where you'll meet lots of other travellers.

You'll gain a tremendous sense of achievement from exploring far-flung places alone. Each country conquered will increase your self-confidence, self-esteem and independence. You knew you could do it!

The drawbacks of travelling alone are that there's no one else to keep an eye on your belongings if you're nipping off to the toilet or to buy a bottle of water. It can be more expensive if you don't have anyone to share the cost of a room with. Sharing a dormitory is cheaper (and a good place to meet people) but it's less secure and there's only you to watch your possessions. And there's nothing worse than falling ill when you're on your own with no one to bring you an aspirin or a drink.

If you're planning to travel alone, but feel nervous about it, you could join an organized overland trip (see p26). At the end of the tour, you'll probably have built up enough confidence to strike out on your own if you want to travel further. There may even be fellow passengers who are going your way whom you can link up with. This is a particularly good idea if you want to travel in countries that might be politically unstable or considered 'difficult' to travel in.

Solo women travellers obviously face different problems from men – but there are masses of them out there and we've yet to meet a solo woman traveller who didn't have a wonderful time. You may be concerned about safety but a few simple precautions will reduce the dangers (see Chapter 10).

FINDING A TRAVEL COMPANION

If travelling alone still doesn't appeal, you could consider joining one of the travellers' societies that aim to match you up with possible companions. It's obviously more of a gamble going with a stranger than it is with someone you know, so you should devote even more time and thought to making sure you and your prospective companion are compatible. Meet up several times and discuss every aspect of your trip to make sure you agree on the route, how long you want to spend in each place, how much spending money you're taking and any other points that need clarifying.

Travel Companions
2 Coxhill Cottages, Boldre, Lymington, Hants SO41 8PS
01590 683005
E-mail: coxhill@btinternet.com
Membership fee: £63. Caters mainly for short-haul trips for travellers in their thirties and older.

Travel Mate
52 York Place, Bournemouth, Dorset BH7 6JN
01202 431520
One year's membership: £35. Once you find a travel companion, you can suspend your membership until you're ready to use it again. Send details of your intended trip and they'll provide a list of people whose travel plans match yours.

Women Welcome Women
88 Easton Street, High Wycombe, Buckinghamshire HP11 1LT
01494 4654 413
Aims to foster international friendship by putting women in touch with women in different countries who will provide accommodation. There are almost 3,000 members in more than 60 countries. Suggested minimum donation of £20, which covers the cost of the membership list and three newsletters.

TRAVEL CLUBS

There is also an increasing number of travellers' clubs you could join. While these don't aim to fix you up with a travelling companion, they're good places to meet like-minded people, who might well be interested in a bit of globetrotting with you. Some charge a modest membership fee.

The Amazonians. Founded by travel writers Dea Birkett and Sara Wheeler, this is a club for professional women travel writers. They meet on the last Friday of each month in a central London pub to network and exchange travel ideas and information. For further information, contact Dea Birkett on 020 7608 3953.

Birmingham & Midlands Travellers Club. Meets regularly for slide shows, talks and social events. Contact Mike on 0121 356 5086 or Louise on 0121 449 5909.

Bristol Travellers Club. Meets on the second Tuesday of the month (7.30 p.m.) at the YHA International Centre, 64 Prince Street, Bristol BS1 4HU. Run by the Marco Polo Travel Advisory Service (an independent travel agent), which also organizes seminars for women travellers. Ring 0117 929 4123 for further information.

Globetrotters Club (The Friends Meeting House, 52 St Martins Lane, London WC2; no telephone number; www.globetrotters.co.uk). Holds monthly meetings with slide talks in central London, provides a travel query service and publishes a bi-monthly travel magazine, *Globe*.

Guildford Travel Club. Meets twice a month from October to April for talks and slide shows. For information, call 01252 702285.

Leicester World Travellers. Holds regular informal meetings for Midlands-based travellers. Call Shirley Thomas on 0116 270 2308.

Nottingham World Travellers Club. Meets at 7.55 p.m. on most Fridays at the YMCA, Shakespeare Street, Nottingham.

Royal Geographical Society, 1 Kensington Gore, London SW7 2AR (020 7591 3000). The RGS has a splendid map room (the world's largest private collection, with 900,000 maps) that members of the public can use (open Monday–Friday, 11 a.m.– 5 p.m.). Also houses a unique collection of expedition reports.

Royal Scottish Geographical Society, 40 George Street, Glasgow G1 1QE. Holds regular illustrated talks from September to March at venues around Scotland. Members can use their library, housed in Strathclyde University. For information on becoming a member, ring 0141 552 3330.

STEP (Scottish Travellers Exploring the Planet). Holds monthly meetings and invites guest speakers to talk about their travels. Further information from Anna, 0141 423 9796, or Marisa, 0131 229 7141.

Trippers, Trips Worldwide, 9 Byron Place, Triangle, Clifton, Bristol BS8 1JT (0117 987 2626). Meets once a month and organizes special events every two or three months, such as a Latin America Fair, to give you a flavour of different destinations.

Wexas Travel Club, 45–9 Brompton Road, London SW3 1DE (020 7589 3315; www.wexas.com). E-mail: mship@wexas.com. A travel association with over 35,000 members. Full members get discounts on air fares, insurance and car rental among other things, a free subscription to *Traveller* magazine and a free copy of their *Traveller's Handbook*. Membership is currently £43.98; you can join on a one-month 'free trial offer' basis.

You can also advertise for a travelling companion in the Connections page in *Wanderlust* magazine (see Chapter 15); and the Members' Classified column in the Wexas magazine, *Traveller*. *Overseas Jobs Express* (see p57 for details) has a column where travellers can contact other travellers. The Internet, too, is a possible place to meet fellow enthusiasts.

En route, you'll come across noticeboards in backpackers' hostels, cafés and bars with details of trips you can join, travellers looking for people to share car rides, etc. Nairobi's famous Thorn Tree Café is a classic example. It has been a backpackers' meeting place for many years, and around the massive thorn tree it was named after are pinned lots of travel tips, details of items for sale, safari offers and so on.

TAKING AN ORGANIZED TOUR

If you decide you will travel on your own, but still feel apprehensive about it, why not join an organized tour with an overland adventure tour group such as those listed below? Most of these companies attract travellers in their twenties and thirties and tour for anything up to six months in small groups (usually between 12 and 20 people). Many travellers go with a partner or friend, but around half are people travelling on their own. It's a good way to travel in 'difficult' destinations such as some African countries, or, for single women, those countries where it can be hard work for females travelling alone. Collect all the different brochures and check them out carefully to see which company sounds best for you. Compare routes, activities and prices – but bear in mind that what will make or break the trip is not so much the places you'll go to as the people you go with. Look at the type of clients the company attracts, what ages they are and how many passengers are on each trip. Most companies give talks and slide shows (where you can also meet some of the staff and get a look at potential fellow passengers) or have videos you can borrow; they usually provide project dossiers containing detailed information on individual trips that you can check out.

There are two main pricing policies: all inclusive or basic plus kitty. All inclusive means you don't have to take much extra cash with you; you know you can join in the activities and events without wondering whether or not you can afford to shell out. Also, everyone's in the same boat, so you'll all do things together, which can help the group bonding, as you're all on an equal footing. Basic plus kitty means you can pick and choose which activities you want to pay for – but can cause disagreements over money.

Adventure Travel Centre
131–135 Earls Court Road, London SW5 9RH
020 7370 4555
www.topdecktravel.co.uk

Discover the World
29 Nork Way, Banstead, Surrey SM7 1PB
01737 218800
www.arctic-discover.co.uk

Dragoman
98 Camp Green, Debenham, Stowmarket, Suffolk IP14 6LA
01728 861133
www.dragoman.co.uk

Encounter Overland
267 Old Brompton Road, London SW5 9JA
020 7370 6845
www.encounter-overland.com

Exodus
9 Weir Road, London SW12 0LT
020 8673 0859
www.exodus.co.uk

Guerba
Wessex House, 40 Station Road, Westbury, Wiltshire BA13 3JN
01373 826611/858956
www.guerba.co.uk

The Imaginative Traveller
14 Barley Mow Passage, Chiswick, London W4 4PH
020 8742 3049/8612
www.imaginative-traveller.com

Kumuka
40 Earls Court Road, London W8 6EJ
020 7937 8855
www.kumuka.co.uk

Top Deck
131–135 Earls Court Road, London SW5 9RH
020 7244 8641
www.topdecktravel.co.uk

Truck Africa
37 Ranelagh Gardens Mansions, Fulham, London SW6 3UQ
020 7731 6142
www.truckafrica.com

'I went to South America on my own because none of my friends wanted to go – they all had jobs they wanted to keep. I preferred going on my own anyway – that way I could plan my own itinerary and go where I wanted when I wanted. I saw lots of people arguing in the middle of their trip about where to go because they hadn't thought it out beforehand. I travelled round by coach, bus and minibus (or plane when the roads were washed out). They're quite good, especially between cities, but buses in small towns are small and cramped. The roads were safe – apart from a horrible mountain road to La Paz which had an incredibly steep drop and little crosses by the side of the road where cars have gone over the edge.

'There were lots of other travellers around and I joined up with a New Zealander and a German guy and did a bit of travelling with them. I felt lonely occasionally, but I'd listen to my Walkman and drink a few beers and drive those blues away! Going to a bar on your own is a good way to meet people – most of the locals were friendly and would come and chat, so it helps if you speak Spanish or Portuguese. I knew some basics but found it frustrating because I didn't speak enough; if I was going back, I'd make an effort to learn more.

'One tip for anyone going to South America: if you're staying somewhere that's at a high altitude, always leave yourself plenty of time to get wherever you're going. In La Paz, it was a 15-minute walk to the bus station but I only left myself five minutes. I had to run uphill with my rucksack, and when I reached the bus station I passed out. While I was unconscious, someone loaded my rucksack on and my ticket was stamped, so when I came round I was all ready to board – quite efficient really. I just stood up, dusted myself down and got on the coach.'

'I originally left with a girlfriend, but in Thailand we split up for a while and agreed to meet up again later on. Then she broke a bone in her foot in Australia and went to stay with some relatives until it healed, which meant I did a fair bit of travelling around on my own. That did wonders for my confidence – I feel I could go anywhere on my own now.'

'I can't deny that I was apprehensive about travelling as a woman on my own. It was all unknown territory – I'd only ever travelled in Europe before. But I encountered no real problems. You do hear horror stories, but I think staying safe is just a case of being reasonably sensible. We met some women who had had hassle, but it was generally because they weren't dressed properly or weren't sensitive to the ways and culture of the country they were in. I didn't ever feel under threat in any way until I got to Los Angeles – that was probably the most frightening of the places I've visited and it's the most westernized.

'Before I set off I thought, here it is, the big adventure, I'm the only one who's doing this. But as soon as you leave the UK, you realize there are hundreds of people doing the same thing. There seems to be a circuit of people going round and a great camaraderie between travellers. I can honestly say I never felt lonely. In fact, it can be difficult sometimes to have time on your own. Some of the time you can get caught up in the travellers' world and miss out quite a lot on actually seeing the country or meeting the local people.

'I did get a tremendous feeling of achievement out of having made it on my own and getting back in one piece. It sounds corny but it was literally the best decision I ever made, to get up and go. I think the hardest thing of all is actually making the decision to go and taking the first flight. Once you've left the country it all becomes much easier and anything seems possible.'

CHAPTER 4

PASSPORTS AND VISAS

Passports

All travellers from the UK must now be in possession of a full ten-year passport (one-year visitor's passports were abolished in 1996). This costs £28 for a standard passport (32 pages); £38 for a larger one (48 pages).

Passport application forms are available from main Post Offices in Great Britain and from the Belfast Passport Office and most travel agents in Northern Ireland. Form A is for those applying for their first passport (or who've only had a British Visitor's Passport before), their first passport in a new name or a replacement for a passport that has been lost or stolen. Form R is for anyone wanting to replace their soon-to-expire existing passport.

Allow plenty of time for your application to be processed. They're usually turned round within a couple of weeks, but to be on the safe side, apply at least one month before your trip commences – and don't forget to allow extra time if you need to apply for visas, too. Remember that in peak periods (i.e. the run-up to the summer holidays) Passport Offices are incredibly busy and you'd be wise to allow even longer. The Passport Office claims to deal with applications between September and December within two weeks; between January and August within four weeks. In emergencies, applications can be delivered in person, but you'll be charged a £12 handling fee. You also have to justify why you need your passport so quickly and will be asked to provide evidence of travel.

The Post Office has a Passport Application Service: for a charge of £3.20 (on top of the passport fee) they'll check your application through, making sure you've answered all the questions corrrectly, and have included the right payment, then send it by registered post to the relevant Passport Office. Your passport is posted to you at home. The aim is to speed up the issuing of passports – at the moment one in five applications has to be returned because the form hasn't been completed properly or payment hasn't been included.

If you already have a passport, check the expiry date. At the risk of stating the obvious, you need to make sure that it will last until the end of your trip – and probably another six to 12 months beyond that. Many people end up staying away longer than planned, so it makes sense to check that the expiry date allows for you extending your trip. Entry requirements for many countries, including such popular travellers' destinations as Thailand and Australia, insist that your passport has at least six months to run after you plan to leave their country.

If you're planning a big trip, covering lots of different countries, make sure your passport has plenty of blank pages left in it to allow for all the new visa, entry and exit stamps you'll be acquiring. Some border officials are reluctant to use a page with another stamp already on it, which can cause problems as the passport starts to fill up. Memorizing your passport number and date of issue will save time when you're filling out countless forms at borders and signing into hotels. In fact, you'll be writing the information down so often that you probably won't be able to help remembering it!

Bear in mind that some Arab countries, such as Syria, won't let you in if you have an Israeli stamp in your passport. (The Foreign & Commonwealth Office has a list of these countries.)

Remember to fill in the next of kin details in your passport so that your family can be contacted as soon as possible if anything happens to you and you're not able to call them yourself.

Carry your passport with you at all times, rather than leaving it in your suitcase or a safe. If you lose it or have it stolen while you're away, report it to the police and the nearest British Consulate immediately.

Take two photocopies of the last page of your passport (the first five if you still have the old navy-blue one); leave one at home; take the other with you in case the original gets lost or stolen.

N.B. After registering in a hotel in some countries, you must leave your passport with reception until you are checking out. Don't forget to ask for your passport back when you leave!

PASSPORT OFFICES IN THE UK

All passport offices now have the same telephone number. Ring the Passport Agency on 0870 521 0410.

ENGLAND

Liverpool Passport Office, 5th floor, India Buildings, Water Street, Liverpool L2 OQZ

London Passport Office, Clive House, 70 Petty France, London SW1H 9HD (personal applications only; send postal applications to Glasgow)

Peterborough Passport Office, Aragon Court, Northminster Road, Peterborough PE1 1QG

NORTHERN IRELAND

Belfast Passport Office, Hampton House, 47–53 High Street, Belfast BT1 2QS

SCOTLAND

Glasgow Passport Office, 3 Northgate, 96 Milton Street, Cowcaddens, Glasgow G4 0BT

WALES

Newport Passport Office, Olympia House, Upper Dock Street, Newport, Gwent NP9 1XA

Passport Offices are open Monday to Friday 9 a.m. to 4.30 p.m. (8.15 a.m. to 4 p.m. in London). The Passport Agency website (www.ukpa.gov.uk) has details of processing times, office locations, etc.

VISAS

Most visas are stamped into your passport, although some politically sensitive countries still provide a separate document. Visas are normally obtained from a country's embassy, high commission or consulate (see Chapter 17 for a list of addresses) though in some cases travel agents may be authorized to issue them. It can sometimes be less expensive and easier to obtain visas as you travel. In Bangkok, for example, there's no problem picking up visas for travel to surrounding countries such as Vietnam, Cambodia, Laos and Myanmar (Burma). In some cases, it simply isn't practical to get your visas before you travel as they may expire before you even reach the particular country. If you're planning to pick up visas *en route*, don't forget to take plenty of passport photos with you.

Most countries charge a fee for issuing visas and sometimes it can be quite a lot, so take this into account when working out how much the trip is going to cost. If time is short, you may have to pay extra for a visa to be issued faster than normal: in the case of the Russian Federation, for example, it's £80 for a same-day visa.

Allow plenty of time to get your visas. Some places will issue them immediately or within a couple of days and most will do it within a week. Other countries can take a couple of weeks to process your application. Always take great care filling in the application as any errors or omissions can mean it takes longer to process. If you're going to get your visa in person, be patient – you usually have to queue for ages. If you're applying through the post, always send your passport by recorded delivery.

Check whether your visa is valid for single or multiple entry. If you're going to Thailand, for example, and plan a side trip to Myanmar or Cambodia, you'll need a multiple-entry visa to get back into the country.

Visa information is particularly vulnerable to change. Always check requirements with the relevant embassy or consulate (see addresses in Chapter 17) prior to travel. If you're having trouble getting through to them, you could contact the MASTA Visa & Passport Information Line on 0906 5 501 100 who'll be able to give you the information you need, but at £1 a minute it doesn't come cheap.

VISA SERVICES

If you can't face the hassle of getting your own visas, there are agencies who will do the legwork for you – for a fee. The amount will usually be around £11–£15 per visa, on top of the visa fee charged by each country. Occasionally it can rise to as high as £50 for somewhere like the Russian Federation that involves a lot of waiting around. Ring a few agencies to compare prices; look in Yellow Pages to find local services or try the following organizations:

Hogg Robinson Travel
4 Wendle Court, 131–137 Wandsworth Road, London SW8 2LH
020 7622 0757

Rapid Visa Service
135 Earls Court Road, London SW5 9RH
020 7373 3026

Thames Consular
548 Chiswick High Road, London W4 5RG
020 8995 2492

Trailfinders Visa Service
194 Kensington High Street, London W8 7RG
020 7938 3848

Travcour UK
Tempo House, 15 Falcon Road, Battersea, London SW11 2PJ
020 7223 7662

Visa Australia
PO Box 1, Nantwich, Cheshire CW5 7PB
01270 626626
Issues Australian visas by phone, fax or post, seven days a week.
£10 for adults.

The Visa & Passport Service
PO Box 11862, 1 St Stephens Mews, London W2 5GQ
020 7229 1262

The Visa Service
2 Northdown Street, King's Cross, London N1 9BG
020 7833 2709

Children's passports
Since 5 October 1998, children must have their own passport
and cannot be added to an adult's. A child's passport costs £11
and is valid for five years. Children already on an adult's
passport can continue to travel on that until they turn 16, or the
passport expires or is sent in for amendment.

'Arriving in Guatemala involved the worst border crossing of my life. Our bus was stopped by the Guatemalan army and all the men had to get off – I was stuck on the bus with a load of farmers who didn't speak English. The two guys I was with were made to walk up the road away from the bus and, when I tried to go with them, this 15-year-old with a machine-gun stood by the bus and wouldn't let me get off. It was four in the morning and very scary. Some of the soldiers got on the bus. When they found out I was English, they made me get my rucksack out and went through everything, looking for political literature. They went through all my books asking what they were about, and I was desperately trying to explain the finer points of Jane Austen! It was an unpleasant couple of hours but eventually they got bored and let us carry on.'

'Everyone had warned us about how heavy border crossings in South America could be and by the time we did our first one, from Ecuador to Peru, we were terrified about crowds of people waiting to rip us off and evil officials trying to fine us for fictitious misdemeanours. In fact, it was a breeze. There were lots of money changers with rigged calculators but a friendly policeman took us under his wing, went to the bank and made somebody official come out with a briefcase full of money so that we could change our money in the secure environs of the police station. And on the Peruvian side, too, there was a big, smiley welcome. Then there was the crossing out of Peru into Bolivia which was all a bit of a blur as the bus left at 5 a.m. and I was still drinking cuba libres and dancing enthusiastically with some new-found Peruvian friends at 4 a.m. All I remember of it is my friend warning me very strictly at the border not to sing, dance or get too friendly with the guards!'

'I almost missed a flight to Vietnam from Bangkok. Thanks to horrendous gridlock and the fact that the bus dropped us off at the wrong terminal at the airport, we arrived for our flight about 20 minutes before the plane was due to take off and had to run all the way to the check-in desk, which was closed, persuade someone to reopen it and check us in, then carry on running to the plane, with heavy backpacks on and throngs of people blocking our way. The man at passport control stared in puzzlement at my photograph and then at the red, sweaty face in front of him. "Oooh!" he said. "You are not as beautiful as in your passport. Is this really you?" In my frustration, I got redder and redder and more and more sweat ran down my face until he eventually relented and let me through. When we finally got on the plane (as the gate was just closing) a kind steward took one look at us and brought us a pile of cold, wet towels before we had even taken off – only to arrive in Vietnam to find that actually we were 24 hours late and should have been on the plane the day before anyway.'

CHAPTER 5

MONEY MATTERS

HOW MUCH MONEY SHOULD I TAKE?

It depends on your route, how you're planning to travel, what kind of accommodation you stay in, etc. Obviously a week spent living in a straw hut and lazing on a beach will cost next to nothing, while a week in a city or one when you do lots of travelling will be much more expensive. As a general guide, you should probably allow a minimum of £10 a day, but £15 a day will be more comfortable and allow you more leeway.

For what it's worth, we usually budget for $30 (about £20) a day on top of flights and that works for us, and means we can splash out on the odd G&T instead of beer, travel in air-con instead of third class on hot, humid days, and move up a hotel notch if the cheapest one turns out to be a rat-infested, filthy, insecure dump. And we always have our credit cards in case of emergencies or special occasions. That said, we've come across plenty of people who allow themselves as much per week as we do per day – but it has to be said, many of them are pretty miserable. Better to spend longer at home saving up then have a good time while you're away, than to end up a sad, sorry traveller, adding up your small change on a Saturday night to see if you can afford a weekly beer between two.

If you're on a tight budget, aim for countries that you know are going to be cheaper than the UK. India and most of South East Asia, for example, are still cheap destinations (you can find yourself a Goan bungalow or a beach hut on a Thai island for just a few quid per night). North America or Australia will obviously be more expensive – and Japan will probably blow your budget completely. Much of South America (with the exception of Argentina and Chile) is cheap once you get there, but air fares are more expensive. Reading the most up-to-date guidebooks will give you some indication of costs of accommodation, meals, transport, etc. – but you can assume that all prices will have risen slightly since the writer was there.

Allow some extra money or take a credit card for the times (and there will be some) when you've had enough of dormitories and dubious hotel rooms and feel like treating yourself to somewhere more luxurious. There will also be activities and events along the way that you won't want to miss out on – like whitewater rafting or scuba diving on the Great Barrier Reef. This sort of thing doesn't come cheap (though you may get reductions with one of the discount cards mentioned later in this chapter) but it seems mad to miss out on what would certainly be a highlight of your trip – and possibly a once-in-a-lifetime experience.

You can really cut costs and get by on a minimal budget if you turn teetotal for the trip. Alcohol can be expensive in some places and you may sometimes find that your drinks are costing you more than your accommodation and food put together. If, like most travellers, you fancy a few drinks in the evening, remember that local beers and spirits are always cheaper than imported varieties; and as a general rule local spirits are cheaper (and more lethal) than beer.

A BASIC BUDGET

Obviously it's impossible to draw up a definitive budget, but the following is an approximate guide to the sort of money you need to allow for a basic RTW trip. If you plan to work, or will only be away for six or nine months, of course you can reduce the cost substantially. If you include Europe, want to visit every continent, try every activity going and treat yourself to nice meals and hotels now and then, it will obviously bump it up hugely.

RTW plane ticket	£850
Overland travel	£350
Spending money (365 days @ £15 per day)	£5,475
Basic insurance for 12 months	250
Rucksack and other equipment	250
Pre-trip vaccinations and visas	150
Books, toiletries, miscellaneous	100
TOTAL	£7,425

Don't forget to leave yourself some reserves for when you return – coming home is hard enough anyway, without being totally broke, too.

HOW DO I TAKE IT?

There are three main ways to carry your money: traveller's cheques, cash and credit/charge cards. Each has its uses, so the best advice is usually to take a combination of all three.

TRAVELLER'S CHEQUES

Traveller's cheques are safer than carrying large amounts of cash and are (usually) quickly replaced if lost or stolen. They sometimes have a slightly better rate of exchange than cash and you may find they make it easier to keep track of your spending. In much of the world, both dollar and sterling cheques are widely accepted, and taking a mix of both means you can change whichever gives the best rate of exchange on the day. However, in some areas (e.g. the US and South America), sterling traveller's cheques are very difficult to cash and dollar cheques are pretty much the only option. In the US itself, dollar cheques can be used just like cash in shops and restaurants.

The downside of traveller's cheques is that you can be stung for commission both when you buy them and when you change them (though any unused sterling traveller's cheques can be cashed without charge in the UK). It's always best to buy a well-known name (AmEx, Thomas Cook, Visa, etc.), especially if you're going somewhere unused to mass tourism. Take them in a mixture of small and large denominations. Keep a note of the numbers somewhere separate from the cheques themselves (and leave a copy at home, too). And carry your traveller's cheques in something waterproof – when they're in your money belt you could find that sweat makes the ink on the signature run and they might be difficult to change.

If you're travelling with a partner, AmEx and Thomas Cook do two-signature cheques that can be signed by either one of you (US$ cheques only).

Also useful is the new Visa Travel Money card, available from major banks including the Alliance & Leicester , the Royal Bank of Scotland, the Bank of Scotland and branches of Thomas Cook. Described as an 'electronic traveller's cheque', it can be loaded with between £100 and £5,000, then used to withdraw local currency from more than 440,000 Visa cash machines around the world. You get a PIN number for security and once the money has been used up, you simply throw the card away.

CASH

In some countries (e.g. Laos), and in very remote regions, traveller's cheques are not widely recognized, in which case cash is favourite. However, it is obviously riskier to carry and most insurance policies have a limit on how much they will compensate you for stolen cash. Check the cash limit on your insurance policy and don't carry more than the maximum amount they'll refund in the case of theft.

Take enough local currency (if you can) to pay for a taxi from the airport, and drinks when you arrive, but don't change too much here – usually get a better rate when you're away. Check if you'll be arriving at your destination on a holiday or at a time when banks will be closed and, if so, allow extra. Don't let the bank palm you off with all large notes: get small denominations as well, as large ones can be hard to change. When buying your currency, ask for new, or newish, notes from your bank. In some countries, they won't change banknotes which have penmarks on them or which have been Sellotaped together.

Always hold some cash back for emergencies.

CREDIT CARDS AND CHARGE CARDS

Take at least one credit card. Not everywhere accepts all cards but if you have Visa and MasterCard you should be well covered. As well as being invaluable for emergencies, they can be a cheaper way to pay when abroad as they tend to offer competitive exchange rates. They also help to raise your status in the eyes of otherwise suspicious foreign officials who look askance at penniless backpackers. Don't bank on bills taking months to come through, though – they usually turn up on your statement pretty quickly.

Statements will keep coming through every month while you're away, of course, so you need to arrange how you're going to pay for them. One way is to pay money into your credit card account in advance, which avoids interest piling up on your debts. Alternatively, you could ask your bank to arrange for a standing order to pay off a certain amount each month (remember to leave enough money in the bank to pay the bills as they come in). Or you could pay some money into an interest-earning account, set up a standing order from that to pay your bills each month and gain interest on the money at the same time.

Remember to make a note every time you charge something to your card so that you don't overspend.

Before you go, check the expiry date on your cards to make sure they won't run out while you're away; if necessary, apply for a new one in advance. Check your limit too. If you don't think it's enough, ask for it to be raised so you have the security of knowing it's there to fall back on in emergencies – but don't feel you have to use it! You can also use your card to get cash abroad, either as a cash advance over the counter or, if you know your pin number, from cash point machines.

American Express cards are useful, too, and fairly widely accepted. As well as being able to use AmEx offices as a poste restante service, AmEx cardholders can also cash cheques against their personal bank accounts. With a basic green AmEx card, you can cash up to £500 every 21 days; the money can be taken in cash or traveller's cheques. You'll pay commission on the cheques, just as you would if you bought them at home, but it saves you carrying them around for months before you need them. Remember, however, that the amount charged to your card has to be paid off in full each month when your statement comes in.

MONEY TIPS

* Shop around before you buy traveller's cheques and currency. Fees, rates of commission and minimum charges vary from one bank or building society to another – you may think you're getting a bargain if you find somewhere that doesn't charge commission, but you may find they offer a bad rate of exchange. The Post Office now sells foreign currency and AmEx traveller's cheques at many branches. If you work for a large organization, ask if they have commission-free arrangements with any banks.

* Don't leave it to the last minute to sort out your travel money – most banks need at least a few days' notice, especially if you're after a more obscure currency. If you need soft currency (e.g. roubles, dong, Kenyan shillings) you can only get them inside the country itself. Take dollars and change them on arrival.

* Wherever you go, one-dollar bills are useful for tips.

* Some cash cards can be used abroad just as in the UK. Check with your bank.

* Consider signing up with a credit card registration service, such as Card Protection Plan (0800 330 000) or Sentinel (0800 414 717). It will cost £10 to £12 a year, and means that if your cards are stolen while you're away, you'll only have to make one phone call to sort everything out.

* Eurocheques can be used in 50 countries in Europe and the Mediterranean, and even beyond – Israel and some North African countries accept them too. With Eurocheques, you write cheques out in the foreign currency (either to withdraw cash from a bank, or to pay for goods in shops, restaurants and hotels) and the sum is then debited to your bank account at home, just as with a normal cheque. You have to pay an annual fee for your card, a fee for the cheques, plus commission on each cheque.

* The costs of treatment and repatriation if you fall ill or have an accident while you're away can be huge, especially in the USA, so don't even think about travelling without insurance (see Chapter 7).

* If you're planning to buy perfume, alcohol, or other goods in duty free, check out the high street prices before you go – duty free isn't always a bargain.

* Look out in newspapers or magazines for travel bursaries or competitions that could help fund your trip.

* Don't leave home without: the number to call if your credit cards or traveller's cheques go missing; a separate note of your cheque numbers; enough sterling to see you through any transport delays when you leave (and keep some back to pay for a taxi home, a pint of milk, and other essentials when you get back).

TRANSFERRING MONEY ABROAD

If you run out of money while you're away, it is possible to have funds transferred to you quickly and fairly painlessly – for a fee, of course.

Western Union offer an International Money Transfer Service, which they claim is the fastest way to send money worldwide. The person sending you the money from this end can either go into a Western Union agent with cash (sterling) or call them with a credit card number (Visa or MasterCard), and the money should be available at the other end within about 10–15 minutes (for cash) or one to two hours (for credit cards). They cover most countries in the world. The charge varies according to how much you're sending – sending £500 would cost £37 (cash) or approximately £45 (credit cards). For information, call 0800 833 8333.

MoneyGram is another international money transfer service that can transfer funds of up to £5,000 per day, usually in less than 10 minutes, and covers over 90 countries worldwide.

Again, charges are on a sliding scale – to send $1,000 costs $60. The MoneyGram service is available at main Post Offices and travel agents.

Thomas Cook also operate a telegraphic transfer service that allows you to send funds to almost anywhere in the world, usually within 24 to 48 hours. The money can be paid into a bank account abroad or sent to a Thomas Cook branch or agent. Contact your local branch for details.

Banks will also transfer money abroad – ask your local branch for information. The Royal Bank of Scotland Royworld Budget, for example, is a payment system that allows you to send up to around £2,000 to a bank account in one of 18 countries (including Australia, New Zealand, the US and Canada as well as European countries). It costs £9 per transaction and takes about six days to reach the other account.

Another way to get access to money abroad would be to have someone deposit the money in your credit card account at home. This will avoid the bank charges incurred by transferring money abroad and the hassle of trying to arrange it.

BANK ACCOUNTS

Before you go away, let your bank know what you're doing and how you're arranging for your money to be handled. They may be able to offer you help and advice. You could arrange for a relative (a trustworthy one!) to become a signatory on your bank account, which will enable them to pay bills for you.

If you know you're going to be spending any length of time in a particular country, find out about opening a bank account there. In Australia and New Zealand, for example, this is easy and popular among travellers, because it means you don't have to worry about carrying round too much cash or too many traveller's cheques. At one time it was relatively easy to open your account in England before you left and deposit money in it so it would be waiting for you when you got there. This has now been tightened up, but you can still open an account once you get there, deposit a nominal sum, then get someone back in the UK to transfer funds to you.

DISCOUNT CARDS

There are a number of different cards available that can save you money while you're away, entitling you to good discounts (anything from 10 to 30 per cent) on all sorts of things from coach travel to car hire, skydiving to snorkelling, museum entrance to hostel accommodation. Some of the main ones you can get before you go are listed below. In addition, look out for discount cards available once you arrive in different countries, particularly in Australia and New Zealand, which are so well geared up to backpacker travel.

International Student Identity Card (ISIC), issued by ISTC (International Student Travel Conference). Available to full-time students. As well as qualifying for discounts on a variety of things, holders may also get commission-free currency and have access to a free 24-hour emergency Helpline from anywhere in the world. The card (which runs for 15 months from September to December of the following year) costs £6. Find application forms at student unions, or branches of usit CAMPUS and STA. ISTC also have an International Youth Travel Card for those who aren't students but are under 26. It offers similar benefits to an ISIC card. For details of both visit www.istc.org

Under 26 Card (called Young Scot Card in Scotland). Part of the Euro <26 Youth Card network, and supported by the British Council. Holders are entitled to discounts on fares, goods and services in 25 European countries, including the UK; they also receive a regular magazine and have access to a free travel advice line. Cost: £7. For information, write to Under 26, 52 Grosvenor Gardens, Victoria, London SW1W 0AG, or call 020 7823 5363. In Scotland, call 0131 313 2488, or order on the credit card hotline, 0990 134 936.

VIP Membership Card, from VIP Backpackers Resorts International. Membership (Aus$25; valid for one year) gives you discounts on hostels, travel passes, shops, etc. in Australia, New Zealand and a number of other countries. You can buy them in most student or backpacker travel specialists, at any VIP hostel or via www.backpackers.com.au.

Youth Hostel Association Card. Open to people of any age, a YHA card entitles the holder to use the YHA's worldwide budget accommodation network and gives discounts on a wide range of other goods and services, especially in Australia. In the UK, YHA members get a 10 per cent discount on all purchases at YHA Adventure Shops. Costs: £12 (18 and over); £6 (under 18).

NATIONAL INSURANCE

If you're out of the country for a long period of time your National Insurance contributions will be affected, reducing your pension rights and other benefits. If you go away part way through a tax year, during which you've already been paying contributions, 18 months after the end of that tax year, the computer will check your account. If your contributions for that year are below the required level, and if they have a note of your current address, you will be sent a Deficiency Notice, notifying you of the amount you need to pay to make the year count towards your pension. If, however, you are away for a full tax year (from April to April) you won't be contacted automatically; you will need to contact the Department of Social Security and ask to pay voluntary contributions if you wish to. You are allowed up to six years to pay up (though you will pay more after the first two years); after that, you can't pay for the missing year at all.

It's a confusing system so if you know that you're going to be out of the country for a full tax year or more, it's probably best to contact the DSS and ask for advice. Write to them with your date of departure, a rough idea of where you're going, your contact address in the UK, how long you plan to be away for and what you'll be doing, your expected date of return to the UK, and your National Insurance number. They'll forward it to the relevant section to deal with. The address is DSS, Contributions Agency, International Services, Newcastle Central Office, Newcastle upon Tyne NE98 1YX; 0191 213 5000.

WHILE YOU'RE AWAY

* Don't forget to haggle for goods and services – nearly everything is negotiable. Be patient (haggling takes time), stay calm and be prepared to compromise – the aim is for both of you to come away happy, not for you to beat the seller down completely. It's very easy to get carried away and then feel slightly shamefaced later that day when you realize you were arguing furiously for the sake of two pence.

* If you're staying somewhere for longer than a few days, try to negotiate a discounted rate on your accommodation – most places will let you have a room cheaper if you're going to be there for a few weeks or months. If a hotel looks pretty empty, it's also worth asking for a discount on the first price they give you.

* Banks almost always give a better rate of exchange than hotels. Try to avoid changing money at airports, border posts and tourist traps, etc, where a captive market means the exchange rate is often low.

* Don't call home from hotels as they charge hugely inflated rates. Use the local post office or pay phone instead.

* Remember that you pay over the odds for a drink with a view – side-street and off-beach prices are lower. In some countries drinking at the bar is cheaper than sitting down.

* If you're treating yourself to a night in a good hotel as a change from huts and dives, remember that you'll pay through the nose for any food or drink in a mini-bar. It's cheaper to sneak in your own supplies (and sneak the empty bottles out again).

* Keep all receipts when changing money in case you need them to change money back or take money out of the country when you leave. You should also keep receipts for any major purchases (if you buy a camera in Singapore, for example) in case customs ask for them.

* Don't carry all your money in one place – spread it between body and bag. Leave any valuables in the hotel safe, or, better still, leave them at home. As a rule, if you couldn't bear to lose it, don't take it. (See Chapter 10 for more advice on money and safety.)

* Always keep a note of all purchases made with your credit card so you can check it against the statement when you get home.

* Don't change too much money if you're leaving a country in a few day's time – you may find you can't spend it and lose out when changing it into the next currency. Have some traveller's cheques in small denominations.

* Each time you arrive in a new country, don't do too much spending (especially on souvenirs) until you've got a feel for prices. It's easy to get ripped off in the first few days before you've had a chance to learn what things should cost.

* Don't make the mistake of thinking that if all goes wrong and you run out of funds, you can simply go to the nearest British Consulate and be popped on a flight home. The Consulate is there to help you in emergencies, but won't dole out money or free flights home at the taxpayer's expense. In an emergency they may be able to cash a personal cheque drawn on a British bank for up to £100 (with a guarantee card), or help you get money on your credit card. They can also help you contact relatives, friends or banks at home to transfer funds to you. Only in the very rarest and most extreme of cases will they advance money to get you home – but it's a loan, not a gift, and once you return to the UK your passport will be impounded until you have paid back the money. There will probably also be a charge for any consular service.

* In each country, remember to check before you arrive at the airport to leave what departure tax, if any, is payable. Otherwise you can find yourself without the right amount of local currency (which nearly caused us to miss a flight on one occasion) or having to change far more than you need just to pay it.

BLACK MARKET

Changing money on the black market is widely practised in many countries and can help your money go a lot further. Most travellers will change money this way at some point, but you should remember that it is illegal and not without risk. Dealing in currency seems to thrive in countries that are dirt cheap anyway, so even the official rate is good value. Using unofficial money changers leaves you open to scams: you could be given old, devalued currency (well, do you know what a 20,000-dong note is supposed to look like?), forged notes or wads that are bulked up with cut-up newspaper. You might be cheated on the exchange rate by some nifty calculator work. In extreme cases, you can be mugged, or even arrested. Don't say we didn't warn you.

However, if you do decide to risk it (and most travellers, attracted by the prospect of up to double the exchange rate offered by banks, do), always keep your wits about you. Listen to other travellers' recommendations as to the best money changers. Usually, the more money you change, the better the exchange rate. Change money in shops and restaurants rather than with dodgy-looking men on street corners. Never allow yourself to be led into a deserted side street. Don't flash too much cash around, and be discreet. Change some money officially first so that you know how genuine notes look and feel. Always make sure that you are the last person to count the foreign currency before you hand over your money: sometimes the changer will hand it to you to count and it will all be there but he'll then ask for it back to check once more and will pocket some of the notes so skilfully you won't even notice until it's too late (if he gets nasty if you don't give it back to him, it's a sure sign that he's trying to pull a fast one).

'I took eight months off after finishing university and bought an RTW ticket. I visited India, Nepal, Thailand, Malaysia, Indonesia, Australia, New Zealand, Hawaii and finally Los Angeles. I didn't follow a rigid schedule, I followed other backpackers' recommendations as I went along and went where the fancy took me. I was with another guy, but we ended up travelling with some other people we met along the way, which was fun. My favourite country was Nepal. It's so different from anywhere else and the people were exceptionally friendly.

'I worked for five months before the trip to get some money, then borrowed the rest from my parents. My flight and travel insurance came to about £1,300 and I guess I spent about £4,000 on top of that. It was hard to stick to a budget as the prices were so different from country to country. We could live quite happily on £35 a week in India, but spent a lot more in Australia. That was because we wanted to do so much while we were there, such as diving, bungee jumping, whitewater rafting. It seemed a shame to miss out on anything.'

'While travelling round Australia, I decided to do a diving course in Byron Bay. It was the first time I'd been diving, and it was awe-inspiring. After qualifying, I did some pleasure dives in the Whitsundays and on the Great Barrier Reef, then I went to Cairns and did an advanced course there, spending three days on the outer Reef. This made me decide I wanted a complete change of career (helped by the fact that I didn't have a job to go back to). When I got home, I applied for a Career Development Loan and trained as a scuba diving instructor, which is what I do now.

'The trip was too short – only five months – but I hadn't really planned it properly and ran out of money. If you're travelling round Australia, you need to budget for fun things. Everyone plans how much they'll spend on food and accommodation, but there's more to it than that. You need to allow for things like whitewater rafting, parachute jumps, scuba diving – in Australia there's so much to do.'

'I saved madly for a year to do my trip and spent about £10,000. I know that sounds a lot, but I'm a shopaholic and was determined to buy anything I wanted to. I bought tons of things and shipped them all home – everything arrived safely. I didn't mind spending the money because the trip was the treat I'd always promised myself when I turned 30. Also, my company had agreed to hold my job open for me, so I knew I'd be financially secure when I got home.'

'When I was in South America, it was common practice to change money on the black market, which was done quite openly on most street corners. In some cases, you could double the exchange rate offered by banks, making a huge difference to a tight budget. It was also handy to be able to change small denomination traveller's cheques (or, even better, dollars) as $50 or $100 converted into some local currencies meant a rucksack full of notes.'

'Travelling around Chile on a fairly limited budget, I met two girls who were great fun and joined up with them. They had a bit more spending money than I had, and were out for a good time. They were happy to stay in backpackers' accommodation, but it was cuba libres, piña coladas, clubs and taxis home every night and I was going through my money at an astonishing rate. By the time we got to Santiago, Eileen was celebrating her 30th birthday. She booked us into the Sheraton Hotel and insisted on putting everything on her credit card – weeks' worth of filthy laundry, gin and tonics, lunch by the swimming pool. I have to admit, I did enjoy seeing how the other half lived! The next day, I made them come to a hostel I'd read about in Lonely Planet at £1 per night – bit of a contrast! I spent about four times what I would have done if I hadn't met them, but then I also had four times the fun!'

CHAPTER 6

WORKING ABROAD

If you need to make your money go further while you're travelling, the best way is to pick up work as you go. It's also a great way to meet other people.

While permanent jobs can be hard to find and require cutting through masses of red tape, casual work such as fruit picking, bar work, dishwashing and cleaning is usually easy to find (with or without a work permit). If you're a qualified nurse, secretary, chef or hairdresser, you'll always be in demand. If you are working illegally (and many travellers do), be discreet about it. Telling everybody could get both you and your employer in trouble.

One of the best countries for finding work is Australia, especially if you're under 26 and can get a working holiday visa (although the Australian government, faced with a deluge of young Brits, now limits the numbers issued). New Zealand also has a working holiday visa scheme, open to UK citizens aged between 18 and 30.

Europe, too, is more open than ever and UK nationals can work freely anywhere within the European Economic Area (EEA), which consists of the 15 member countries of the EU (Austria, Belgium, Denmark, Finland, France, Germany, Greece, Ireland, Italy, Luxembourg, the Netherlands, Portugal, Spain, Sweden and the UK) plus Norway, Liechtenstein and Iceland. The Overseas Placing Unit (OPU), a department of the UK Employment Service, publishes factsheets on 'Working in...' (covers EU countries, plus USA, Canada, Australia and New Zealand). They're available free from JobCentres or from the OPU, Rockingham House, 123 West Street, Sheffield S1 4ER; 0114 259 6051/2.

As far as working visas for America go, forget it, unless you start off going through an official working programme (see Working in America, overleaf).

If you're thinking of looking for work for which you'll be expected to dress fairly smartly (office work or teaching English, for example) remember to pack suitable clothes. You'll need to be reasonably neat, too, for approaching potential employers. Take with you a copy of your CV and any references or qualification certificates to show to potential employers.

TEACHING ENGLISH

English is used as an official or semi-official language in more than 70 countries, so teaching English offers more job opportunities than almost anything else. Those with TEFL (Teaching English as a Foreign Language) qualifications are greeted with open arms around the world, but are particularly sought after in Japan and other Asian countries, especially China. In addition to an official TEFL certificate, many employers look for two years' teaching experience.

However, there are also plenty of others willing to take those without experience (and sometimes even without qualifications). Eastern Europe and the Baltic States are crying out for English teachers and it's not difficult to pick up work, even without a TEFL certificate. Generally, the further you are from the UK, the less you need an official qualification. Bear in mind, though, that you'll earn less than someone who's qualified and you'll probably have more pupils, but fewer teaching materials.

A comprehensive guide to the huge array of TEFL courses on offer, both in Britain and abroad, is contained in the *ELT Guide*, which gives details of costs, starting dates, venues and duration of courses. It costs £12.95 from good bookshops.

i to i International Projects Ltd.
1 Cottage Road, Headingley, Leeds LS6 4DD
0870 333 2332. Offer intensive TEFL courses designed for travellers hoping to work along the way. Their free magazine, *Inspired*, has lots of travel/work ideas.

JET programme (Japan Exchange and Teaching) Administered by the Council on International Educational Exchange, Jet Programme Desk, 52 Poland Street, London W1V 4JQ; 020 7478 2010.
Although they concentrate mainly on teaching job opportunities in Japan, they also have information on placements in China, Finland, Korea and Thailand.

For additional information on teaching opportunities, EFL courses and publications, contact The British Council, Information Services Management, Bridgewater House, 58 Whitworth Street, Manchester M1 6BB; (0161 957 7000).

SUMMER CAMPS USA

American summer camps employ student counsellors to look after children and teach them new skills. Counsellors usually spend eight to nine weeks at a camp, from June to mid-August. There are also positions available as camp support and maintenance staff, but these are usually open only to students. The bonus of going through an organized programme is that as well as receiving a (small) salary and free food and accommodation, your return flight is paid for and you get the chance to travel after camp has finished. The following organizations all operate working programmes.

Au Pair America
37 Queen's Gate, London SW7 5HR
0800 413116
Open to 18 to 26-year-olds who are willing to commit to working a full year and have a valid driving licence.

BUNAC
16 Bowling Green Lane, London EC1R 0BD
020 7251 3472
www.bunac.org.uk
The BUNACAMP Counseller programme is open to students and non-students; interviews start in November and early application is advised. In addition, BUNAC also operate other work/travel programmes in America, Canada, Australia and Jamaica, though they are either open only to students (or those taking a gap year) or carry age restrictions.

Camp America
37a Queen's Gate, London SW7 5HR
020 7581 7373
www.campamerica.co.uk
As well as a counsellor programme, also offer a Family Companion Programme, assigning people to work in American homes looking after children during the summer break.

Camp Counselors USA
6 Richmond Hill, Richmond Upon Thames, TW10 6QX
020 8332 2952

(Scotland and Ireland)
27 Woodside Gardens, Musselburgh EH21 7LJ
0131 665 5843
www.campcounselors.com
Operate a similar scheme to BUNAC.

KIBBUTZIM AND MOSHAVIM

You could also work on a kibbutz or moshav in Israel. Volunteers on a kibbutz are given free accommodation and board and pocket money in return for their work. You must commit yourself to working for at least five weeks. On a moshav (a kind of capitalist version of a kibbutz), you'll be paid more. Neither will make you rich (though on a moshav you may be able to accumulate some savings) but both are good ways to make friends who might then want to travel on with you (but see note about Israeli passport stamps in Chapter 4). For more information, contact the following organizations:

Kibbutz Representatives
1a Accommodation Road, London NW11 8ED
020 8458 9235
Open to those aged 18–32.

Project 67
10 Hatton Garden, London EC1N 8AH
020 7831 7626

Transonic Travel
10 Sedley Place, London W1R 1HG
020 7409 3535

TOUR OPERATORS

Another way to earn money while travelling is by working as a representative for a tour operator abroad. Travel and tourism is one of the world's largest industries (if not *the* largest), so there are plenty of opportunities. You'll usually be expected to be aged between 18 and 35, have a knowledge of the relevant country and preferably a second language, though this isn't always necessary. Depending on the organization, your duties can include anything from appearing in cabaret to lecturing on historical sites in Europe, from erecting tents on campsites to babysitting for clients. Look out for adverts in national newspapers two or three months before the season starts (January/February for summer jobs; August/September for ski resort work). Here are a few contacts to get you started; you could also try the overland travel companies listed in Chapter 3. If you're going out to look for work on spec, it's best to go just before the season starts, when bars and restaurants are gearing up for the tourist invasion.

Canvas Holidays
12 Abbey Park Place, Dunfermline, Fife KY12 7PD
01383 644000

Eurocamp Travel
Hartford Manor, Greenbank Lane, Hartford, Northwich, Cheshire CW8 1HW
01606 787878
www.eurocamp.co.uk

Keycamp Holidays
Address as Eurocamp, above
01606 787522
www.keycamp.co.uk

Mark Warner Ltd
61–65 Kensington Church Street, London W8 4BA
020 7761 7300

OTHER USEFUL ADDRESSES

Africa & Asia Venture
10 Market Place, Devizes, Wiltshire SN10 1HT
01380 729009
Offer school-leavers over $17^1/_2$ the chance to work for four months in Uganda, Kenya, Malawi, Zimbabwe, India, Nepal and Tanzania. You pay around £2,500 but are given a living allowance, food and accommodation.

usit CAMPUS (Work Abroad Department)
52 Grosvenor Gardens, London SW1W OAG
0870 240 1010
www.usitcampus.co.uk
Have a Work to Travel Australia Programme for those aged between 18 and 25. It costs £69 for the package, which includes two nights' accommodation in Sydney, airport transfer, handbook, e-mail address, phone card, maps, harbour cruise and discounts. A working visa costs £60, plus £25 handling fee. They also run Work and Travel USA, an American working holiday programme for students over 18.

The Daneford Trust
45–47 Blythe Street, London E2 6LN
020 7729 1928
www.danefordtrust.fsnet.co.uk
Recruit volunteers between 18 and 25 to work as assistant teachers of English in Asia, Africa and the Caribbean. Cost varies according to destination and how long you stay, but reckon on around £2,000.

Gap Activity Projects
Gap House, 44 Queens Road, Reading, Berkshire RG1 4BB
01189 594914
www.gap.org.uk
Offer school-leavers the chance to spend six to nine months overseas in the gap year before university. Most volunteers teach English as a foreign language, help with the disabled and underprivileged, assist in schools and activity camps or participate in farming and conservation work. You pay a fee of around £1,000 plus air fare, in return for which you get free board and lodging and usually some pocket money.

Health Projects Abroad
PO Box 24, Bakewell, Derbyshire DE45 1ZW
01629 640051
www.hpauk.org
Run three-month Community Development Programmes in Africa for young volunteers. You pay a fee of around £3,000 to participate. Write for their free leaflet, *In Partnership with Africa*.

Project Trust
The Hebridean Centre, Isle of Coll, Argyll PA78 6TE
01879 230444
www.projecttrust.org.uk
A junior version of VSO, with a wide variety of voluntary, one-year work placements overseas for 17-to-19-year-olds in full-time education. You pay a fee of £3,250. Operates in 26 countries worldwide.

Raleigh International
Raleigh House, 27 Parsons Green Lane, London SW6 4HZ
020 7371 8585
www.raleigh.org.uk
Send 17- to 25-year-olds on ten-week expeditions in many parts of the world. Those over 25 can also join expeditions as volunteer members of staff.

Teaching & Projects Abroad
Gerrard House, Rustington, West Sussex BN16 1AN
01903 859911
Have 1,000 placements a year in 12 countries, either teaching English or working on projects ranging from medical work to tourism and conservation.

VSO
317 Putney Bridge Road, London SW15 2PN
020 8780 7200/7500
www.vso.org.uk
Accept qualified volunteers aged between 20 and 70 to work in areas such as teaching, surveying, nursing, building and journalism.

FURTHER INFORMATION

We have space to give only a brief idea of the type of work available. For more details, read the following books, all published by Vacation Work and readily available in good bookshops: *Work Your Way Around the World*; *Kibbutz Volunteer*; *Working in Ski Resorts*; *Working on Cruise Ships*; *Summer Jobs Abroad*; *Summer Jobs USA*; *Emplois d'Eté en France*; *Teaching English Abroad*; *Teaching English in Asia*, *The International Directory of Voluntary Work*. Call 01865 241978 for a Vacation Work catalogue or visit www.vacationwork.co.uk

OTHER PUBLICATIONS

How to Find Temporary Work Abroad
How To Books Ltd; 01752 202300

Working Holidays 2000; A Year Between
Central Bureau for Educational Visits & Exchanges;
020 7389 4004/4880

NEWSPAPERS

Overseas Jobs Express is a newspaper for international job-hunters and carries ads for permanent and temporary jobs, as well as articles of interest to anyone planning to work abroad. A three-month subscription (six issues) costs £29.95. For details, call 01273 440 220, write to Premier House, Shoreham Airport, Sussex BN43 5FF, or visit www.overseasjobs.com

'My girlfriend bought me a yachting magazine one day and when I read it I saw an ad from someone looking for people to help crew a yacht across the Atlantic. Although I didn't have much sailing experience I'd always fancied doing something like that, so I applied – and got taken on. I flew to Florida, where I met up with the owner of the yacht, his girlfriend and two other guys who were helping crew. We didn't get paid for it – in fact, we had to contribute money for our food. We spent a week in Florida getting everything ready, then sailed across the Atlantic, stopping off in Bermuda and the Azores and spending some time in each, before ending the trip in southern Portugal. It took about two months and was brilliant fun.

'Once we got to Europe the two guys and I travelled round Portugal and Spain, then I headed down through Italy and Greece to meet up with my girlfriend, who was working on one of the islands. I ended up getting work there too, then took off to Egypt and travelled down the Nile. I ended the trip with some snorkelling on the Red Sea, then flew back to England. It wasn't a problem with work because I've always worked freelance anyway, so I just slipped back into it when I returned.'

'I very much wanted to travel in America, but couldn't afford to do it on my own so I took a job on the BUNAC scheme and worked in a children's camp in Maine for ten weeks. Most of the English staff were employed on the kitchen and maintenance programme. They prepared meals, washed up, and worked an eight-hour day. I was a cleaner, which wasn't the most desirable job in the camp, but I only had to work a two-hour day, which left me lots of spare time. The camp was in the middle of nowhere, but there were lots of sports facilities I could use, such as swimming, tennis and archery. At the end of my contract, I joined up with some other girls and spent six weeks travelling around America by train, from New York to San Francisco, then down to San Diego, along the bottom of the States and back to New York. I'd highly recommend the BUNAC scheme. I enjoyed working in the camp, and it's a very cost-effective way of seeing the country.'

'I spent four months working in Greece one summer. After coming home, I fancied doing some more travelling so my girlfriend and I jumped on a plane to Tenerife where a friend of ours was already working. We found a cheap apartment in Playa de las Americas and our friend fixed us up with jobs selling timeshares. We became the sort of people I hate when I'm on holiday, harassing people and persuading them to visit timeshare resorts. We worked from nine to five, walking up and down the streets and beach, seeking tourists out everywhere (there was no escape!) and giving them the spiel. I didn't like doing it but I wanted to stay in Tenerife. The work was commission-based and paid well if you were good at it. The best ones approach everyone, but I only went to people who looked quite kind and wouldn't shout at me, so I didn't do very well.

'After three months, I got a job driving the minibus taking people back from the timeshares. I was on an hourly wage and worked long hours so I was earning quite well. Then I got more involved with the administrative side and ended up as the supplies person – picking up stationery, catering supplies and equipment for the villas. I had an excellent time – Playa de las Americas is definitely for young people and the evenings were wild. It was just party, party until I ran out of steam and came home – it took me two years though, so that's not bad!'

'I wanted to go travelling but didn't have much money, so working my way round seemed the only option. I went to France and met up with a friend in Paris. She had a child-minding job which came with free accommodation in the form of a garret room, so I slept on her floor. I found work pretty quickly and ended up with one cleaning job and two jobs that were a mix of child-minding and English teaching. The pay wasn't great, but it was enough to live on (especially as I wasn't paying for accommodation). We became experts at finding the cheapest places to eat, the days museums were free and the best places for cheap clothes and second-hand books.

'We spent four months in Paris, then moved to Greece, and ended up in Paros, where we stayed for six months, working in a little sea-front bar. At first they paid us just to sit in the bar so that it wouldn't look empty and other customers would come in. We'd chat and play backgammon and the drinks were free – it's a tough job but someone's got to do it! We were living on the campsite so we got to know lots of other travellers who started coming down to our bar in the evenings to see us and that, in turn, attracted more people so the bar ended up really lively. As the season hotted up we began working behind the bar too. It was great fun, though very exhausting, working all night; we spent the days just lying out on the beach, recovering.'

'I backpacked around Australia for a year. I had the most amazing time, meeting wonderful people and getting an insight into a unique country and the great Aussie lifestyle. After my year was up, my funds had run out and my parents were fed up with the "I need some more money" telephone calls so I decided to return to Sydney to look for work. I had met a girl who had told me she would always have a floor for me to sleep on. Not only did she have the floor, but the law firm where she worked needed a floating secretary.

'I was temping for a junior lawyer who worked with a senior partner. At the end of the first week, there was an office party. After a couple of glasses of Aussie champagne, I was in a very sociable mood and ended up spending the whole night chatting with the senior partner. The following week we went out for dinner and got on very well. We had several dates together, then he organized a weekend at the coast in Noosa. We stayed in the penthouse suite of a luxury hotel. After backpacking, it was nice not to be sharing a bathroom with 50 other people! I only had two months left on my visa, so I moved in with him to make the most of our time together.

'I came back to England and applied for Australian residency. We moved in together and stayed in Australia for four years, then moved to London. We've now been married for five years and have just had our first baby. We still laugh when we think of our first meeting and I feel so lucky to have him – even if I did have to travel 14,000 miles to meet him!'

'We spent about three months in Guatemala, setting up a co-operative making rugs. We designed them and chose what colours to dye them; the Indians in the highlands wove them. We rented a house in Antigua, the cultural capital, and I stayed there during the week learning Spanish. Then at weekends we went up to the highlands and stayed in the weavers' houses. There was no electricity or water or anything to do, so after half seven or eight everyone went to bed because you couldn't see to do anything.

'The administration side of shipping the rugs and getting money was a complete nightmare. The exchange rate was horrific and we made very little money at the end of the day. We were doing it on a fair-deal basis, so we paid the weavers over the odds for the rugs and put 20 per cent of what we made back into the community. We set up a school teaching the local kids their language because the government was trying to stop the Indian language and make everyone learn Spanish.'

CHAPTER 7

INSURANCE

Although millions of pounds are spent on travel insurance every year, it's one item that some backpackers think they can skimp on: according to a Campus Travel survey, 40 per cent of students travel abroad without insurance. Our advice is, wherever you're going, and however long you're going for, don't even think about saving a couple of hundred pounds by not taking out medical or personal insurance. It's the biggest false economy there is, and you won't be able to relax all the time you're away. If you have an accident, the cost of evacuation and repatriation can be astronomical. An injured person might need four airline seats, plus two more for medical staff, as well as ambulances at each end. One patient who was evacuated from the Himalayas to Singapore was faced with a bill of more than £30,000. If you're including America in your itinerary, medical insurance is essential – you should be covered for up to £5 million.

* Take out insurance cover as soon as you book your ticket. This means you're covered if you have to change or cancel your travel plans for any reason.

* It's important to check exactly what your insurance covers (and what it doesn't cover). If you're planning an Indiana Jones-type of trip with lots of paragliding, whitewater rafting, scuba-diving, off-piste skiing or bungee jumping, you must mention this at the time, as most insurance policies don't cover 'dangerous' sports.

* Check, too, that you're covered for unexpected losses or expenses incurred if you miss a flight, have cash and credit cards stolen or lose your passport. And is there a 24-hour emergency back-up service or number that you can contact if necessary?

* Bear in mind that if you go anywhere that the Foreign &

Commonwealth Office has issued a warning against visiting, it could invalidate your insurance altogether.

* Once you're on the road, you may decide to prolong your trip. Find out how easy it would be to extend your period of insurance cover while you're away and ask if someone else, such as a parent, can arrange to do this for you. Some insurers don't allow it.

If you are travelling within the EU, you can get some medical cover by filling in form E111 (see p89 for details). However, you should still take out extra insurance, because even when there are reciprocal health service agreements between countries, you won't always get the full cost of treatment back. Some insurers waive their excess charge if you've used an E111.

WHAT TO LOOK FOR IN AN INSURANCE POLICY

Don't just go automatically for the cheapest policy – it's not necessarily the best. Boring as it is, you should read the small print and check exactly what you're covered and not covered for.

Cancellation or curtailment

This insures you in case you have to change your travel plans. It should cover the following:
* being called for jury service or as a witness
* you or a close family member becoming ill
* being made redundant
* your home being severely damaged by fire, flood or storm.

Delay

* Compensation is paid if your departure is delayed by a specific number of hours or cancelled altogether. The amount depends on the length of delay but is usually no more than £200.

Personal accident

* Money will be paid to you if you are permanently disabled, or to your next of kin if you die.

Personal liability

* This will cover you if someone makes a claim against you for injuring or damaging them or their property. Look for cover of at least £1 million, or £2 million in the United States.

Medical and emergency expenses

* Your policy should pay for emergency medical treatment, as well as hotel and travel expenses incurred because of sickness or injury. Look for cover of at least £1 million.

* Medical insurance should also cover your repatriation costs because of illness, injury or death of a friend or relative. In Europe, the normal minimum payment is £250,000; maximum payout is up to £2 million. In America, however, it could be as high as £5 million. Check that it also includes the cost of accommodation and travel costs for a friend or relative to stay behind or fly out to help look after you.

* Check that emergency dental work is included. And are you covered for lost contact lenses or glasses?

* You must let your insurer know if you have any permanent or recurring illness. If you don't, it will invalidate your policy. They may ask for a doctor's note confirming that you are fit to travel.

* Most insurers provide 24-hour emergency service and telephone advice lines. Take a copy of the policy and a note of the UK telephone number with you.

Baggage and personal belongings

* If you've bought a new, expensive rucksack, it's probably worth insuring it. If it's ten years old, and you're not worried about losing it, going for a policy that doesn't include baggage will save you money.

* Most policies allow up to £150 for the emergency purchase of essentials if your baggage is in Nantucket and you're in Nairobi.

* Check if your passport comes under personal belongings. You may have to pay a supplement to cover loss of passport.

* Valuable items, such as cameras, are usually subject to a limit. Bear in mind, also, that most insurers will make a deduction for wear and tear when paying your claim – you're unlikely to get the full replacement value.

* If you have a personal possessions or all-risks extension for certain belongings (such as a camera) on your house contents insurance, these will be covered if you take them out of your home, as will any money you're carrying. Check the cash limit, however: the limit for all forms of money is usually between £200 and £500, and the limit for cash itself can be half this. Check, too, that the policy covers you for where you are going and for the length of your stay away. (Some policies will cover you only for 30 or 60 days outside the UK.)

Sporting activities

* Planning a bungee jump while you're away? You'll probably have to pay a supplement to be covered for this activity – the cost will depend on how many jumps you plan to do and the level of supervision. Ask your insurer for details.

* Many other adventurous activities such as parachuting, mountaineering, scuba-diving or whitewater rafting may also be excluded from your policy. Even some things that don't seem particularly wild, like hiring a motorbike or snorkelling, are sometimes excluded. Always check the small print to see what's covered.

Working abroad

* Will you be insured if you have an accident while working abroad? Tell your insurer before you go if you're planning to look for work en route.

DON'T FORGET: Many insurance policies have an excess of around £35–£50, which means you have to pay the first £35–£50 of any claim yourself. It's vital you check if this sum is applied separately to individual sections of your policy, meaning you could end up paying out more. For example, if you were the victim of a mugging and needed to claim for medical costs as well as loss of money and possessions, you could have to pay three excesses, totalling more than £100. This is clearly unfair, since your claim would arise from a single incident. Read the small print carefully. If you're not sure about excess charges, ask your insurer to explain the policy in detail. It may be possible to pay an excess waiver – an extra £25 or so added to your premium – which means that any claims you make won't be subject to an excess charge.

Also, don't be misled by the term 'worldwide', which very rarely means what you'd expect it to. In insurance terms, it usually means everywhere except the USA and Canada. Including these two countries makes a policy more expensive.

FLEXIBLE FRIENDS

If you pay for a holiday with a credit or gold card you can claim a refund from your credit card company if your holiday company goes bust. Most credit cards also give you some form of insurance if you use them to pay, but not enough to rely on. Check with your credit card company.

WHERE WILL I GET THE BEST DEAL?

Insurance is a competitive business and mainstream insurance companies, banks, building societies, private health care companies, some high street stores, and post offices all offer insurance services, as do most of the travel agents featured in this book. Below, you'll find some contact numbers and basic prices to get you started, but it's impossible to provide an exact quote for every policy, because prices vary greatly according to your age, destinations, length of time away, whether or not you'll be working or indulging in 'dangerous' sports and numerous other variables. Shop around, stating your precise requirements, to get the policy that suits you best on price and cover.

LONG-STAY TRIPS

There are hundreds of insurance companies around, but the following are particularly geared up to backpackers' needs.

Austravel
(for addresses see Chapter 2)
020 7730 6525/3402
Offer Great Escape cover, a no frills policy for backpackers. Worldwide cover (but including only 31 days in the USA and Canada) is £155.

Boots the Chemist (branches around Britain).
Their Gap Year Travel Cover costs £199 for six months; £365 for 12 months. Pick up a leaflet and pay in store or call 0845 840 2020. www.thegapyear.co.uk/health/insurance.html

usit CAMPUS
52 Grosvenor Gardens, London SW1W 0AG
020 7730 3402
www.usitcampus.co.uk
Also have regional branches. Their Go Banana Travel Insurance, for students and under-35s, offers three levels of cover. Worldwide cover for 12 months costs £270 (excluding baggage), £339 (including baggage and some hazardous pursuits) or £433 (their most comprehensive cover). European cover for a year is £149, £174 or £209. Policies available for up to 24 months.

Club Direct
Dominican House, Freepost PT577, Chichester, West Sussex PO19 1YQ
0800 074 4556

www.clubdirect.com
They offer a Discovery travel insurance for backpackers and
long-term travellers and will also insure anyone wishing to work
while travelling. Basic premiums start at £200 per year. If you
come home early, they'll refund the unused part of your
premium.

Columbus Direct Travel Insurance
17 Devonshire Square, London EC2M 4SQ
020 7375 0011
www.columbusdirect.com
Columbus offer three levels of cover: fully comprehensive;
standard, which doesn't cover loss of camera, cash or
documents; or Globetrotter, which is basically just medical
cover. The Globetrotter rate for six months is £107.10.

Endsleigh Insurance Services Ltd
Endsleigh House, Ambrose Street, Cheltenham, Gloucestershire
GL50 3NR
01242 258 258
www.endsleigh.co.uk
For 12 months' worldwide cover (including the USA), Endsleigh
have a Standard policy for £350 or a Premier policy for £486.
Premier offers higher levels of cover and also covers money up
to £250, transport delays, missed departure, luggage delay, legal
expenses and hijack of aircraft.

Preferential Direct
01702 423280
www.worldtrekker.co.uk
Have a worldwide travel policy which costs £264 for a year with
baggage and will even cover you for repayment of your student
loan if anything happens to you.

STA Travel
(for addresses see Chapter 2)
Offer three levels of cover: Backpack (essential medical and basic
luggage cover), Standard, and Premier. Premier offers higher
levels of cover, which are advisable for travel in the US and
Canada. Annual worldwide policies for 12 months cost £278.50
(Backpack), £344 (Standard) or £537 (Premier). STA also run a
24-hour international helpline which you can call from
anywhere in the world if you have problems.

Trailfinders
(for addresses see Chapter 2)

Provide personal travel insurance cover from four days to 12 months. They have a 24-hour medical emergency service, Voyagers Assistance. Premiums (worldwide, including North America) start at £249 for six months; £399 for 12 months. They also have a policy that covers just Australia and New Zealand: six months' cover is £185; 12 months' is £299. Further information from individual branches.

Travelbag
(for addresses see Chapter 2)
Offer a basic backpackers' insurance for £199; or a more comprehensive 365-day, round-the-world policy for approximately £365.

Wexas International
(for address see Chapter 3)
Offer members a fully comprehensive, 12-month worldwide policy, including North America, for £504.45, which gives medical cover and additional expenses up to £10 million.

Worldwide Travel Insurance Services Ltd
PO Box 99, Elm Lane Offices, Elm Lane, Tonbridge, Kent TN10 3XS
01892 833 338
www.wwtis.co.uk
Their Long Stay Travel Insurance gives cover for up to 18 months and covers anyone who wants to take up work (excluding manual labour). There's a 24-hour emergency service and their medical cover goes up to £5 million. Also, if you pay for 12 months' cover (£192) but return after nine months, they'll refund the difference. Policies from £16 per month (medical only) or £27 per month (medical and baggage).

SHORT TRIPS

We appreciate that not everyone can take as long as a year off to travel. If you can only go away for two or three months at a time, it's worth checking out the growing range of annual insurance policies on the market. Don't be misled by the name – annual insurance policies don't actually cover you for a whole year away, but they do cover you for multiple trips within a 12-month period. If you're planning, say, a three-month trip with maybe the odd fortnight or weekend away in the same year, then annual policies are much more cost-effective than buying separate insurance every time. It's important, though, to check out what the maximum length of each stay is – some policies only allow for 30–45 days, while others allow for trips of up to three months at a time. Try the following for starters:

American Express
0870 600 1060
Annual worldwide policy costs £99. Maximum stay per trip is 45 days with no limit on the number of trips per annum.

Boots
0845 840 2020
Annual policy costs £99 for worldwide cover. Maximum stay per trip is 45 days and cover is limited to a total of 183 days away a year.

BUPA Travel Services
0990 858585
Annual policy costs £104.50 for worldwide cover. Maximum stay per trip is 45 days and cover is limited to a total of 183 days away a year.

Club Direct
0800 074 4556
www.clubdirect.com
Annual worldwide policy costs £75 for Prima; £99 for Premium Plus. Maximum stay per trip is 31 days for Prima; 90 days for Premium Plus.

Columbus Direct
020 7375 0011
www.columbusdirect.co.uk
Annual policy costs £82 for worldwide cover. Maximum stay is 60 days per trip.

Trailfinders
020 7938 3366
www.trailfinders.com
(see Chapter 2 for addresses).
Annual policy costs £99 for worldwide cover. Maximum stay is ten weeks.

World Cover Direct
0800 365121
www.worldcover.com
Annual policy costs £89.10 for worldwide cover. Maximum stay is 93 days.

Worldwide Travel Insurance Services
01892 833 338
www.wwtis.co.uk
Annual worldwide policy costs £75 for Standard, £89 for Super and £121 for Elite. Maximum stay per trip is 31, 45 and 62 days respectively.

WHILE YOU'RE AWAY...

* Leave a photocopy of your insurance documents at home with parents or whoever is looking after your affairs. Take another copy with you in case you lose the original.

* However insecure the hotel safe looks, use it rather than leaving valuable belongings in your room. Most insurance companies will refuse to pay up if items are stolen from your room when there was a safe available.

* If you're robbed, you must report it to a police station immediately (i.e. within 24 hours) and obtain a police report. Even if you think they'll never catch the culprit or get your belongings back, you'll need their report to present to your insurers back home when you make a claim. Check your insurance documents to see if you need to contact them immediately or if it can wait until your return.

* If you need to buy new things as a result of loss or theft, be careful to keep all the receipts.

WHEN YOU COME HOME

* If you do need to make a claim on your insurance policy, do it as soon as you get back to the UK because it's often a condition of the policy that claims be submitted within one calendar month of your return.

* Keep all receipts for any treatment, prescription drugs, services and other expenses and submit them with your claim form, together with any back-up documents such as police reports. (Keep photocopies of everything, in case of any dispute.)

* If your claim is rejected, the insurers must tell you why. If you don't agree with their decision, take your complaint to the highest level within the insurance company. If you're still not satisfied, seek advice from the Insurance Ombudsman Bureau (08456 006666) or the Chartered Institute of Arbitrators (020 7837 4483), who run a personal insurance arbitration scheme.

THINK IT COULDN'T HAPPEN TO YOU?

Here are some of the claims which have been submitted to insurance companies:

* A couple visiting the Rock of Gibraltar had their camera stolen by one of the apes.

* A couple buying petrol in India were attacked by a tiger.

* A holidaymaker in the US went for a midnight swim and was bitten by a vampire bat.

* An alligator swallowed a tourist's glasses in Jamaica.

* A safari group in Africa lost all their equipment when a hippopotamus capsized their boat.

The insurance companies paid up in every case.

'I spent three months travelling through Brazil, Bolivia and Argentina, and had a great time everywhere. South America is very exciting: it seems more unexplored than other parts of the world, and I felt very intrepid.

'About a month into the trip I had lots of stuff stolen in Salvador, in Brazil. I went out for the evening and, because the hotel "safe" was just a locked cupboard that everyone knew about, and looked really easy to get into, I left everything in my room. I hid valuables in my rucksack and under my mattress. I locked the windows and door and took the key with me, but when I got back everything was gone. They took my camera, film, Walkman, cash, electric razor – anything they could sell. I think it was an inside job because the room was locked when I got back, but I couldn't prove it. I spent all day getting a police report, but the insurance company in England wouldn't pay out because my belongings weren't in the safe. So no matter how dodgy the safe looks, always use it or you won't get any compensation.'

'I hadn't travelled widely, and hadn't travelled on my own, when I decided to go to Australia for a while. I was due to change planes at Hong Kong but just before we arrived they announced that we couldn't land there due to a typhoon so, after flying around in circles for a while, we ended up landing in Taiwan. We were kept waiting at the airport for eight hours. No one told us what was happening and we couldn't understand the language, so it was a bit worrying. Eventually our passports were taken from us and we were informed that we'd be staying the night in a hotel in Taiwan. At the hotel I was told I'd be sharing a room with two elderly women who'd also been on my flight, which was fine until we got to the room and there was only one bed. We were told it was big enough for three! The next day, we were put on a flight to Hong Kong, where I had to wait 11 hours for the next flight to Sydney. When I arrived I was exhausted and had already missed a day of my trip. I had pre-booked a hotel from England, fortunately, so went straight there and had a good sleep. I had a great time in Australia and hope to go back. One word of warning though: I had taken out insurance, but it didn't cover me for the delay, or for missing my first night's accommodation at my hotel, because the typhoon was considered an Act of God.'

'A friend and I went diving in Honduras, but didn't know that the diving school was a bit of a cowboy outfit. They didn't train us properly, and took us into water that was too deep. My friend's equipment was faulty, and he ran out of air. He surfaced quickly while holding his breath, which is the worst thing you can do. One of the instructors got him back to the beach, but a couple of hours later he started coughing up blood. A doctor told us he should go into a decompression chamber, but the nearest one was in Florida.

'They said, "If he's going to die it will be in the next 20 hours, so you'd better get him to hospital quickly." We tried to get off the island and eventually managed to get a charter flight on a dodgy old plane, then a bus back to Guatemala and went to the nearest hospital. He was kept in for observation because he had problems with his lungs, but it all turned out OK in the end. He was incredibly lucky.

'Before leaving the UK we'd taken out medical insurance, and I'd complained at how expensive it was. But once that happened, I was so thankful we were covered. Who knows what would have happened if we hadn't been?'

CHAPTER 8

HEALTH MATTERS

An alarming number of travellers leave the country without bothering to take any medical precautions, yet many travel health problems can be avoided with a bit of foresight and sensible planning before you go and by following a few simple rules while you're away.

VACCINATIONS

First step towards a healthy trip is booking an appointment with your GP or travel clinic to sort out which vaccinations you need and when. You should do this at least a couple of months before you go. Don't leave it to the last minute: some vaccinations take time to become effective; some have to be administered in stages or can't be given at the same time as others. You need to provide the doctor with the following information:

* Which countries you'll be visiting and when

* How long you'll be there

* What kind of areas you'll be visiting (rural or cities?)

* What your living conditions are likely to be (tents, straw huts or five star hotels?)

* What existing allergies or illnesses, if any, you have

* Whether or not you're pregnant (or likely to be soon)

* What medication (including the Pill) you're already taking.

In exchange, the doctor should tell you which vaccinations you need (both to meet official requirements and for your own health), how much they'll cost, how long they'll protect you and what possible side-effects there might be.

Keep a record of all the vaccinations you receive and when. Some places give you a 'health passport' or form on which details of vaccinations and dates are recorded for easy reference and for showing to officials. Carry the form with your passport.

The cheapest source of jabs is your GP. Some vaccinations (e.g. typhoid, hepatitis A and polio) are available on the NHS, so your GP should provide these free (or just for the cost of the prescription charge). Other vaccinations (e.g. rabies, diphtheria, Japanese B encephalitis) are not available free on the NHS and whether or not your GP charges you for them (and how much) seems to be down to the luck of the draw – it differs from one to the next. Some GPs may also charge a small fee for entering your vaccine details on your form; others will do it free of charge.

You can also have your jabs at a travel clinic (see the end of this chapter for contact addresses or look in Yellow Pages). Prices vary greatly, so shop around. Having all the required vaccinations can cost a hefty whack, especially if you're going to a developing country (you can easily end up spending £100 plus), so it really is worth checking out all the options rather than booking into the first travel clinic you find. When you're comparing prices, remember that some vaccines are given in two or three doses, so check whether the price quoted is per dose or per completed vaccination. Some clinics may charge you a consultation fee if you're asking for advice, though this may be refundable against the cost of your vaccinations if you have them done there.

POTENTIAL HEALTH PROBLEMS

This is a selective list of some of the more common or widely publicized travel ailments or worries. It's not exhaustive but you may still feel, looking at it, that perhaps the world's too dangerous a place for travelling. However, you should remember that the chances of catching some exotic disease are actually very remote – most travellers return home having experienced nothing more serious than the occasional bout of diarrhoea.

Remember, though, that just because you've had a full course of jabs it doesn't mean you're invulnerable. In fact, the illnesses you're most likely to come into contact with are those caused by consuming contaminated food and drink and for many of these there is no vaccine. It's therefore important to take care of your health while you're away, both by watching what you eat and drink (see p93) and by guarding against insect bites (see p88).

Altitude sickness can occur above 10,000 feet (3,000 metres) and can be fatal. Symptoms may include dizziness, sickness, headache, lack of coordination, breathlessness, fatigue, sleeplessness, loss of appetite and coughing. If you're affected, there are drugs you can take (available on private prescription before you leave the UK), but it's better to take preventive action. It takes your body a while to acclimatize to high altitude so you should avoid going straight off on a mountain trek, especially if you've just flown in somewhere that's already at high altitude. Spend a few days getting used to the height, and when you do start to ascend, do it gradually. Any trek should ascend no more than about 1,000 feet a day and include rest days to allow your body to adapt. Even then you may be affected. Don't let yourself be pushed by peer pressure further or faster than it's safe to go. The simplest remedy is to descend to a lower level. If you have respiratory or heart problems, you should avoid spending much time at very high altitude. Even if you are in perfect health, allow yourself some time to acclimatize. Remember also that the thin air at high altitude will give you little protection against sunlight. Take plenty of sunblock and apply it frequently.

Bilharzia (also known as **schistosomiasis**) is caused by tiny larvae found in freshwater lakes, canals and rivers. Water close to human habitation is particularly likely to be infected but it's not a problem in salt water so the sea is OK. It's found in most of Africa, but also in parts of the Middle East, South America and South East Asia. Larvae can penetrate the skin and once in your body develop into worms which produce eggs. You can help reduce the risk by frequent application of waterproof insect repellent and drying yourself thoroughly and rapidly as soon as you leave the water (the larvae can't survive out of water). No vaccination is available but the disease can be treated.

Cholera is spread via contaminated food and water and is a problem in any area where sanitation is poor, especially in Asia, Africa, South America and the Middle East. The best way to avoid it is to take care over what you eat and drink (see p93). A vaccination is available but is not very effective. Some GPs won't give it; some may (for a fee) give you a vaccination certificate without actually giving you the jab. Although immunization is no longer officially required by any country, this can be useful to have, as the authorities in some countries may still, very occasionally, ask for proof of vaccination. If there is a cholera outbreak, they may also administer compulsory vaccinations – better to have it done in the UK where you don't have to worry about how clean the needle is or how often it's been used before. Given as a single injection, the vaccine's effectiveness, such as it is, lasts for three to six months.

Cuts and scratches. Take care with minor injuries in hot climates, as they can become infected more easily than they would at home. Clean well, put antiseptic on them and cover with a plaster or dressing.

Dengue fever, a viral infection carried by day-biting mosquitoes, occurs throughout the tropics, in Asia, the Caribbean and Central and South America. Increased outbreaks of dengue were one of the after-effects of El Niño in 1998. The disease lasts between a week and ten days but has no long-term effects. Although not usually fatal, it is extremely painful and there is no vaccine or known treatment so it's even more important to avoid getting bitten in the first place (see p88).

Diarrhoea. All the vaccinations in the world can't protect you against the illness you're most likely to fall victim to. Delhi belly, Montezuma's revenge, the Turkey trots – call it what you will, diarrhoea affects most travellers at some time, to a greater or lesser extent. However, you can take sensible precautions (see p93). If you get diarrhoea: drink lots of water to prevent dehydration; eat only plain foods; stay out of the sun; forget alcohol and milk. It usually clears up on its own after a couple of days, but if necessary (if you have to make a long journey, for example) Imodium is an effective remedy and a rehydration solution (e.g. Dioralyte) replaces lost minerals. If the diarrhoea is accompanied by fever and the passing of blood or mucus, seek medical advice. If you're on the Pill, remember that diarrhoea or vomiting can reduce its effectiveness, so you should take extra precautions for the rest of your cycle. For more information, call the London School of Hygiene and Tropical Medicine's recorded telephone information line on diarrhoea: 0900 1600 272.

Diphtheria is caught by close contact with an infected person and is found especially in tropical countries (Asia, Africa, Latin America) with overcrowding and poor sanitation; also in parts of Eastern Europe. You were probably vaccinated against this as a child but that doesn't give lasting immunity, so if you're going to an infected area and planning to spend time with local people, you should consider having a booster, which is effective for ten years. Diphtheria may sometimes be given in a combined vaccine with tetanus.

Dysentery. There are two types of dysentery – amoebic and bacillary – both spread via contaminated food and water and common in the tropics, especially India and Africa. There is no vaccine against either form but they can be treated with antibiotics. The most important thing is to take steps to prevent dysentery by taking care over what you eat and drink (see p93).

Giardiasis is caused by the giardia parasite in infected food and water and seems to be on the increase. It is common in North Africa but is also found in other parts of Africa, Iran, India and even Eastern Europe. It may start like traveller's diarrhoea but will last much longer if not treated. No vaccine is available but it can be treated with antibiotics. The best ploy is to take great care eating and drinking.

Heatstroke or **sunstroke** is brought on by overheating, so take things easy and don't do anything too active in the hottest part of the day (do as the locals do and have a siesta instead). Early warning signs include nausea, headache, hot red skin, and light-headedness. Get into the shade straight away. If possible, lie down in a cool room, with a fan or air conditioning. Loosen any clothing and use water to cool your body. Drink plenty of water.

Hepatitis A (also known as **infectious hepatitis**) is spread via contaminated food and water or from person to person in areas of poor sanitation. It is more common among backpackers and hikers than 'normal' tourists, yet it is preventable with a vaccination. A gamma globulin vaccination (a big jab in the bum) shortly before travelling takes effect immediately and helps protect you for three to six months. However, if you're away for longer or travel frequently, two injections of the Havrix vaccine (a small jab in the arm) four to six weeks apart will protect you for a year; if followed by another six to twelve months later, it will give you protection for up to ten years. The Havrix vaccine takes two to four weeks to become effective so if you leave it to the last minute you'll have to go for the gamma globulin. Vaccination is recommended for anywhere outside northern and western Europe, North America, Australia and New Zealand. You should also take great care over what you eat and drink and personal hygiene (see p93). A combined Hep A and Hep B vaccination is now available free from GPs: a series of three jabs (the second and third at five weeks and six months after the first) gives you immunity for ten years. Another new vaccine, Hepatyrix, protects against Hep A (for up to 15 years) and typhoid (up to three years) in one injection.

Hepatitis B is more severe than Hepatitis A, highly infectious and can be fatal. It is transmitted, like HIV, via infected blood or body fluids, and most British travellers catch it when being given medical treatment after an accident. A vaccine is available (given as three injections over a period of six months, and providing protection for five years) but can take six months to become effective. It's recommended for travellers who will be living for long periods in high-risk areas (which include parts of Asia, South America, Africa and Eastern Europe). You should protect yourself by not engaging in high-risk activities (such as unprotected sex, using infected needles, having a tattoo or acupuncture). There is also a joint Hep A and Hep B vaccination – a series of three shots to be started six months prior to departure.

Hepatitis C. Like Hepatitis B, this can be contracted via contaminated blood products, the use of poorly sterilized surgical equipment or needles and unprotected sexual contact. There is no vaccine. Travellers should be vigilant when receiving hospital treatment and ask for their personal sterile equipment to be used.

HIV/AIDS. HIV is widespread throughout the world and there is no vaccine or cure for either HIV or AIDS, so it's important to be aware of the risk of contracting it when you're travelling. It's easy to get carried away when you're out in a hot climate, meeting attractive fellow travellers from around the world and drinking the night away together. Excessive alcohol consumption on holiday can blur your normally good judgement and you're much more likely to make silly mistakes while you're travelling than you would at home. Don't get so carried away by holiday romance that you forget the rules of safe sex – always use a condom. In countries like Australia and America, reliable condoms are readily available but take a supply with you for countries where the local versions might be suspect. Visiting prostitutes, especially in places like Thailand and East Africa, is highly risky and just asking for trouble.

If you're travelling in developing countries where medical facilities are sparse, carry a sterile medical kit to reduce the risk of HIV contamination through dirty needles, syringes and other medical equipment (see p92). In the unlikely event that you need a blood transfusion, ask for screened blood. Reduce your risk by avoiding unnecessary medical or dental treatment. Remember that tattooists' needles can be infected too – don't have a tattoo or get your ears, nose or anything else pierced unless you're absolutely sure the equipment is sterile.

Japanese B encephalitis is a viral inflammation of the brain, spread by daytime-biting mosquitoes. It occurs in rural parts of Asia and can be fatal, so you should consider vaccination if you're going to be travelling in such areas, especially during the monsoon. Three jabs, taken over a four-week period (and sometimes followed by a booster a year later), provide protection for up to three years. The course should be completed two weeks before travel to allow time for the vaccine to take effect.

Leishmaniasis is transmitted by sandflies and can be fatal. Although rare, it occurs in parts of Asia, Africa, South America and the Middle East. It can cause skin scarring or various internal infections. No vaccination is available but it can be treated. The best thing is to guard against being bitten in the first place (see p88).

Malaria is transmitted in tropical areas by mosquito bites. As long-haul travel has boomed, so has the incidence of malaria in the UK. Each year at least 2,000 British travellers return having contracted malaria abroad – and some of them die. The number of travellers returning home with malaria increases each year. It's essential to take precautions if visiting an affected area. This includes much of Asia, Africa and South America (and even some places you might not expect, such as parts of Turkey). Having said that, many areas where you might expect to need malaria tablets (e.g. much of Thailand, Malaysia, Indonesia and South Africa) are actually malaria-free, so don't just assume that if you're going somewhere hot and tropical, you must take them. As most malarial prophylactics have some side-effects, you don't want to take them unless you have to. Lariam/mefloquine, in particular, has had much criticism – we know many people who've experienced problems with it (ranging from nightmares to panic attacks to paranoia) – and doctors are now much more cautious in prescribing it.

Which anti-malarial tablets to take will depend on where you're going. Strains of malaria vary in different parts of the world, and mosquitoes in some areas are developing resistance to certain drugs, so always get up-to-the-minute advice from your GP or travel clinic – don't just listen to what your friends say. Some malaria tablets are available over the counter, including chloroquine (Avloclor/Nivaquine) and proguanil (Paludrine) but mefloquine (Lariam), now being prescribed for areas where mosquitoes have become resistant to chloroquine, is available on private prescription only and costs a bomb (around £30 for a box of eight, plus a fee for your doctor for writing a private prescription).

Start taking the tablets, after a meal, a week or two before you reach the malarial area, and follow instructions on how long to continue after you leave (usually a further four weeks).

Always ask your doctor about potential side-effects (which, depending on the tablets, can include hair loss, skin problems, disruption of sleep patterns and nausea) and find out if there are alternatives.

Even anti-malarial drugs aren't 100 per cent infallible – the best protection of all is to avoid being bitten in the first place (see p88). You should be particularly vigilant between dusk and dawn, which is when most malaria-carrying mosquitoes are active, but remember that you can be bitten at any time. However careful you are, there are no guarantees that you won't be bitten so if you fall ill with flu-like symptoms after you've been travelling in a malarial zone (even as long as six months or a year after you left it) contact a doctor and let them know where you've been.

The London School of Hygiene and Tropical Medicine has a recorded telephone information line on malaria medication on 0900 1600 350.

Meningococcal meningitis, found in much of Africa and parts of Asia, Central America and the Middle East, is spread by close contact with an infected person and can be fatal, but is treatable with drugs. Vaccination (one injection) takes two weeks to become effective and gives three to five years' protection.

Natural hazards

Corals and anemones. These can give you a nasty graze, which can become infected, so look out for them. If they are present you may need to wear shoes in the water.

Jellyfish. In Europe these are generally not lethal but can give you a painful sting, so check with the locals before you swim. If you are stung, there's little you can do other than rub the area with dry sand and neutralize the sting by bathing the affected part in vinegar or alcohol. Poisonous jellyfish are found in Australia, parts of Asia and the Pacific; if stung, you need to get medical attention. In Australia during stinger (poisonous box jellyfish) season, make sure you swim only on beaches that have nets to protect bathers.

Sea urchins have sharp spines. If you know they're there, wear shoes when swimming. If you tread on one and get a spine stuck in your foot, remove it as soon as possible, using ointment or olive oil to soften the skin and spine first.

Sharks are many people's big fear but hardly anyone dies from a shark attack – only a couple a year even in Australia. Always heed local advice on when and where it's safe to swim.

Wear flip flops or sandals when you're in the shower or wading in a stream to prevent burrowing thingies getting into your feet.

Snakes are generally more scared of you than you are of them and won't attack unless they feel under threat. You're highly unlikely ever to come across one, but if you're walking in snake territory, keep your feet and legs covered with thick boots and trousers and make plenty of noise as you walk so any nearby snakes are warned in advance. Don't stick your nose into undergrowth or trees. In the unlikely event that you are bitten, keep the limb as still as possible or you'll increase the blood flow. Put a splint or bandage on to help immobilize it and get to a doctor. Try to give a description of the snake so that they know what anti-venom to give you. Don't take aspirin as that will also increase the blood flow. Remove any rings in case of swelling.

Spiders can lurk in all kinds of places (under the toilet seat, in your empty shoes, etc.) but again, most will scuttle a mile from you given the chance and very few are dangerous (though you may feel happier always checking the toilet first and shaking out shoes before you put them on). If bitten, get to a doctor as soon as possible, and, as with snakes, try to give a description of the beast.

Polio (poliomyelitis) is spread via infected food and drink or contact with an infected person. Most of us are immunized against polio as children but you should have a booster (taken orally) if you are travelling to areas where the disease is still found, which means anywhere outside northern and western Europe, North America, Australia and New Zealand. The vaccine (either the full course of three doses or one booster) is effective for ten years.

Prickly heat is a nasty and maddening rash that occurs when your sweat glands are blocked and it can be a problem in high humidity. Guard against it by wearing loose clothing, preferably in natural fibres. If you get prickly heat don't scratch, however desperately itchy you are. Take a cool shower, soothe the skin with calamine lotion, talcum powder or 1 per cent hydro-cortisone cream, and cover up so that you can't scratch.

Rabies occurs in all continents except Australia and Antarctica, though individual countries on other continents are rabies-free or low-risk. A vaccine is available: given as a course of three jabs over 28 days, it gives you two to three years' protection but does not, however, give you total immunity. If you're bitten by a rabid animal, you'll still have to have another two injections. If you don't have pre-exposure jabs, you'll need a course of seven injections over a period of months. (Either way is a huge improvement on the old treatment, which was a horrendous course of needles in the stomach!) Avoid strange animals, however cute and tame they look – and that applies to all mammals, not just dogs. Remember, also, that you don't have to get bitten – even just a lick or a scratch can be enough to infect you. The World Health Organisation claims over 20,000 rabies-related deaths a year in India; it has also been estimated that between 4 and 7 per cent of street dogs in Thailand are infected. If bitten or scratched, wash the wound immediately and put alcohol on it if possible. The most important thing is to get medical help straight away if you think you've been at risk. If treatment is given immediately, the disease can usually be prevented from developing, but once the symptoms of hydrophobia start to show, it's too late and the disease is fatal.

Tetanus is a dangerous disease caused by bacterial spores entering the body through a cut, scratch or other wound. The spores are found all over the world so you should make sure your tetanus protection is up to date wherever you're going. It's particularly important if you're likely to be in remote areas with no access to medical facilities. You were probably vaccinated against tetanus at school, but you will still need a booster dose if you haven't had one in the past ten years. The vaccine (either a full course of three injections at one-month intervals, or one booster) is effective for ten years.

Tick-borne encephalitis is an inflammation of the brain caused by a bite from an infected tick. It can be a problem in forest areas of northern and central Europe, Austria and Scandinavia, especially where there is heavy undergrowth. It's most common in late spring and summer. Make sure you keep well covered up in affected areas and take precautions not to be bitten (see p88). A vaccine is available.

Travel/motion sickness. Whatever form of transport you're using (train is favourite), try to get a seat in the area with least movement – in the middle of the middle decks on a boat, for example (and the larger the boat, the better); in between the wings on a plane. If possible, lie down and close your eyes. Alternatively, keep your eyes focused on something fixed, like the horizon. Sit near the front of a bus or in the front seat of a car, look forward rather than out of the side windows and don't read books or maps. Fresh air helps, so keep the window open.

Avoid eating greasy or rich foods before you travel. Indeed, don't eat or drink too much of anything (even water) as the more you have the sicker you'll feel. Steer clear of alcohol altogether. If you're taking any travel sickness medication, remember that most of them include drowsiness among their side-effects, so you should not drive after taking them. Check the packet to see how far in advance of the journey you need to take them (usually two to four hours); they're unlikely to be much use if you leave it until you start throwing up. You could also try elasticated wrist bands that work on your acupressure points and have no side-effects. Ginger in various forms is also said to be an effective remedy, as are fresh lemons and peppermint tea. (See Chapter 9 for more travel tips.)

Tuberculosis is on the increase worldwide. You were probably immunized against it at school (it's the BCG immunization); if so, you don't need a booster. If not, and if you're planning to spend a month or more in Asia, Africa or Latin America (especially if you're going to be in close contact with the local people), you should consider getting immunized. You should talk to your doctor at least two months before you go because you'll need to have a skin test first to see if you're already immune.

Typhoid is transmitted via contaminated food and water, so is particularly prevalent in countries with poor standards of hygiene. Typhoid jabs used to be particularly unpleasant, with side effects such as headaches, fever, vomiting and diarrhoea (a brief taste of the disease itself). However, the new vaccines don't have the same side-effects. Available as an oral dose or as an injection, they provide one year's or three years' protection respectively and need around ten days to take effect. Typhoid vaccination is recommended in most of Africa, Asia, and Central and South America.

Yellow fever is a viral infection transmitted via bites from insects such as mosquitoes, ticks and flies. It can be fatal. Vaccination may be compulsory for visitors to some African and Latin American countries, where the disease is endemic. Other countries may also insist on proof of vaccination from travellers coming from an infected region. The vaccination (a single jab) must be given at a designated Yellow Fever Vaccination Centre, who will issue an internationally recognized certificate as proof you've had the jab. To allow time for it to take effect, it must also be given at least ten days before you travel – if it isn't, your certificate won't be valid. Immunity lasts for ten years.

REPELLING INSECTS

Diseases such as malaria, dengue and Japanese B encephalitis are spread by insects in tropical climates. Even in cold countries, mozzies and gnats can be a nuisance and give you a nasty bite. So it makes sense to take all precautions to avoid being bitten.

* Use a good-quality insect repellent, both indoors and out. Repellents come in a range of forms: lotions, gels, creams, sprays, sticks and soaps. Recommended makes include Autan, Repel, Jungle Formula and Ultrathon. The most effective repellents are those containing DEET but it's powerful stuff so treat it with respect, especially if it's in a high concentration. Use sparingly, keep it away from the eyes, and avoid it if it causes a skin rash. If you have sensitive skin, repellents without DEET include Alfresco (mail order: 020 8348 6704) and Mosi-guard Natural. Some swear by Avon's Skin-So-Soft bath oil or taking a daily Vitamin B supplement.

* Wear repellent day and night – you can be bitten at any time, not just dusk.

* Your repellent will last a shorter time if you are sweating profusely, in which case wrist or ankle bands impregnated with repellents can be useful. Cotton clothing can be impregnated with DEET and should be kept in a plastic bag when not being worn.

* Mozzie coils are usually widely available as you travel, though good repellent can be hard to find, so it's worth taking a stock with you.

* Try to ensure that your accommodation is mozzie-proof. Look for rooms with insect screens on the windows and check that the screens are intact. If there are holes or gaps, plug them with sticking plaster or similar. Clear your room every evening with a knock-down spray containing pyrethrum. Overnight, you can get protection from burning mosquito coils or using small electrical hot-plates fitted with tablets which vaporize slowly for up to ten hours. These work best in sealed rooms; otherwise, place them upwind. Electrical buzzers have been proven in tests to be totally useless.

* At peak biting times (from dusk to dawn for malarial mosquitoes), wear thick cotton trousers and long-sleeved tops as a barrier against bites (light colours are better than dark).

* Look for rooms with a mozzie net round the bed or carry your own (you can buy them in travel stores and clinics), preferably impregnated with a repellent. An impregnated net will also keep out sandflies, whose bites can cause leishmaniasis. It can sometimes be a problem finding somewhere to fix your own net up, so carry some sticky hooks to use if there aren't any hooks on the wall already. Take care the net is not torn, fill any gaps with cotton wool and tuck it in well all round. Try not to touch nets. If there is no net, a fan blowing over the sleeper can help, as can a heavy cotton sheet. You're also less likely to be bitten in an air-conditioned room.

* Avoid camping by stagnant or slow-moving water as this is where mosquitoes and other insects lay their eggs.

If you are bitten, don't scratch your bites – they'll just get more swollen and inflamed and may become infected with bacteria. Put tiger balm or tea tree oil on as soon as you're bitten. We've also heard that rubbing wet soap on them is effective.

MEDICAL TREATMENT ABROAD

If you're travelling within Europe, get hold of Form E111, a certificate which entitles UK nationals to free or reduced cost emergency medical treatment in other EEA (European Economic Area) countries – namely, EC members, Iceland, Norway and Liechtenstein. You should be aware, though, that it doesn't cover repatriation and is no substitute for a proper insurance policy. You'll find an E111 application form in the Department of Health leaflet T6 *Health Advice for Travellers*, available at health centres, post offices and travel agents or by calling Freefone 0800 555 777.

There are about 30 more countries around the world with which the UK has reciprocal health care agreements that entitle you to emergency medical care. These include Australia, Malta, New Zealand, most ex-Soviet countries, some Caribbean islands and some East European countries. The Department of Health leaflet T6 has full details of what the agreement covers in each one.

For the rest of the world (indeed, most of the world), however, you're on your own – and that includes such popular destinations as the US, India, the Far East, Africa and Latin America – so you must take out full medical insurance if travelling to these areas (see Chapter 7). You get so used to free treatment on the NHS in the UK that it's easy to forget that falling ill or having an accident abroad can end up landing you with a bill for thousands of pounds.

BEFORE YOU GO

Dentist. If you haven't been to the dentist for a while and you plan to be away for a long time, have a check-up a month or so before you leave. You can buy dental emergency kits to take with you, but it's better to get any potential problems sorted out before you go. Dental treatment abroad can be costly and/or risky.

Optician. If you wear glasses or contact lenses, ask your optician to tell you what your prescription is so you can replace them while you're away if they're lost or damaged. If you can afford it, treat yourself to a pair of prescription sunglasses. Take a spare pair of lenses or glasses with you, or buy yourself a cheap pair somewhere like Bangkok or Hong Kong. Even if you usually wear lenses, take glasses with you as a back-up because there are times (on dusty desert roads or at altitude, for example) when wearing lenses can be uncomfortable. You should also take eye drops in case of minor eye infections (fairly common among travellers in hot countries). The big pain about contact lenses is the weight of the solutions you have to carry. If you're going off the beaten track you'll need to take enough to see you through, but if you'll be visiting plenty of big cities along the way you should be able to pick up solutions as you go. Alternatively, you could consider getting disposable lenses.

GP. If you don't already know your blood group, get your GP to test it and find out what you are before you go; it will save time in the event of accidents.

First aid. Consider taking a basic first aid course before you go, especially if you're going to be spending much time away from major population centres and medical facilities. Contact the St John Ambulance Brigade or St Andrew's Ambulance in Scotland for details.

ARE YOU FIT TO TRAVEL?

Consider how fit you are before you embark on anything too ambitious. Trekking through the Himalayas, walking the Inca Trail or rafting down the Colorado River call for a great deal of physical exertion and if you're planning anything active, you should start preparing at least a few months before you go. If you don't already have one, establish a regular exercise routine and work your way up to the trip gradually. Swimming, cycling and other aerobic exercise will boost the efficiency of your heart and lungs and increase your stamina, while weights will help build up strength in your legs and arms.

Even if you're not out there conquering the great outdoors, travelling can be exhausting. Sleepless nights, long journeys, soaring temperatures and humidity, extremes of temperature and altitude, can all take their toll. Some people cope better than others but the better your general fitness, the greater your enjoyment will be.

If you have a medical condition such as angina, asthma, diabetes or epilepsy, carry an identity card or wear a tag giving details and names of any medication you're taking.

WHAT TO TAKE WITH YOU

If there are any regular medicines you need, take a supply of these with you (pack them in your hand luggage in case your baggage goes astray). Your doctor may only be able to prescribe a limited amount so check whether or not they will be available in any of the countries you're going to. Keep a note of their generic names (rather than particular brand names) because they may be sold under different brand names abroad. Some medicines available in the UK may be restricted abroad; if in doubt, check with the relevant embassy or high commission or call the Home Office Drugs Unit on 020 7273 3806. (It may also be the case that any medicines you're given abroad are illegal to bring back into the UK, so if you're carrying anything you're not sure about when you come back home, declare it at customs.)

Make sure all medicines are clearly labelled and keep them in their original containers rather than decanting them into smaller, unmarked ones which may look suspect to customs and border officials. You should also carry a doctor's letter explaining that you require these medicines for personal use (your doctor may charge for writing this). Wrap clear Sellotape round the labels so they don't fade or fall off.

Take a sterile medical kit if you're going to be travelling in countries where hygiene is poor, and needles and other medical equipment are reused. You can get these in travel shops, chemists and from MASTA (see p97). You can buy sterile equipment separately, but ready-made kits will have a selection of the necessary items and will also look less suspicious to customs officials than a few loose syringes and needles in your washbag. Get a doctor's letter explaining that they are for use in case of emergency. If necessary, they should be handed to a doctor or nurse to use.

If you're on the Pill, ask your doctor for an extended prescription so you'll be covered for the time you're away. Remember to take time differences into account when working out when to take your Pill – if you normally take it when you go to bed, you may have to change to breakfast instead. If you do get sick while you're away, remember that it will reduce the effectiveness of the Pill. Take condoms as a back-up.

You should take a mini first-aid kit. Either make up your own or buy a ready-made one and add to it. You should include the following items:

* a broad spectrum antibiotic (ask your doctor's advice on which to take and when to use it)
* anti-diarrhoea remedies (e.g. Imodium)
* antihistamine cream (for bites and stings)
* antiseptic or antiseptic wipes (for cuts and scrapes)
* aspirin or paracetamol (painkiller)
* bandages and safety pins
* dressings
* blister kit (if trekking)
* indigestion tablets
* malaria tablets
* multivitamins
* plasters
* oral rehydration powders (e.g. Dioralyte). In an emergency you can make your own by dissolving 1 level teaspoon of salt and 8 level tablespoons of sugar in 1 litre of safe water.

* sore throat lozenges
* travel-sickness tablets
* eye drops
* some means of water purification
* tiger balm (for insect bites, aches and colds; easy to buy en route)
* tea tree oil (for bites and burns)

If you're prone to cold sores, they can often be triggered off by hot climates, so take some Zovirax or other cold-sore cream. You might also like to consider an antifungal powder as athlete's foot can be a problem in tropical countries.

WHEN YOU'RE AWAY

WATCHING WHAT YOU EAT AND DRINK

The best health precaution you can take when travelling is to keep a careful eye on what you eat and drink. Many diseases, including giardiasis, hepatitis, cholera, typhoid and dysentery, are spread via contaminated food and water, and following these precautions should help safeguard you to some extent.

* Always wash your hands before eating.

* Avoid tap water. Use only bottled water for drinking and even for cleaning teeth. Bottled water is available in most places but check the seal is intact before you buy (if you go for fizzy water you can be absolutely sure it isn't tap water). Don't have ice in drinks (you can cool them by packing ice outside the glass).

* Boiling water kills germs so you're usually OK with hot tea and coffee. There should also be no problem with bottled soft and alcoholic drinks.

* Be wary of salads (which may have been washed in tap water).

* Only drink fruit juice if you're sure it isn't diluted with water.

* Water in rivers, lakes, swimming pools and the sea can also be contaminated so try not to swallow any water when you go swimming.

* If you're vegetarian you should be wary of dishes using pulses or legumes that have been soaked in water and cooked slowly at a low heat – the bacteria may not have been destroyed.

* Yoghurt is generally safe to eat (and eating a little when you first arrive will help accustom your stomach to the local bacteria) but avoid ice cream and other dairy products made from unpasteurized milk.

* Fish and shellfish can be dodgy, especially if eaten raw (e.g. oysters).

* Steer clear of food that has been reheated or kept warm – buffets in particular are a breeding ground for bacteria. Go for food you know has been freshly cooked such as omelettes, piping-hot fried or deep-fried dishes, or something cooked in boiling water, and eat it while it's still hot.

* It's better to have meat well-cooked, even if you normally prefer it rare.

* Avoid uncooked foods and only eat fruits you can peel yourself.

* Don't assume that food in posh hotels will automatically be safe, and avoid dishes that involve a lot of handling to prepare.

* Look at the place you're thinking of eating in – is the food covered or is it swarming with flies? Does it look fresh or has it obviously been sitting around for a while?

WATER PURIFICATION

If you're heading off the beaten track, where bottled water won't be available, make sure you have some means of purifying water, either tablets or tincture or a portable purifier or filter, or a combination. These are some of the pros and cons, but ask the staff in a specialist outdoors shop for the most up-to-date advice.

Tablets are small and light to carry. They're also convenient if you want to purify water in a café, though some (especially the chlorine-based ones) leave an unpleasant taste. If you're using water-purifying tablets follow the instructions closely and bear in mind that you should not take iodine-based tablets for a prolonged period of time.

Alternatively, you can take a filter or a purifier which pumps water through a chemical filter to render it instantly drinkable. These are more thorough than tablets but also more expensive and bulkier to carry.

Boiling water for two to three minutes (longer at altitude) is the most effective way to make it free from infection; if you cool it in a clean, covered container it will stay safe for several days. However, it means you have to carry a cooker and have access to fuel.

HANDLING THE HEAT

It's been said a million times before but we'll say it once again: go easy on the sun. A Health Education Authority survey in the late 1990's found that 75 per cent of women under 25 had suffered sunburn in the previous year, even though 94 per cent knew it could cause skin cancer (where on earth had the other 6 per cent been?). Sunstroke is no joke; neither is skin cancer. And, on the level of pure vanity, do you really want to have that leathery look later in life? Even in the UK, UV rays can damage your skin, and the nearer the equator you go, the stronger those rays are, so the more careful you need to be. Bear in mind also that sun can be reflected off sand, water and snow.

* Don't set straight out for some serious sunbathing the minute you hit a hot climate – work up gradually. The joy of extensive travel is that there's plenty of time for you to build up a golden suntan, so there's no excuse for succumbing to the kind of suntan panic that hits people when they have only one week to go brown.

* Make sure you always protect your skin with a high factor sunscreen (SPF15 at least) or sunblock. If you'll be in and out of the water a lot, make sure to get one that's water resistant. You may already have your own favourite suncare product but, after years of trying different ones, the one we swear by is Clinique's Oil Free Sun Block. You can also buy sunscreens that contain an insect repellent, which will help cut down on the number of bottles you have to lug around. If you're feeling self-conscious about being glaringly white (which marks you out as a beginner) put some fake tan on before you leave.

* Whichever sunscreen you use, reapply it frequently, paying particular attention to sensitive areas like your neck, nose, ears and, if you're lying on the beach, nipples and the soles of your feet.

* Sun lotions are readily available in most places but the choice may be limited so if you have sensitive skin or prefer a certain brand, take enough supplies with you.

* If you're sunbathing, set sensible limits and stick to them: don't 'just give it another 15 minutes' and don't be fooled by hazy or cloudy weather or breezes – you can still burn, and surprisingly quickly. Remember, however bad you think your pasty skin looks, it looks a hell of a lot worse when it's beet-red and peeling.

* Always stay out of the sun between 11 and 3 when it's at its fiercest.

* Follow the Aussie slogan of 'Slip, Slop, Slap': slip on a shirt, slop on the sun lotion, slap on a hat.

* Buy a decent pair of sunglasses (with a UV filter) to protect your eyes.

* Remember that you can burn even in water so if you're going snorkelling wear a T-shirt to protect your back and use waterproof lotion on exposed parts of your body.

* Always drink plenty of fluid in hot climates so that you don't get dehydrated (don't wait until you're thirsty). If you notice that your urine is dark in colour, that means you need to drink more water. Other early warning signs of dehydration include thirst, lethargy, nausea and weakness.

* Make sure you're eating enough salt to compensate for the amount you're losing in sweat.

PACING YOURSELF

Friends can be one of the biggest health hazards on holiday. It may be grossly unfair (OK, it is grossly unfair) but just because your mate can lie all day in the sun without burning doesn't mean you should follow their example. And the fact that your friend has a cast-iron constitution that allows them to feast on shellfish and ice-laden drinks from day one, doesn't mean you can too. Your friends may have no problem swimming out to that little island but if you know you're a weak swimmer don't even think about it. Never feel pressurized to keep pace with others: stay safe and healthy by knowing your own limits and sticking to them.

WHEN YOU COME HOME

Remember that some diseases don't produce symptoms immediately. If you feel unwell or notice unusual symptoms after your return, visit your doctor and explain where you've been travelling.

TRAVEL CLINICS AND ADVICE LINES

British Airways Travel Clinics
There are about 30 BA Travel Clinics around the UK – call the Location Line on 01276 685040 for details of the one nearest you. You can also find the British Airways Travel Clinic Web page on www.british-airways.com/travelqa/fyi/health/health.shtml

Hospital for Tropical Diseases Travel Clinic Healthline
2nd Floor, Mortimer Market Centre, Grafon Street, off Tottenham Court Rd, London WC1
For advice and information call the Travel Clinic's pre-recorded Healthline on 0906 1337733 (calls cost 50p a minute at all times). For appointments only, call the clinic on 020 7388 9600.

Liverpool School of Tropical Medicine
Pembroke Place, Liverpool L3 5QA
0151 708 9393 (pre-travel advice and queries) or 0906 7088807 (recorded travel advice line; calls cost 50 p per minute).

MASTA (Medical Advisory Services for Travellers Abroad)
020 7837 5540.
For detailed advice on health abroad, call the MASTA Travellers Health Line on 0906 8224100. A recorded message talks you through your itinerary, and a Health Brief tailored to your journey is then drawn up and sent by return first class post. It includes any Foreign & Commonwealth Office advice as well as information about immunizations and malaria. The line is open 24 hours a day, seven days a week; calls cost 60p a minute. If you're planning to visit more than six countries, call 01705 553933 first to find out which countries to leave on the answering service. You'll also find MASTA on the Web at www.masta.org

Pro-Choice Traveller is a service offered by high street chemists and some Tesco in-store pharmacies (look for the traveller health information sign in the window). You give them the details of your trip and they give you a personalized advice print-out with current medical recommendations, plus general health tips.

Berkeley Travel Clinic
32 Berkeley Street, London W1X 5FA
020 7629 6233

Birmingham Hartlands Hospital
Tropical and Communicable Diseases Department
45 Bordesley Green East, Bordesley Green, Birmingham B9 5SS
0121 766 6611

Vaccination Clinic
131 Earls Court Road, London SW5 9RH
020 7259 2180

Nomad Travellers' Medical Centre
3–4 Wellington Terrace, Turnpike Lane, London N8 0PX
020 8889 7014

and 40 Bernard Street, Russell Square,
London WC1N 1LJ
020 7833 4114
Travel Health Line: 09068 633414 (60p per minute)

Thomas Cook Vaccination Centre
32 Berkeley Street, London W1X 5FA
020 7629 6233

Trailfinders
194 Kensington High Street, London W8 7RG
020 7938 3999

Leeds Overseas Travellers' Clinic
Leafield Clinic, 109 King Lane, Moortown, Leeds LS17 5BP
0113 305 5223

(See Chapter 16 for addresses of health sites on the Internet.)

USEFUL BOOKS

Travellers' Health ed. Richard Dawood
Oxford University Press

Health Information for Overseas Travel
Department of Health; available from HMSO, 0870 600 5522

Healthy Travel – Bugs, Bites and Bowels Dr Jane Wilson Howarth
Cadogan Books

TEN FOODS YOU DON'T GET AT HOME (USUALLY)

Roasted guinea pig (South America)
Cold fried ants in chocolate sauce (Brazil)
Monkey brains (China)
Bear's liver liqueur (Hong Kong)
Sheep's eyes (Middle East)
Double-boiled deer's penis (China)
Dried antelope (South Africa)
Kangaroo steak (Australia)
Pig's uterus (Vietnam)
Goat's bone stew (Ethiopia)

'I spent six weeks travelling around India and fully expected to lose lots of weight. However, I'm proof that you can travel around India and actually come back fatter! Yes, I got the occasional bout of diarrhoea, but that's inevitable. I'm always very careful about what I eat when I'm travelling, especially at the start of a trip before my body's had a chance to acclimatize. I'm vegetarian, which probably helped in India – some of the meat looked decidedly dodgy and my meat-eating friend certainly got sick more often than I did. Even if you're usually a meat eater, it might be best to become a vegetarian during your stay in India. I was also very wary of anything cloaked in mysterious sauces and tended to go for the drier curries. I was careful with what I drank too, sticking to bottled water and beer most of the time. We ended up in Goa, where the food was absolutely delicious – fabulous fresh seafood and great vegetable sizzlers. We ate anything we liked there and had no problems at all.'

'I got nits really badly in South America. I had waist-length hair and picked up nits from hell. It took months to get rid of them. In Venezuela we stayed in one hotel and I felt something moving in the bottom of the bed, and it was lizards. Other places, we slept in rooms with rats under the beds or in huts where the roofs were covered in tarantulas. You'd wake up in the night with people screaming because a spider had landed on them. If you can pay over £5 or £6 a night for accommodation you can get a nice clean hacienda, but we were on a tight budget and it made a big difference.'

CHAPTER 9

TRANSPORT TIPS

PLANES

Planes are undoubtedly the fastest and most convenient way to get from A to B but they take their toll on you physically, with the combination of changing time zones, lack of sleep, tension, dry cabin air, and cramped conditions. Follow our tips to make sure you reach the other end in the best possible shape.

* Set your watch to the time at your destination the minute your flight takes off, and try to adjust to the new times. If you can fall asleep easily, you'll be fine. If you're having trouble getting to sleep, earplugs and an eyeshade may help. In extreme cases, a sleeping tablet – available on prescription from your doctor – can help. Some doctors may be reluctant to prescribe them, but they should be more understanding if you explain the situation. You need to take them half an hour or so beforehand and the effect lasts for six to eight hours.

* Jet lag can be a problem, particularly if you're flying long distances from west to east. You can feel tired, spaced out and below par, and your body clock will be completely out of sync so that you don't feel like sleeping or eating at the right times. Some experts suggest that it takes a day to recover from each time zone you fly through. So, if you fly from the UK to India, six hours ahead, you'll be affected for six days. It helps if your flight lands in the afternoon local time, so you just have time to relax, settle in and have a meal before you go to bed. Arriving in the morning means you have to struggle through a whole day feeling awful. Different people have different ways of fighting jet lag but there's no guaranteed cure. However, great claims are being made for melatonin supplements, which are only

available on prescription in the UK but can be bought over the counter in the US. Other homeopathic remedies include arnica and camomile tea. The more rested you are, the quicker you'll recover, which is why some people swear by sleeping tablets.

* Don't forget to reconfirm all flights three days in advance or you'll be bumped off if the flight's busy. If you can't speak the language, the hotel or hostel staff may do it for you, or visit the office in person (most airline offices are downtown). You should also double-check that any special meals (vegetarian or kosher, for example) have been ordered.

* If there's a particular part of the plane you want to sit in, most scheduled airlines will accept prebooking of seats on long-haul flights as much as six months ahead, so you don't have to take potluck at the check-in desk. Ask your travel agent to do this for you, then double-check with the airline that the request has gone through.

* A seat next to the window gives you more chance of getting to sleep as you have something to lean against. An aisle seat makes it easy for you to come and go without disturbing anyone else, but isn't good for trying to sleep as people in the inside seats will want to get past. Seats next to the emergency exits are best for legroom. The worst seat to have is a middle seat in the middle block – unless the flight is almost empty, in which case it gives you the chance to stretch out over four seats and get some sleep. Avoid seats near the toilets if you don't want to be constantly disturbed.

* If you want to watch the movie, try not to get the seat right behind the bulkhead where you'll be sitting directly under the screen.

* Always wear loose, comfortable clothes and shoes. Even if you're travelling to or from somewhere hot, take something warm to wear – the air conditioning can be fierce.

* Sucking sweets, chewing gum, yawning or swallowing does help to clear your ears when the pressure changes, especially on take-off and landing. Flying with a cold can be very painful, so take a decongestant shortly before take-off to help.

* Walk round the plane now and again to stop yourself getting stiff, and do regular exercises: stretch your arms and legs, rotate your ankles, roll your shoulders.

* Every travel expert around recommends that you avoid

alcohol when you're flying and there's no doubt that that's the sensible thing to do. But we have to come clean and admit that, for us, one way of coping with the tedium (and, for one of us, the fear) of long-haul flights, is to hit the duty free as soon as the trolley comes round. And if you're setting off on a big adventure, it seems miserable not to take advantage of the free champagne on offer. That said, moderation is, as ever, the key word. Flying is already dehydrating and alcohol makes it worse (which makes jet lag worse) so make sure that you drink plenty of water (still, not sparkling; aim to drink one pint per hour) and fruit juice too. Don't smoke and don't take sleeping tablets if you have had any alcohol.

* Take your own big bottle of water on board, so that you don't have to keep calling the flight attendant or getting up every ten minutes.

* Take an inflatable neck cushion to help you get into a comfortable sleeping position. Eyeshades and earplugs may help too.

* If your ankles and feet tend to swell, take some of the Body Shop's Cooling Leg Gel to soothe them. Removing your shoes and putting your feet in brown paper bags is said to prevent swelling. Avoid fizzy drinks.

* To counteract the dehydrating effects of flying, moisturize your skin throughout the flight. Regular spritzes with a mineral water spray are wonderfully refreshing.

* If you wear contact lenses, the cabin air will dry them out. Remove them for the flight and wear glasses instead. Keep your lens case and solutions in your hand luggage.

* Fear of flying is widespread. If you're a nervous flyer, try to distract yourself by taking a really gripping book with you, listening to your favourite calming music, watching the in-flight movie or listening to the comedy channel. Learn some relaxation or deep breathing techniques before you go and use them on the plane. Sleeping tablets can help, but never mix them with alcohol. You could also try homeopathic remedies such as argent. nit. to calm you, or aconite. Or try pure essential oils: put one drop of lavender and one drop of geranium oil on a tissue and hold it to your nose.

* You know how disgusting airline food can be, so make sure you take some healthy snacks with you, especially if it's going to be a long flight.

* Always remove luggage tags and airport stickers each time you arrive somewhere new – if you leave them on as souvenirs, you run the risk of baggage handlers getting confused and sending your bags on somewhere else.

* Finally, make it easy on yourself by booking in somewhere comfortable for the first couple of days so that you can come round gently (most travel agents will do good deals on accommodation). When you get there, try to take a brisk walk or swim to boost your energy.

TRAINS

Trains have to be the most civilized form of transport. They're also (outside Europe) one of the cheapest and definitely the most fun. You'll meet lots of people and have the chance to see some marvellous countryside and scenes of rural life that you would miss if you travelled by plane.

* When buying a ticket, try to go with a local or someone who knows what they're doing. The system can be confusing, especially if you don't speak the language. You may have to queue at three different windows before you get your ticket. (Or, as we did in Guangzhou, spend three days going to every single window and still not manage to work out how to get one. Travel tip: it's easier to get out of Guangzhou by boat!)

* If people approach you trying to sell you a ticket, be careful. If you can't read or speak the language, it's easy to be palmed off with a ticket that's out of date, or going to a destination other than the one you want.

* Arrive early to make sure you get a seat, and to allow for the inevitable problems in finding out which platform the train is leaving from and if it really is the train you want.

* In most developing countries, people besiege the train at every stop, selling food, drink and fans. We've also been offered slightly more unusual items such as live chickens and caged rats on an Indonesian train. On the Trans-Siberian, we could have snapped up a patchwork leather jacket or fluorescent tracksuit from one of the Chinese traders on board but opted instead for Russian champagne at $2 a bottle.

* Unless you're on the most minimal of budgets, avoid third class – or save it for the shortest of journeys. Carriages are inevitably crowded, uncomfortable, noisy, smelly and dirty, and

it can be harder to keep your belongings safe.

* For information on train times around the world, check out the Thomas Cook rail guides: *Overseas Timetables* (railway, road and shipping services outside Europe) and *European Timetable* (railway and shipping services throughout Europe), both of which are regularly updated.

CARS

* Many travellers, especially in Australia and America, buy a car on arrival and sell it at the end of their trip. When buying a vehicle, don't admit you're a traveller who'll only be around for a couple of months. If the seller thinks you've come to live for a while (and will therefore be able to come back if anything goes wrong), you're less likely to get ripped off. Choose a car that's in good working order and take it for a test drive before you buy. If you're going down under, get hold of a copy of *A Traveller's Guide* from the Australian Tourist Commission (see p216), which contains hints on buying a car in Australia.

* You can also contact hire car companies and ask if they need a car delivered to another city. All you have to pay for is the petrol and accommodation costs en route, which makes it a very reasonable form of transport, especially in America, where petrol is cheap. Find companies listed in the American Yellow Pages under Automobile Transporters and Driveaway Companies. You will need to be over 21, with an International Driving Permit (see below).

* If you get a campervan, it provides you with accommodation and kitchen as well as transport, so the extra you pay out, you'll save on hotels and restaurants. It also gives you the freedom to go where and when you want without worrying if you'll find somewhere to stay. On the down side, though, it means you'll miss out on the backpacker network.

* If you're planning to drive while you're away, make sure you get an International Driving Permit before you go because very few countries will accept your British driving licence alone. They're available from the AA (0990 500 600) and the RAC (0990 722 722) price £4, and are valid for one year. You'll need your passport, a passport photo and your driving licence.

* If you suffer from travel sickness, lemon drops and peppermints are said to help combat nausea. (See also Chapter 8 for more tips.)

(See Chapter 10 for advice on staying safe on the road.)

BOATS

* Seasickness can be a real misery. If you're prone to it, make sure you carry a remedy such as Dramamine. It also helps to remain in the centre of the ship where there is least movement, avoid looking at the water (keep your eyes closed or fix them on the horizon instead) and be very careful about what you eat and drink. Other than that, all you can really do is lie down and pray for sleep. As a general rule, big boats are better than small ones. (See also Chapter 8 for travel sickness tips.)

* In some developing countries boats are potential death traps – the Philippines have a particularly poor reputation. You may not always have a choice, but if possible try for the one that looks most seaworthy and has plenty of lifejackets. (If you can't see any, ask where they are.) If you think the boat is getting dangerously overloaded (they'll try to cram on as many paying passengers as possible) get off and take the next one.

BUSES

Buses are usually the cheapest form of public transport – with good reason. In some countries, they transport not only people, but live animals, bales of hay, pots and pans, enormous bags, beds, turkeys, sacks of oranges – it's amazing how much can be squeezed in...They're also the least reliable mode of transport. Road conditions in many developing countries are appalling and even the word road is an imaginative description of the pothole-filled, muddy track you find yourself juddering along. However, there are many small towns and villages that are only accessible by bus, so you're bound to spend quite a bit of time on them.

* Try to keep hold of your luggage rather than letting someone whip it off you and put it up on the roof. If it's going into a luggage compartment under the bus, wait to see the compartment closed before you get on, and keep an eye on it at stops.

* Avoid catching overnight buses. You don't get to see any of the scenery, there's more risk of theft, and you're unlikely to get any sleep. Also, the mad driving in some countries is even more dangerous on unlit roads.

* If you do have to get a night bus, check whether or not it's a video bus – if you're not careful you could find yourself

subjected to endless action movies at maximum volume. On one unfortunate South American odyssey, we endured three Jean Claude Van Damme films followed by two Arnies – no chance of sleep.

* On overnight trips in Australia, try to get two seats to yourself so that you stand a chance of being able to curl across them and get some sleep. Even if you're travelling with a friend, book yourself into solo seats rather than side by side. If the bus gets too packed, you can always give up the tactic and sit next to each other. (Of course, it would be great to get two seats to yourself wherever you are, but Australia's the only country where we've ever found it likely – everywhere else you're lucky to get one seat to yourself!)

* If you're prone to travel sickness, avoid the back seats. Sit near the front and keep your eyes on the road ahead rather than looking out of the side window. Or put your Walkman on and close your eyes until you reach your destination. Don't read. Eat only lightly and avoid anything greasy. (See also Chapter 8 for travel sickness tips.)

* If you're a nervous passenger, don't take a window seat, especially in India, where the roads are littered with crashed or burnt-out wrecks.

* If you're busing it round Asia, you'll find a lot of your fellow passengers suffer badly from travel sickness (especially on mountainous, twisting roads) and throw up for much of the journey. It's wise to keep the windows shut, however hot you are. Otherwise, when the person in front of you is sick out of the window, it will blow back in your window. We speak from experience on this one (much as we wish we didn't).

HITCHHIKING

* Basics first: never hitch alone, especially if you're a woman. Don't hitch at night. And if you're at all unsure about a driver, turn the lift down and wait for the next one.

* Read guidebooks and ask around to find out if hitching is both accepted and generally safe in the country you're going to. In New Zealand, for example, it's very much the norm and millions of travellers have hitched safely there. In Islamic countries, and parts of South America and the States, it's probably not such a good idea.

* In less developed countries, hitchhikers are often expected to give the driver some money.

* Check that you know the correct sign to make – a thumbs-up sign is considered very rude in some countries. You may have to point down and waggle your hand. Better yet, hold up a sign with your destination written on it.

CYCLING

Cycling is a great way to get to out-of-the-way villages and places that can be hard to reach by public transport. It's also a good way to meet people, who'll be intrigued and probably highly amused by the sight of a foreigner pedalling by on a bike.

* Travel light. Cycling can be hard work, especially in hot climates and hilly countryside. The more you can keep your baggage down, the better. That said, you must have enough tools with you to carry out emergency repairs, and enough clothes to keep you warm if you get stranded in the middle of nowhere.

* Make sure you always have plenty of water with you.

* Remember that you don't have to cycle everywhere. If you fancy a break, you can load your bike on to trains, buses or planes.

* Make sure you have a comfortable saddle, wear padded shorts and take overtrousers for rainy weather.

* Don't do any strenuous cycling in the heat of the day. Take a siesta instead and get back on the bike when the sun is less fierce.

* The Cyclist's Touring Club (CTC), Cotterell House, 69 Meadrow, Godalming, Surrey GU7 3HS (01483 417 217; www.ctc.org.uk), produce information sheets on cycling itineraries worldwide, including the Karakoram Highway, Panama to Tierra del Fuego and London to Tanzania. Membership (£25 a year for over-18s) entitles you to advice on technical problems, specialist insurance, a free bi-monthly magazine and a handbook with accommodation, technical and touring advice. There's also a mail order service.

'My friend and I wanted to travel across the States and decided the cheapest way to do it would be to do a driveaway – you pick up a car in one city and deliver it to another. You don't pay for any rental; all you pay for is the petrol, which is very cheap in America. We went to a driveaway agency in New York (we found the address in our guidebook) and they had about five long-distance driveaways to choose from. Most of them were to Florida but we decided to take one to Seattle instead. We stopped off at a few places en route – Chicago, the badlands of North Dakota, Yellowstone, Banff National Park in Canada and Mount Ridgemore. The trip was cheaper than we expected. Unfortunately when we got to Seattle we parked the car illegally and it was towed away. We had to spend two days trying to find it – and £300 to get it out of the car pound.'

'I was meeting friends in Dali, a small town in Yunnan, South-West China. At the time, the only way to get there was to take a 14-hour bus ride from Kunming along the old Burma Road. My guidebook said the scenery was spectacular, but I didn't see any of it. The road was narrow and twisty with heart-stoppingly sheer drops, and far below us we could see the mangled wreckage of buses that hadn't made it. The buses were ancient – they were sent from Poland when the Poles considered they were no longer usable! Few had glass in the windows, so if it rained you got wet (we wondered why the driver was wearing one of those little umbrella hats when he got on). To make things worse, the Chinese are very bad travellers and suffer from motion sickness. Half of them were sick on the floor; the other half were chomping chicken feet and God knows what else and spitting the bones out on to the floor. The bus halted a few times for a toilet stop, but there was no toilet, just a field where everyone, men and women, squatted down together. I had a great time in Dali, a very lovely little town – but couldn't help thinking about having to endure the trip again at the end of my stay.'

'I adore trains, so for me the highlight of a recent trip round South-East Asia and China was coming home on the Trans-Siberian. We left Beijing at 7.30 on a Wednesday morning and arrived in Moscow the following Monday afternoon. The people on the train were a real mix of personalities and nationalities and we all got on very well. The buffet car was the social centre of the train. Everyone would meet there in the morning and spend the time swapping travel stories, playing cards and drinking cheap Russian champagne. We got off to stretch our legs and take photographs at Ulan Bator, Novosibirsk and Irkutsk. From Moscow, I travelled on by train to Warsaw, then to Berlin and Amsterdam. My aim was to travel from Beijing back to Glasgow by train all the way but I ran out of time in Amsterdam (I had a job to go back to) and had to fly from Amsterdam to Glasgow.

The most interesting thing about the trip, from a personal point of view, was that I was a bit older than other backpackers. But travelling's a great leveller – I was amazed at how easy it was to get on with people of all ages, backgrounds and nationalities and I kept in touch with quite a few people afterwards.'

'If you're in Africa and time is short, you'll find it difficult to get everywhere you want to go by local buses and trains. Remember that Africans are used to a journey taking days rather than hours, so there's no point in getting annoyed if a bus is delayed by a week or so. Travelling on a suspensionless bus is a wonderful way to get a feel for the country and strike up conversations.'

'In America, we got the Green Tortoise bus from Seattle down to San Francisco. The bus is brilliant – it's a hippy coach full of travellers, with seats that convert into beds at night. They stop at a kind of hippy commune camp half-way there and you have a big meal and sit round the campfire with guitars and try to sing and feed the ducks and get stoned. The worst coach journey of my life was Kansas City down to Houston by Greyhound. One little old lady got left behind in the middle of nowhere because the bus driver wouldn't wait for her to come out of the toilet.'

'It's worth bearing in mind how enormous some countries are. If you're going to India, for example, and you only have a few weeks rather than a few months to explore it, it's better to concentrate on one specific area and see it properly rather than spend all your time on trains and buses. I only had four weeks to spend there, so I decided to concentrate on exploring Rajasthan.

'Travel and accommodation are exceptionally expensive in Japan, but you can save money by hitchhiking. It's very safe and easy, provided you have a board with your chosen destination written in English and Japanese. Ask someone where you're staying to write it for you with a marker pen. If you're travelling long distances, make sure you have one board for each major town or city along the way, as drivers won't stop for you if they're not travelling as far as your final destination. If you're planning to travel round by train, buy a rail pass before you leave the UK because it's much cheaper than buying it in Japan. And never blow your nose in public – it's considered the height of rudeness.'

'I hate flying more than anybody else in the entire world. I worry about any flight for weeks beforehand, I cry when we take off, and spend the whole flight tense, nervous and downing as many large gins as I can get my sweaty mitts on. I love travelling, so I know I have to do it, but I try to go overland as much as possible, and to avoid internal flights in Third World countries or on dodgy airlines. However, in Peru my friend persuaded me it would be fine to fly from Arequipa to Cuzco, as the overland alternative would have taken ages. But I could have killed her once we were up in the air and even she, not a nervous flyer, was quite scared as we were buffeted around by strong winds over the Andes – not that I had any time to sympathize because I was too busy screaming! But the most stupid thing of all is that when we were in Cuzco, a couple of mates took us out to see a film one night, which turned out to be *Alive*. You know, the one about the plane crash in the Andes, where the survivors ended up eating the dead bodies. That was it – no more South American flights for me until we had to go home!'

TEN SUREFIRE TOPICS OF CONVERSATION

The British Royal Family
Football (especially Manchester United) (or, if you're in Argentina, dodgy refereeing decisions)
The Beatles/Michael Jackson
Your husband/wife
Your tragic lack of husband/wife
Your age
How much you earn
Why you don't have children
Your curly hair/freckles/big feet
What you think of the country you're travelling in

CHAPTER 10

STAYING SAFE

There has been much debate about the risks faced by young travellers. After all the publicity over recent years about tourist kidnappings and murders in places like Cambodia, Kashmir, Thailand and Australia, potential backpackers and their parents may be feeling a bit nervous. But you have to remember that the reason these events get such a huge amount of publicity is precisely because they are rare occurrences. If they happened every day, you'd hardly hear about them. And when it comes to violent crime, statistics from the Foreign & Commonwealth Office show that the most dangerous destinations for British tourists are the US, South Africa and Spain.

Common sense is your biggest asset when it comes to staying safe abroad. Most crime is opportunistic and by following a few basic rules you lessen the risk of falling prey to thieves or muggers. Remember, though, that no matter how tight a budget you may be on, you're rich compared to most of the people you meet in many countries, so you're an obvious target. Be particularly vigilant during the first week or two as you're at your most vulnerable when you've arrived in a strange country tired, jetlagged and not yet in the travelling groove.

Reassure friends and family by talking through your route, showing how much thought and planning you've put into it, how aware you are of safety concerns, how sensible you're being and what your plans are for keeping in touch.

YOUR BELONGINGS

* Keep a close hold on your daybag (even wearing it on your chest instead of your back to stop anyone snatching it). Never leave it hung over the back of a chair or lying at your feet.

* A bicycle lock is useful for attaching backpacks on to racks on trains and buses.

* Some travellers recommend lining your rucksack with plastic-coated chicken wire to thwart thieves who try to slash it. You can also buy Saklocks, especially designed for rucksack buckles (see Chapter 12).

* Unfortunately, fellow travellers are among the main culprits when it comes to theft. Keep a close eye on your possessions when staying in dorms and campsites and don't leave valuables lying around. Don't leave anything unattended on the beach.

* Keep your camera in your daypack rather than around your neck.

* Budget accommodation often means faulty door locks or windows that don't close properly. To make your room more secure take a padlock with you and add it to the one supplied by the hotel whenever you go out. There are also various security devices available from travel shops that secure the door from within, or a simple door wedge jammed underneath will help. Don't leave belongings within reach or sight of the window. Avoid rooms on the ground floor.

* Don't wear expensive jewellery or pull out wads of cash. Don't take items of jewellery that have sentimental value. The rule is: if you can't bear to lose it, don't take it.

* If you leave any valuables in a hotel safe, first put them in a plastic bag, then wrap it round with tape and write your name across the tape and bag. That way you'll be able to tell instantly if anyone has tampered with it.

* One of the worst things to lose is exposed film with all your precious souvenir photos on it. Rather than carrying it around, consider sending it home (by mail or with a fellow traveller returning to the UK). Alternatively, have it developed en route, then send the prints home (they're too heavy to carry). You can then keep the negatives, or send them home separately (in case one packet goes astray).

* Watches are very nickable, so don't bother taking a valuable one with you. Digital watches are said to be less tempting to thieves.

* It's not unheard-of for seemingly friendly strangers to offer travellers food and drinks, which turn out to be drugged. The

first you know about it is when you wake up hours later to find your belongings gone. Be careful about what you accept from others.

* Thieves love trains. The Foreign & Commonwealth Office advise that anyone travelling on long distance or international train services, particularly in Eastern Europe and Russia, should keep their train carriage door securely locked from the inside by tying it shut with wire or strong cord.

YOUR MONEY

* Don't carry your money in one place – spread it around your body and pack.

* Count money in private.

* A cotton money belt that ties round your waist, or a wallet that hangs round your neck, under your clothes, is the safest place to keep your passport, money and valuables. Some travellers recommend you hide money in an elasticated bandage worn round your thigh.

* For everyday spending, always keep some money in a pocket or purse, so you don't reveal your money belt every time you buy something.

* Avoid getting caught up in crowds – they're heaven for pickpockets.

* Remember that children, however appealing or pitiful they might look, are as likely to make off with your money as adults.

* Don't wear a shoulder bag on the shoulder nearest the road – someone on a bike or in a car could snatch it off.

* Watch as your credit card vouchers are printed and make sure only one copy is taken. Don't let anyone out of sight with your card – they could be running off multiple copies. Always fill in the total box clearly.

* Take care if you decide to change money on the black market (see page 47). You should be particularly alert in big cities.

SCAMS TO LOOK OUT FOR

* Foreigners are an easy target in some countries. Here's how some con artists attempt to part travellers from the cash.

* A policeman asks to see your passport, which you left in your hotel. He says he'll have to fine you. If he's only after a small amount of money, pay up. If he asks for an outrageous sum, say you're happy to pay it but you'll do so only at the police station. Chances are, he'll settle for less and you can go on your way.

* Another trick of policemen is to fine you for an imaginary offence such as walking on the wrong side of the road. The same rule applies as above.

* A taxi or cyclo driver persuades you to hire him for an hour or more but won't agree the fare in advance. 'Whatever you think,' he'll tell you. At the end of your journey, what you think the fare should be and what he thinks it should be are two very different things. You'll have to spend half an hour wrangling about it. Always prearrange the price.

* Having just got off a bus or train, your tuk-tuk/cyclo/cab driver tells you the hotel you want to go to is full, but he can recommend somewhere else that's very clean, not too expensive. He's probably getting a rake-off. Take his advice if you like – but if you insist on being taken to your original destination – it probably won't be full.

* Someone throws or spills something on you. A sympathetic passer-by stops to help. In the confusion, one of the two makes off with your valuables.

* As you're walking down the street, a woman walking past you stumbles and falls. Naturally, you stop to help her get up. Later on, you reach in your bag to find your camera, only to discover the bag has been slashed and all valuables removed by the faller's accomplice.

'While strolling in the park in the middle of Connaught Place in New Delhi, my husband and I were accosted by a young man who offered to shine our shoes. As we were both wearing brown suede hiking boots which would not have looked any the better for being covered in black polish, we politely refused. He persisted, but we still refused. "But your shoes very dirty," the shoeshine wallah said in a final attempt to persuade us. "There's poo on your shoes!" "No there isn't," I replied impatiently, but, as some doubt had been cast, I decided to take a sneaky look. To my horror I discovered that one of my boots was indeed completely covered in a huge cowpat. As a bit of spit and polish wasn't going to help matters, and as I harboured dark suspicions as to just how that offending material had landed on my boot (can holy cows fly?), I scraped off the dung with a stone and stalked off. Imagine my delight then when, on returning to our hotel, I discovered that I'd accidentally put on my husband's boots that morning. Five years later we were again walking in the same park and were highly amused to see a Japanese tourist with a cowpat on one of his trainers vainly trying to assure a shoeshine wallah that he did not want his spanking new Nikes bootblacked.'

'Entering the grounds of Wat Arun in Bangkok, my friend and I were approached by a young man who informed us it was 100 baht (about £2.50) each to enter. He asked us to sign our names in a book and gave us a ticket. We did think it was rather expensive (most temples are free; though you are expected to make a small contribution towards their upkeep) and there was no mention of a fee in our guidebook. A few minutes later, we arrived at the temple proper, where a woman in a booth requested the admission fee – 10 baht each! We told her we had already paid and she simply raised her eyes in an "Oh no, not that old scam again" kind of way and explained that the man was in the business of ripping off tourists and was nothing to do with the temple. We went back to see if we could find him but, of course, he was nowhere to be seen. It was only a few pounds, but we were irritated that we had been caught out so easily and were a bit more canny from then on.'

YOURSELF

* Read about the culture and traditions of the country before you go, so that you don't unwittingly offend people. Check up on any unusual laws that may affect you: in Thailand, for example, you can be arrested for joking about their Royal Family, while defacing the currency is a criminal offence in Kenya and Tanzania.

* If you are warned against travelling in a certain area, take heed. Insurrectionist and guerrilla groups are increasingly targeting tourists as a means of getting their voices heard internationally, so venturing into areas you've been told are high risk isn't a good idea. Keep abreast of the news when you can. Talk to other travellers so you're aware of events that might affect your travel plans. Don't travel into restricted areas (e.g. the Punjab area bordering Pakistan) without a permit.

* Steer clear of public demonstrations – crowd behaviour is unpredictable and things can quickly turn nasty.

* When you're due to arrive in a strange town, study the guidebook before you get there and work out a route to your

prospective accommodation before you set out walking. Try not to stand out as a stranger or make it obvious that you're lost. Reading a map in the middle of a busy street advertises the fact that you're new in town. Walk confidently, as if you know where you're going.

* Try to avoid arriving in a strange city late at night. Always double-check the local arrival times of flights and whether or not there will be facilities open at the airport (toilets, cafés, bureaux de change). If you catch a taxi, make sure it's an official one and don't share it with strangers.

* Learn at least a few words of the local language so that you're not totally at the mercy of others.

* Avoid dark or badly lit streets. Steer clear of deserted beaches, alleys and parks at night.

* Only camp in offical campsites.

* Don't try to fight muggers and thieves, especially if they're wielding weapons. Better to hand over your cash or whatever they want than to resist and risk losing your life.

* Don't go trekking without checking the weather conditions and forecast first. Always make sure someone knows where you're going and when you're expected to arrive or return.

* Don't take part in hazardous sports without first checking that good emergency medical facilities are available. Check that your insurance covers you for accidents (see Chapter 7). Always follow any instructions or safety guidance the experts give you. And remember that activities like whitewater rafting and bungee jumping do involve an element of risk. (See also Water Safety, p121.)

* However bolshie or unpleasant they're being, always keep your patience with officials.

* Be careful about what you photograph. Ask people's permission before snapping them. If you're in a politically sensitive area, don't even think about taking pictures of airfields, barracks, borders, bridges, etc., unless you want to be whisked off on suspicion of spying. Ask permission, too, before taking pictures in religious buildings.

* Remember you're bound not by the laws of the UK, but by the laws of the country you're in, however restrictive or ridiculous you may find them.

* You're more likely to be endangered by local transport than by the local people. Generally speaking, trains are safer than buses (especially overnight buses and especially in India, where the roadsides are littered with overturned vehicles). Any journey in a tuk-tuk or bemo means taking your life in your hands.

* If you change your travel plans, remember to let the folks back home know.

* Be sensitive to the local dress code. If they cover up, so should you, and that applies to men as well as women. Don't wear army-style clothes as they're viewed with suspicion by some officials.

* Don't drink too much alcohol – you're an easy target if you're drunk. Remember that in some countries (e.g. Egypt) you can be arrested for drunkenness. In Islamic countries such as Iran and Saudi Arabia, drinking any form of alcohol (if you can find it!) is a serious offence.

* Consider investing in self-defence classes before you leave.

* *World Wise: Your Passport to Safer Travel* by Mark Hodson and The Suzy Lamplugh Trust (published by Thomas Cook and available at bookshops and Thomas Cook branches) includes general advice on staying safe while abroad, plus a specific guide to more than 200 countries. The up-to-date version of the country guide section is on the Net at www.brookes.ac.uk/worldwise

---

JUST SAY NO!

In many countries, possession of drugs is a very serious crime, so the only sensible advice is to steer clear of them completely. Carrying even a small amount of drugs through customs, especially in countries such as Singapore and Thailand, is a huge risk and punishments can be far more severe than in Europe, regardless of the quantity or type of drugs involved. Never agree to carry someone else's bags through customs or put anything belonging to them in your rucksack. Life imprisonment or the death penalty can be the price you pay. In some places, such as Goa or Ko Pha Ngan, the widespread use of drugs may lull you into a false sense of security, but remember that just because they're readily available doesn't mean they're legal.

ON THE ROAD

Travelling round by car or motorbike can be one of the best ways to see a country and gives you the freedom to get to places you can't reach by public transport. However, according to the Department of Health, traffic accidents are the major cause of death and injury among travellers so make sure you stick to the basic rules of staying safe on the road.

* Don't drink and drive. Check the laws on alcohol limits for drivers in the relevant country. In some places, even one beer will put you over the legal limit.

* Always wear your seatbelt, whether or not it's a legal requirement.

* If you're on a motorbike, always wear a crash helmet – yes, it's great to feel the wind in your hair but it's not worth the risk. Make sure that your arms and legs are well covered – if you hit a pothole and come off your body will need as much protection as possible.

* Keep an eye open for wildlife. According to Richard Dawood's *Travellers' Health*, one survey of motorcycle accidents abroad found that 20 per cent involved collision with an animal.

* Before setting out, check that you're insured and that you're aware of the local driving laws. Take great care driving – conditions and habits differ abroad.

* Don't venture into the outback without plentiful supplies of water, food and spare cans of petrol.

* Keep the car in good condition so there's less risk of a breakdown. You should either have some basic knowledge of car maintenance or travel with someone who has. Make sure you carry tools and a spare tyre. A reflective warning triangle is also compulsory in many countries.

* Always lock car doors when you get out and when you're driving, especially in cities.

* Don't keep valuables on the seat where thieves can reach in through open windows (or smash closed ones). Never leave anything of value in a parked car.

* Keep the petrol tank as full as possible and don't leave it until the needle's in the red zone before stopping to get more.

* If anyone flashes you, or overtakes and signals that there is something wrong with your car and you should pull over, ignore them – it could be a scam. Keep driving until you reach a garage or other safe place to stop.

* When approaching your car, carry the keys in your hand and keep an eye out for other people around you. Check the back seat before you get in.

* If you think you're being followed, drive to a busy area where there are plenty of people around, or to a police station. Do not lead the person back to where you're staying.

* Invest in a really good map, especially if you're going into rural areas.

* Learn the local words for petrol, oil, puncture, etc.

* Look out for specialist publications such as *The Off-Road 4-Wheel-Drive Book* by Jack Jackson (Haynes Group).

WATER SAFETY

Most travellers' accidents are caused through carelessness, especially when it comes to being in and around water. Staying safe is largely a matter of using your common sense.

* Never go swimming or take part in watersports or other activities when you've had too much to drink.

* Don't swim alone or at night. Midnight dips sound fun but are dangerous.

* Don't go swimming after a meal – you're more likely to get cramp.

* Don't dive into water without first checking how deep it is. Many people are paralysed every year as a result of diving into water that's too shallow.

* Before swimming in a strange sea, always check with locals or someone who's been there longer than you. Are there dangerous tides or a fierce undertow you should be aware of? Is the water heavily polluted? Is it stinger season?

* Never swim where there is a red flag flying.

* If using a lilo, take care not to drift out to sea.

* If you go scuba-diving while you're away, make sure you go with an operation that's recognized by a major diving

association such as PADI (Professional Association of Diving Instructors), BSAC (British Sub-Aqua Club) or NAUI (National Association of Underwater Instructors).

WOMEN TRAVELLERS

Outside Western societies, a woman, or women, travelling unaccompanied by a male will generate interest and, in rare cases, harassment. People of both sexes will immediately enquire as to the whereabouts of your husband. If you don't have one, the best defence is to invent one and say he's back at the hotel or you're on your way to meet him. Try saying he's on government business to scare persistent men. Wearing a 'wedding' ring will help, as will carrying a photograph of a friend or relative's child and pretending it's yours. The status of wife and mother is often a form of protection.

Male-dominated Muslim countries, including parts of the Middle East, Africa (especially North Africa), Pakistan and areas of India, can be hard going for women travellers. Some Latin American countries are also rather macho in their approach to Western female travellers. To avoid attracting unwelcome attention:

* Don't wear skimpy shorts or tight skirts. Cover arms and legs when entering a temple or any other place of worship. Watch how much the local women cover up and follow their lead.

* Be careful with make-up – even a small amount is the sign of a 'loose' woman in some countries, as are smoking and drinking alcohol.

* Keep sunglasses on when talking to men and avoid making eye contact – they may construe it as a come-on. In some cultures it is also considered a sign of lack of respect.

* Without being rude, do not be over-friendly – it's open to misinterpretation.

* Walk confidently and speak assertively.

* Avoid night-time travel on your own.

* Don't discuss issues such as divorce, cohabitation or pregnancy with foreigners – your ideas may make you appear 'promiscuous'.

* The best thing to do with 'whispering' and groping is to ignore it. If you start to get worried or scared, tell the person in a loud

voice to leave you alone. Other people, especially women, will chastise him for being rude to a foreigner.

* If you're going camping on safari, or somewhere like northern Canada where there may be bears, try to go when you're not menstruating. Animals can smell your blood, so you need to be particularly cautious when out in the wilderness. You should also avoid wearing perfume and perfumed cosmetics.

ARRESTING MOMENTS

A student survey conducted by STA Travel and British Airways found that 4 per cent of respondents had been arrested while travelling. Reasons included:

* Dancing in the nude in India

* Freeing lizards from a cage in a North African market

* Urinating behind a tree near the Kremlin

* Trying to cross the Swiss border in a caravan which was one inch longer than regulations permit

* Throwing tomatoes in Bulgaria

* Eating cookies on a bus in Texas

'A girlfriend and I spent New Year in Goa. We'd heard about it being a good place for young people, with lots of parties, dancing on the beach, etc. What we hadn't heard is that the main part of tourist Goa is visited by the so-called Bombay Boob Bus, in which Indian men pay to come down from Bombay to see topless Westerners. Apparently they get their money back if they don't see any! They don't actually touch you, or even talk to you, but it was very irritating. Even if you're wearing a swimming costume, they'll sneak up and take your photograph. Because the drinking laws are more relaxed in Goa compared to other parts of India, things could get pretty heavy at night, though. Eventually we had to ask two British guys we met to pretend to be our boyfriends as it was the only way we could get any peace. Be warned!'

'I spent a year travelling on my own in southern and eastern Africa, five months of it in Zimbabwe. If you have only one big adventure during your time in Zimbabwe, make it a canoe trip down the Zambesi. It really is the best way to see wildlife and to be at one with nature. It's important to choose a reputable company with highly trained guides, because they will make or mar the trip. A good guide will open your eyes to all the marvels around you and alert you to the dangers, because a canoe safari is admittedly not without risks. Hippos, crocodiles and submerged tree stumps are the things to look out for. Hippos kill more people than any other mammal in Africa. On an expensive trip, meals will be cooked for you and sundowners served. If you're roughing it, you'll all have to cook in rotation and set up your own camp. Either way, don't expect a toilet in the bush, or anything more than a bucket shower.'

'When you're away, especially in Australia, you get into this thing of doing all the adventure sports, like diving, whitewater rafting, and so on. And it is exciting – but some people do it who aren't really suited to it. They underestimate the risk, and because everyone else is doing it, they get swept along and think they can do everything and everything is safe. But it isn't; there's always a risk, and you have to be sure you can cope. When we went white-water rafting, I was tipped out of the raft, hit a rock and was swept a long way downstream under water. I love water and am a strong swimmer but this was way out of control and it was terrifying. All I could keep thinking was thank God it was me and not my friend, because she's not confident in water and I don't know what would have happened if it had been her. Things like rafting are exhilarating, but no one should forget that they're potentially dangerous.'

'The guy I travelled with in Central America had done a degree in politics and development studies and was very into revolutions. So wherever there was a possibility of a revolution, we had to go there and sit around waiting for one to happen, hanging out in bars with Che Guevara types. We tried to get into the Guyanas but they were having coups and wouldn't let us in. Then we got caught up in a coup in Venezuela – it happens about once a week in the place we were in. I was tear-gassed for the first, and I hope the last, time in my life. It's completely debilitating and it took me about three days to speak normally again. It was very scary. We sought refuge in a nice hotel but people were throwing petrol bombs and bricks at it.'

CHAPTER 11

KEEPING IN TOUCH WITH HOME

Setting off on your big adventure, you may think the last thing you want to do is keep in touch with home – apart from sending postcards from exotic locations to make everyone feel jealous. But it doesn't have to be an emergency or a disaster that propels you towards a telephone. It could be a parent's birthday, for example, or when you know your best friend is due to have a baby, that you feel the urge to get in touch. And, of course, it's important that friends and family can contact you in case of an emergency.

Alternatively, if you're sentimental, you may worry about being so far from people you love for so long and missing them. But global communications are now so sophisticated that there's no reason for you to feel out of touch.

POST

The simplest and cheapest way for you to keep in touch with friends and family back home is to send letters and postcards – they'll never forgive you if you don't. Don't feel you have to write a six-page letter every week, though, or it can start to feel like a chore. Quick postcards are just as good to reassure your family that everything's going well.

Don't take your address book with you because it would be a disaster if you lost it. Copy the addresses out into a notebook instead, or take photocopies of the pages.

It's also easy for friends and family to send letters and cards to you while you're away, even if you have no fixed address, using Poste Restante or American Express. Poste Restante is an international service that is available in all the main post offices in most of the world. Ask people to address mail as follows: your name (surname should come first, in capitals and underlined), Poste Restante, Central Post Office, Bangkok (or wherever you're staying). The central post office will then hold it until your arrival (there's usually a time limit of one or two months, but some hold mail much longer). There's usually no fee. When you go to collect mail, take along proof of your identity. Either a clerk will check if there's anything for you, or you'll be handed a box of letters or a list and allowed to check for yourself. Remember to look under your first name as well as your surname because letters can easily be misfiled. In the USA, the words Poste Restante should be replaced with General Delivery, and in South America with Lista de Correos, but it's the same system.

Type up a list of your destinations and approximate dates you'll be there and copy it to your friends and family. Drum into everyone the fact that mail can take weeks to reach its destination overseas and it's really not much use leaving it until three days before your birthday to post your cards to Bali.

If you have an American Express card or are carrying AmEx traveller's cheques, mail can be sent to you at any AmEx office (you'll find them all over the world) and held until you collect it. This is sometimes more efficient and the offices are generally less chaotic than most main post offices. Ask AmEx for an up-to-date list of their branches abroad before you go. Speaking from experience, it can be extremely frustrating to turn up at a branch only to find it has moved. Be warned that most AmEx branches will only accept normal letter-size envelopes and won't take parcels. Call AmEx on 020 7930 4411 for details.

If you're planning to stay in one place for a minimum of one month and know your address, the Royal Mail will redirect your mail anywhere in the world. Costs are £12 for one month, £26 for three months and £60 for a year. You can get an application form at any post office or telephone 0345 777 888 to order a form or make a credit card payment. If you're going away for less than two months, ask the post office about its Keepsafe service, which holds your mail for you, so that envelopes don't pile up behind your letter box advertising the fact that you're not around. Cost for up to two weeks is £5; for two months, it's £15. You can contact Royal Mail Customer Services on 0345 740 740.

If you want to send small gifts home (or send back guidebooks or clothes that you no longer need) surface mail is cheap and reliable, if slow. If you're staying away for a while, the fact that packages take up to three months to reach Europe shouldn't be a problem. Outside post offices in rural areas, there's very often a person who will take your parcel and wrap it up for you to comply with the local regulations, using lots of paper and intricately tied string, all finished off with a splendid seal. All you have to do then is get it weighed and attach your customs declaration form, stating exactly what you're sending and how much it's worth.

PHONE AND FAX

Some people believe the easiest (and cheapest) way to stay in touch is to ring home and reverse the charges. However, if parents and friends are unwilling, or unable, to pay for your calls, you can take advantage of one of the increasing number of phone cards now available for travellers.

Most of them work on more or less the same principle. You are given a card, an account number and a PIN number which can be used in most countries. Each country will have a Freefone number which will connect you to an English answering service. All you have to do then is tap in your account number and PIN number, followed by the telephone number of whoever you're dialling. BT Chargecards allow you to specify which telephone numbers (up to nine) can be dialled using the card, so it's no use to anyone else if lost or stolen. Calls can be made from private telephones, telephone boxes and most hotel phones. (Some hotels have cottoned on to this, however, and will add a few dollars' charge for using your card.)

The cost of calls depends on your card and where you're calling from. Some companies charge by the minute (so if your call lasts two minutes and seven seconds, you'll be charged for three minutes); others charge by the second. If you think you're going to be making lots of telephone calls, ring all the numbers given below and compare prices.

Different companies have different methods of payment. With BT and Mercury, charges can be put on to your normal home telephone bill (or that of your parents!). Interglobe, World Telecom, Sprint and AT&T insist that you pay on a previously authorized credit card account. VisaPhone calls are charged to your credit card.

CONTACT NUMBERS

AT&T WorldPlus Service
020 7880 6500

BT Chargecard
0800 345144; www.chargecard.bt.com/consumer/index.htm

Global One Calling Card
0800 289751

Interglobe Phonecard
020 7972 0800

Mercury Calling Card
0500 100505

World Telecom Global Calling Card
020 7384 5000

VisaPhone
details from card issuer

Don't promise anyone that you'll ring home at specific times, i.e. every second Friday, or the last day of every month. Chances are you'll find yourself paddling up the Orinoco that Friday, or on a bus in rural India, a hundred miles away from the nearest town. If you can't get to a phone, the person waiting for your call will worry that something's happened to you. Explain that you'll ring when you can and that it probably won't be frequently.

Airports and hotels often now have Business Centres from where you can send a fax. This is useful if you're in a different time zone and don't want to disturb the person at the other end. It's also cheaper than telephoning, but watch out for hotel surcharges. Ask the cost before you send anything.

EMAIL

Email has made it easier than ever to stay in touch with home and setting yourself up with a personal email address is very simple to organize. You don't have to have your own computer; as long as you can get access to any computer connected to the Internet (e.g. in cybercafés, libraries, hostels, Internet kiosks, airports) you're laughing.

Lots of companies offer email services but two of the most popular with backpackers (both free) are Hotmail (www.hotmail.com) and Yahoo! Mail (www.yahoo.com). Just visit their websites and register, then, wherever you are in the world, you can log in your name and password and collect mail from any computer linked to the Internet. No more worries about mail being thrown away if you don't get to the post office in time, or missing it if you leave early. Also check out www.totallyfreestuff.com/email for more free email suppliers.

CYBERCAFÉS

Cybercafés are springing up all over the place. Find them in *Cybercafés: A Worldwide Guide for Travelers* by cyberkath@traveltales.com (Ten Speed Press)

You can also find a list of cybercafés around the world at www.netcafeguide.com. Most will help out if you're new to the Net. Some will even scan in photos so you can send some holiday pics home.

VOICEMAIL

Voicemail is another useful service. It's a system whereby you are given a personal phone number on which you can leave and retrieve messages at any time of the day or night and from any touchtone telephone in the world. Friends and family at home can call you up, hear the latest message you've left telling them where you are and what you're up to, and leave their own message in return. Some also accept fax messages.

COMMUNICATIONS CONTACTS

Various companies offer communications services, but they change all the time, so check travel magazines for details. One of the latest services is Lonely Planets' eKno, which allows you to upload your important documents, visas, passport, tickets, phone numbers etc onto a secure website. It also offers free email and cheap phone cards and voicemail. For details, visit www.ekno.lonelyplanet.com

THE MEDIA

The BBC World Service, Voice of America and Australia Today are the three main international broadcasting stations that can be picked up on shortwave radios to keep you in touch with the wider world. *Worldwide*, a monthly magazine published by the BBC, gives listings.

CHAPTER 12

GOOD KIT GUIDE

RUCKSACK/BACKPACK

Your choice of rucksack is vital – it's your key piece of equipment. You're going to be inseparable from it for months, maybe years, to come, and you'll be carrying it for hours at a time, sitting on it, stuffing it into bus holds and on to train luggage racks, scrabbling through it...If you choose one that's uncomfortable to carry, fiddly to use or too flimsy to cope, you'll be cursing it all the way.

Don't cut corners on this one. It's worth investing in a high-quality pack that's durable and hard-wearing. Good names to look out for include Lowe Alpine, Berghaus, Karrimor and The North Face. Make sure that the straps and zips are sturdy (they'll be taking a battering) and check that the pack has a hip strap and chest strap, which help take the weight off your shoulders and distribute it more evenly. The pack should sit high on your shoulders, not slumped down on your lower back. Compression straps that will reduce the size of the pack when it's not full are useful as they make the pack neater and less bulky, and help relieve the strain on zips and seams.

Try on several packs for size and comfort; they all vary in fit and size. If possible, put something in the pack to weigh it down so that you get a more representative idea of how it will feel. Ask the sales assistant to adjust the frame so that it's properly fitted to your body. The hip belt should sit snugly on your hip bone; the shoulder straps should curve round the shoulders (not sit above them). Watch carefully as it's done (write the instructions down if you don't get any given to you) so that you'll know how to adjust it yourself if necessary.

Don't buy an enormous pack. Remember, you have to carry it

around and, if you have the space, it's terribly tempting to fill it. Rucksack capacity is measured in litres and most packs are between 55 and 100 litres. The averagely built man or woman going away for a year shouldn't look at anything bigger than 65 litres. If you're small, go for something below that. Even for a bloke, 75 litres would be pushing it. As a general rule of thumb, it's recommended that you carry no more than one-third of your body weight. If you're going to be camping and will be carrying a tent, sleeping bag, mat and cooking utensils, you'll obviously need more space than you will if you're going to be staying in hostels and hotels all the way (as many do).

If you're going to be doing a lot of trekking or will be carrying your pack for long periods, you should go for a conventional framed backpack. Some come with fixed back systems; some with adjustable ones. If you can find a fixed back system that happens to fit you, it will be stronger and leave less room for things to go wrong. Otherwise, go for one with an adjustable back system and adjust it to fit your frame (this type is also useful if you ever want to lend your rucksack to anyone else later or sell it on). Special 'ladies' packs are available, with a shorter back. You may find some packs have an indication on the label as to what they're suitable for, e.g. Inter-Railing or adventure backpacking.

It's useful to get a rucksack with two separate compartments rather than one big one. It makes it easier to find things or means you can divide them into wet and dry, clean and dirty, etc. Or you can keep your sleeping bag in the bottom compartment. (It's always best to keep as much as possible inside your pack rather than strapped to the outside – that way it's less likely to be damaged or stolen.) Side pockets are useful but can also get in the way. Once your rucksack is fully loaded, you may find you can't fit through doors, onto trains and buses without a real struggle.

If your trip doesn't involve much trekking, you may decide to go for one of the increasingly popular convertible rucksacks or travelpacks instead, which is what we both use and prefer. A travelpack zips around the front and sides like a suitcase; it has comfortable padded frames and straps like normal rucksacks but, if necessary, the straps can be zipped away behind a cover so that it turns into a soft suitcase, which stops the straps getting caught in luggage carousels and looks smarter if you're checking into somewhere a bit upmarket or going through tricky border posts. One of the biggest advantages is that it's much easier to find things in a travelpack than in a conventional rucksack. Some travelpacks come with zip-off daypacks attached but when zipped on full they make your backpack very bulky and are tempting to thieves. You're probably better off just getting a separate daypack.

You can buy a special big bag to put your rucksack into for protection when travelling. It keeps all the buckles and straps tucked away and also provides extra security (price around £15–£30). When not in use, it folds up small. There are also bags that will cover up your pack but allow the shoulder and waist straps to be threaded through. These protect against wear and tear, keep out dust, dirt and water, and provide an extra barrier for thieves – and if you're trekking through the Borneo jungle, they will stop straps snagging on trees and creepers (prices vary according to your rucksack specifications but are around £25). Alternatively, some people just wrap their packs in an extra strong bin liner or old sack.

Most packs have waterproof fabric but you can't make a pack wholly waterproof. Water tends to come in through stitching and zips. The bags mentioned above can help keep things dry, as can a rucksack liner (you can buy cheap plastic ones for a couple of pounds; more durable nylon liners are around £10–£15). Or you can just make sure to pack everything in plastic bags.

Prices for backpacks start at around £60 and go up to £225, but you should expect to spend about £120 for a pack to take you on a year-long trip. Some packs come with a standard guarantee (which is basically your statutory rights); others may have a lifetime guarantee (but that applies only to you – if you sell it on to someone else the guarantee is negated).

You should also ensure that you can lock your bag. Look out for double zips that can be padlocked together, and when you're buying a luggage padlock, go for one with a combination lock (around £7) rather than a key (too easy to lose). You can also buy devices called Saklocks, which are specially designed to fit rucksack buckles and stop people just clicking them open (around £7.50 for a pack of two locks) or the new metal Universal Saklock (around £11).

DAYPACK

You'll also need a daypack, a mini rucksack in which to carry the day-to-day essentials: camera, water bottle, guidebook, etc. Always keep a tight hold on your daybag – they're eminently nickable and are best carried in front of you rather than slung over your shoulder or on your back. Expect to pay around £25–£35 for a sturdy one, though prices range from around £15–£70. A small pack (say, 20 to 25 litres) would be OK for most travellers but if you plan to go on any short treks (say, three to four days on the Inca Trail), leaving your main pack behind, you might consider getting a bigger daypack.

SLEEPING BAG

Whether or not you think it's worth lugging a sleeping bag around depends on where you're going and when. If you're travelling through the Far East in the dry season, for example, you'll never take it out of its bag. The disadvantage of taking one is the weight and the amount of space it takes up. That said, it can be immensely comforting if you have to rough it for example, sleeping out in the desert where temperatures can plummet at night, or if you're doing overnight bus or train journeys where no bedding is provided. If you decide to go on a trek or organized tour while you're away, there are companies that hire out tents and sleeping bags.

Sleeping bags can be filled either with down or with synthetic material and each has its advantages and disadvantages. Down is one of the best insulating materials available and provides maximum warmth for minimum weight and bulk. High-quality down bags are unbeatable on insulation, are light and will pack up small. However, it's a problem if they get wet. Good synthetic bags, on the other hand, are catching up on down all the time. They're a bit heavier but also cheaper and are not such a problem if they get wet, which is useful if you're travelling in very humid or rainy places – and they'll dry faster.

It's important to keep your bag dry all the time, especially if it's down-filled, so make sure it's well protected in a waterproof bag. Hang it out to air when you get a chance and when storing it for long periods, take it out of the stuff sac and keep it loosely folded, somewhere dry. If squeezed into its sac it will lose its 'loft', the ability to trap air, which is what keeps you warm. If well cared for, a down bag may be good for 15 to 20 years' regular use; a synthetic bag for five to six years.

The type of sleeping bag you buy depends on where and when you're going and you should consult the staff of specialist shops for their advice. Bags come with a 'seasons' rating: 1-season (suitable for summer use); 2-season (summer/spring); 3-season (spring/autumn); 4-season (winter); 5-season (for serious polar explorers!). Remember that it's usually better to be too warm than too cold, as if you're too hot you can just unzip the bag, but if you're too cold you'll have a miserable night. Tapered, 'mummy'-shaped bags keep you warmer but can feel a bit claustrophobic, especially if you're a restless sleeper. You can even find special women's sleeping bags, which are shorter (why carry extra length you don't need?), slightly differently shaped, and come with extra lining at the bottom of the bag for cold feet.

Most travellers want something that's small, light, warm, and not too expensive – which can be tricky. As a general rule, small and light means high-tech materials and therefore a bigger price tag. And if a bag is small and light it's hard for it to be as warm as a bigger bag. Down bags are a good investment if you're a serious hiker and camper. However, synthetic bags are much cheaper and perfectly adequate for most backpackers. Two ranges of bags that would fit the bill for most travellers are the Snugpak Softie and Ajungilak Kompakt ranges. The Softie 3 weighs 750g and costs around £65; the Kompakt Ultra weighs 750g and costs around £80.

It's a good idea to use a sleeping bag liner as this will keep the bag cleaner and is much more easily washed than the bag itself. It also adds a bit of extra warmth, or, on hot nights, can be used on its own, like a sheet sleeping bag. If you've got a mummy-shaped bag, remember to get a mummy-shaped liner, too.

If you already have a bag and can't afford to splash out on a new one, you can buy compression bags (stuff sacks) or harnesses that can reduce the bulk of your bag by up to 40 per cent.

SHEET SLEEPING BAG

This is an essential. If you're travelling somewhere hot, this will probably be all you need to sleep in. If you're staying in budget hotels where the sheets are less than pristine, it's preferable to have your own, and some youth hostels insist that all travellers use a sheet sleeping bag. They cost around £10–£12 or, if you want to splash out, you can buy a silk version for around £35.

SLEEPING MAT

This is probably best left at home unless you're doing a lot of camping out – but if you are camping out, you'll need something to protect you from the cold ground. A sleeping bag is only as good as the insulation beneath it and a sleeping mat has a big effect on how warm you are at night. Foam rolls are cheap (from around £6) but big and bulky to carry. An increasingly popular choice now is a Therm-a-rest self-inflating mat. They're a bit heavier than a foam mat (and, at £60–£65, pricier) but they pack up smaller. They also come in different lengths so if you want to save a bit of weight and space you can get a three-quarter-length one.

TENT

A lightweight tent can be useful in Europe, where accommodation is often expensive, or in places like Australia and Canada, where it allows you to go off the beaten track. However, many travellers, especially in Asia, will probably find a tent unnecessary. It means extra weight and less space, and cheap hotels and hostels can usually be easily found.

Don't buy a tent without putting it up first to see how it works and how simple (or otherwise!) it is to do. Would you be able to do it in the dark? Would it go up quickly in the rain or when your hands are frozen? Can you do it on your own or does it need someone to help you? Is there enough room between the inner tent and flysheet to store your backpack? A-frames, the traditional triangular tents, are fairly stable and reliable but can be bulky to carry. Dome tents and tunnel tents are more roomy than traditional tents, but have lower wind resistance which can be a problem on exposed mountainsides, for example. Geodesic tents are stronger, but probably more than the average backpacker needs. If you're going to be camping in malarial areas, make sure the tent has a mosquito net door.

For travel in hot countries, you'll probably be able to buy something fairly cheap. A basic dome tent, suitable for late spring/summer use, costs around £60–£70. Otherwise, you're looking at upwards of £200.

Once you've bought a tent, practise putting it up and taking it down a few times before you go away. If you're travelling with a friend, split up bits of the tent between you – one can carry the tent, the other the pegs and poles. Try not to pack a tent when it's wet, and always brush off dirt and leaves before you roll it up.

CAMPING GEAR

Most people don't really need to carry stoves and pans around, but if you're planning to do a lot of trekking or camping (outside organized trips), it might be worth investing in some cooking equipment. Bear in mind that some travellers have had stoves confiscated by customs, there's not a lot you can do about it, though some have recommended dismantling them to pack.

Check out what kinds of fuel are going to be available in the countries you're going to. Things like Camping Gaz are widely available in Europe and the US but in developing countries you're more likely to find paraffin and petrol. Gas stoves start at around £20–£30; multi-fuel stoves that can run on different fuels (e.g. petrol, Coleman fuel, paraffin) start at around £60. As a general rule, the more fuels they burn, the more expensive they are. Check airline regulations before trying to take any form of fuel on board. Most airlines ban all types of fuel in both hand and hold luggage.

When it comes to pans, aluminium is lighter and conducts the heat better; stainless steel is heavier and doesn't conduct heat as well, but there's no risk of Alzheimers (which has been linked to the use of aluminium). Best bet is probably to go for aluminium pans with stainless steel liners.

WATER BOTTLE

Water bottles come in plastic and metal. Plastic is cheaper but may leak if not stored upright and can give the water a plastic taste. Metal is stronger and doesn't give an unpleasant taste. Sigg aluminium bottles (from £9) are coated inside and the coating won't crack if you drop or dent the bottle. Nalgene Outdoor Products produce unbreakable plastic bottles (from £6) that have a liquid measure on the side (useful for purifying water), are guaranteed leakproof and can withstand extreme temperatures (so you could even use them as hot water bottles!).

Conventional water bottles take up room even if they're empty but if space is at a premium you can buy collapsible water bottles that squeeze up small when not in use. A Platypus Collapsible costs around £3 for a 1-litre, reusable bottle.

The best size of water bottle to buy is 1 litre, because most chemical water purification works on a 1-litre basis. (See page 93 for tips on water purification.)

MOSQUITO NETS

Mozzie nets are essential if you're travelling in malarial areas. Many hotels will already have them over the beds, but you should carry your own just in case.

Look for a net that's been impregnated with Permethrin. As well as being an added insect deterrent, the impregnation allows the mesh to be wider, which gives a better flow of air through the net and makes it less hot and humid to sleep in. (If the net isn't impregnated, the mesh has to be smaller to keep out sandflies and other insects, which makes it stuffy.) The Permethrin will break down eventually (through a combination of exposure to light and oil from your hands), so if you're travelling a lot and putting your net up and down every day, you'll need to reimpregnate it about every six weeks. (You can buy reimpregnating kits for around £5.) When it's not being used, keep it in its bag.

Nets come in both single and double sizes, and in a variety of shapes. If you're carrying it round, you'll need one that's compact and lightweight. Prices for these start at around £20–£25 for a single.

You won't always find hooks to hang your net on, so some travellers carry their own sticky plastic hooks to use if necessary. Alternatively, Travellers Gaffa Tape (about £3 a roll) can be used to stick your net to the wall – it also has a host of other uses, from sealing tears in rucksacks and jackets to keeping doors closed.

BOOTS/SHOES

Many people find that trainers or walking shoes are perfectly adequate for their trip, so if you've already got a pair and are on a strict budget, stick with those. The only problem is that they're not waterproof.

However, if you know you're going to be doing a lot of serious trekking, invest in a good pair of hiking boots. At one time, these were always leather but now there are fabric boots too. Fabric boots are lighter and cooler to walk in, can be waterproof and are suitable for most travellers. Leather boots are not necessary unless you're planning lots of hill walking and scrambling. Whichever type you go for, they need to be comfortable, provide good support to feet and ankles, cushion the feet from rough ground and keep them warm and dry. When trying boots on wear a pair of thick walking socks. For both leather and fabric boots you can pay anything from around £40–£150 but many are between £60–£90.

Whether you take boots or trainers, make sure you break them in before you go, rather than waiting until you hit the Inca Trail or Milford Track – you don't want to end up with blisters and bruises on the first day. Do a few trial hikes in them. Leather boots will need much more breaking in than fabric. Avoid Gore-Tex boots in very hot, humid or wet conditions (in the jungle, for instance) because they'll take ages to dry out; canvas jungle boots are better. Keep your toenails short to avoid bruising the toes; and after each day's walking, wash and dry your feet thoroughly and give them some fresh air.

Sports sandals or performance sandals are also extremely useful. Basic models are around £30, but higher range models, which are suitable for pretty serious walking, come in at around £40–£70. It may seem pricey but it's worth it – our Tevas are the most comfortable things we've had on our feet. (If you have small feet, it's worth checking out the children's department as the same model can cost up to £20 less.)

OUTDOOR CLOTHING

Fleeces are lighter than wool jumpers and just as warm. They are also easy to wash and quick to dry and, because they absorb so little water, can keep you warm even when wet. Polartec is a popular and effective fleece that comes in different weights; prices start at around £50–£60. An alternative is a lightweight down jacket, which will pack up small, but is more expensive at over £100.

Even in hot countries, it's worth having a lightweight waterproof, preferably one that's breathable. These start at around £30. However, if you're looking for something that will protect you from wind, rain and cold, the price rises to £150 and over (up to £300). Reliable brands include Berghaus, The North Face, Lowe Alpine, Sprayway and Phoenix, but the array of fabrics and fibres on offer is baffling and ever-changing and prices vary greatly. They're getting lighter and more efficient all the time, and the best outdoor clothing for you will depend on exactly what you'll be doing while you're away. It's best to go to an outdoor activity shop and ask for specific advice on the most suitable type for your trip.

BUMBAG

Bumbags are useful for keeping essential items to hand when you're out in the evening, or don't want to be encumbered by a pack. They should be big enough to take sunglasses, lip salve, sunblock, tissues, etc. but don't put all your cash or credit cards in them – valuables should still be kept in your money belt (see below). It's safer to carry the pouch over your stomach than at your back. Costs vary, but there are plenty at around £10–£15. You can also buy Velcro-fastening wristband purses for times when even a bumbag is more than you want to carry.

MONEY BELTS

This is one of the essential items. It's a pain to wear but by far the best way to keep your passport, money, credit cards and other valuables safe. Money belts cost £5–£10. Wear them under your clothes.

You can also buy normal-looking belts, either fabric or leather, with a zip sewn in, in which you can keep an emergency stash of cash; a canvas one costs around £15. Or you could sew pockets in the lining of your clothes.

SECURITY GADGETS

If you're worried about staying in rooms with dodgy locks, there are gadgets to secure doors and prevent them being opened when you're in the room, e.g. the Doorguard or Personal Door Lock (around £6–£8). Or some travellers recommend taking a simple door wedge to wedge under the door.

TORCH

An absolute essential – for finding your way home along pitch-black lanes and beaches, for lighting things up when the inevitable power cuts happen, and finding a toilet spot in the middle of the bush at night. The torch should be small but with a large enough beam to be useful and should also take a common size of battery (AA or AAA are both pretty widely available, especially the former). It should also be water-resistant, strong enough to cope with knocks and bangs, and should have a clip so you can attach it to your clothes and are less likely to lose it. Maglites, which come in several different sizes, are our favourite hand torches and carry a lifetime guarantee. The Mini-Maglite comes, confusingly, in three different sizes; most popular is the one using two AA batteries, which costs around £16–£19; the smaller one, which takes two AAA batteries, costs around £14. One of the useful features of a Maglite is the fact that the head can be completely unscrewed and used as a base on the other end, so the torch becomes a free-standing light.

We're also very taken by head torches. They may look silly but they can be really useful if you're doing something where you need to keep both hands free, like cooking, erecting a tent, mending a car or writing postcards. The Petzl Zoom head torch costs around £25.

Always keep your torch by your side at night, so that you

don't have to scrabble round trying to find it. And remember to take a spare bulb or two with you because you probably won't be able to buy them when you're away.

PENKNIFE

Another absolute essential, wherever you're going. There are lots of makes around but, like most travellers, we swear by our Swiss Army knives. Look for one that includes a corkscrew, bottle opener and scissors as well as the usual blades. Popular models include the Huntsman, at around £24–£26.

CAMERA

Most people like to take a camera so they can record all the sights and faces of the big trip. But cameras are eminently nickable, so you'll have to keep an eye on it at all times.

If you're a real enthusiast, you'll probably want to take a selection of lenses and other paraphernalia, but for most people an automatic compact camera is perfectly adequate and takes up much less space. When you're buying a camera, weight and size are factors to bear in mind. Is it so heavy you'll get fed up lugging it everywhere? Is it small enough to fit in your pocket or bumbag? If you can afford it, go for a camera with a zoom lens. This is particularly useful on safaris or if visiting hill tribes, when you can't always get as close to your subject as you'd like.

If you buy a new camera, shoot a trial roll of film and get it developed before you go, so that you're sure you know how to operate it properly. Take the instruction leaflet with you if you think you'll forget how to rewind, use the timer, etc. Keep your camera well wrapped up at all times – dust and moisture will do it no good at all.

You might also consider taking a single-use wide angle or waterproof camera with you, if you're going somewhere with great scenic vistas or want to record your scuba-diving experience.

Don't worry too much about your film going through airport X-ray machines – most of them are now film-safe. However, if you're entering or leaving a country where the scanning equipment is very old, ask to take the film through by hand. Don't carry exposed film around in hot climates for too long – either process it locally if you're somewhere with good facilities, or post it home.

EQUIPMENT STOCKISTS

There's no shortage of shops selling a wide selection of backpacks, tents, sleeping bags and every little thing a traveller could possibly need. Prices can vary quite a bit, so it's always worth shopping around before you buy. You'll find branches of Blacks and YHA Adventure Shops around the country, but if you don't have a good shop near you, many of the companies listed below offer a mail order service; call them for details.

Blacks have branches in 36 cities nationwide; ring 0191 518 2002 or visit www.blacks.co.uk to find the one nearest you. You can also join their Information Service, which will keep you informed of special sales and offers.

Call of the Wild
21 Station Street, Keswick, Cumbria CA12 5TL
017687 71014

Cotswold have branches in Betws-y-Coed, Glasgow, Harrogate, Kingston-upon-Thames, London (Shepherds Bush), Manchester, Reading, St Albans, South Cerney (near Cirencester), and Southampton.
Call 01285 643434 for a catalogue or to find your nearest branch.
www.cotswold-outdoor.co.uk

Ellis Brigham have branches in Aviemore, Bristol, Capel Curig, Chester, Fort William, Liverpool, London, Manchester, Rossendale and Tamworth.
Call 020 7240 9577 for a catalogue.

Field & Trek have shops in Ambleside, Brentwood, Bromley, Canterbury, Chelmsford, Chester, Croydon, Gloucester, Guildford, London and Slough.
01277 233122

Karrimor International
Petre Road, Clayton-le-Moors, Accrington, Lancashire BB5 5JZ
01254 385911

LD Mountain Centre
34 Dean Street, Newcastle upon Tyne NE1 1PG
0191 232 3561

Nomad Travellers Store
3–4 Wellington Terrace, Turnpike Lane, London N8 0PX
020 8889 7014

4 Potters Road, New Barnet, Hertfordshire EN5 5HW
020 8441 7208
and with STA Travel, 40 Bernard Street, Russell Square, London
WC1N 1LJ
020 7833 4114
www.nomad-travstore.co.uk

Rohan
30 Maryland Road, Tongwell, Milton Keynes MK15 8HN
01908 517900
www.rohan.co.uk

SafariQuip
The Stones, Castleton, Hope Valley, Derbyshire S33 8WX
01433 620320
www.safariquip.co.uk

Taunton Leisure have branches in Birmingham, Bristol, Exeter
and Taunton.
Call 0800 328 7586 for mail order; 01823 332987 for shops.

Travelling Light
Morland, Penrith, Cumbria CA10 3AZ
01931 714488
Also have shops in Bletchingley, Edinburgh, Knutsford, London
and Malmesbury.

YHA Adventure Shops sell a large variety of travelling
equipment (with a 10 per cent discount for YHA members).
There are branches in Ambleside, Birmingham, Brighton, Bristol,
Cambridge, Cardiff, Leeds, Liverpool, London, Manchester,
Nottingham, Oxford, Plymouth, Reading, Salisbury,
Southampton and Staines (call 01784 458625 for your nearest
branch). Alternatively, they have a full mail order service; call
020 7836 8541 for a copy of their catalogue. And they sell gift
tokens if you want to get a present for a travelling friend.
www.yhaadventure.co.uk

FURTHER READING

If you're heading off for some serious trekking through the wilderness, you can find advice on equipment and survival in *The
Backpacker's Handbook* by Hugh McManners (Dorling Kindersley).

'The first time I went on a long trip I borrowed a normal rucksack from a friend, but I got fed up having to unpack it every time I needed something that was at the bottom. The next time I was going away, I bought a convertible one, which makes finding things much easier. I also found it easier to pack. As I like to book into slightly more expensive places sometimes, it makes me look a bit more respectable, too. The other mistake I made the first time was to spend a fortune on very expensive hiking boots – a normal pair of trainers would have been just as good. The one thing I didn't take was a waterproof jacket, and I needed one almost everywhere I went.'

'I've taken my mozzie net all around the world – but never used it. I carry it because I know I should, but I've never actually worked out how to put it up! And everywhere I ever stayed already had one, anyway. I also have a favourite old water bottle that's never seen a drop of water – you can easily buy plastic bottles of water locally – but it has been kept well supplied with brandy or rum and coke to get me through some nightmare journeys. Another old faithful is my head torch. Everyone laughs at it but they always seem remarkably keen to borrow it when they want to find their way to the toilet in the pitch black.'

'If I'm travelling in Europe, I usually take my tent and sleeping bag because hotel accommodation can be so expensive that camping really saves you money. One year a friend and I lived in it for six months while we were working in the Greek Islands. But when it comes to backpacking in Asia or South America, I wouldn't dream of taking a tent and sleeping bag. In those places, cheap rooms and hostels are so easy to come by that it's really not worth lugging them around. If you do decide you fancy doing a bit of trekking or camping, it's usually easy enough to hire equipment. That's what we did in the Torres del Paine national park in Chile. There are lots of places in the nearest town hiring out tents, camping stoves, crampons – everything you could possibly want. The only thing I would say is that you need to check hire equipment really carefully to make sure it's up to the job. You don't want to wait until you're stuck in the middle of nowhere to discover that the last people brought the tent back with just two pegs left.'

TEN THINGS WE WON'T LEAVE HOME WITHOUT

Torch	Water bottle
Swiss Army knife	Sarong
Money belt	Walkman and tapes
Sheet sleeping bag	Camera
Luggage padlock	Addresses

AND TEN WE'D NEVER THINK OF PACKING BUT HAVE DISCOVERED IN OTHER TRAVELLERS' PACKS

Ornamental porcelain clogs

Dressing gown

Fishing rod

Travel iron

Full-sized pillow

Washing line and pegs

Tarot cards

Laptop

Lucky socks

Manicure and pedicure set

CHAPTER 13

WHAT TO PACK

The luggage allowance on most international flights is limited to 20kg per person. However, that doesn't mean you have to pack that much – it's best to keep it light, especially when travelling to hot climates where lugging a heavy rucksack around can be hell. If you're doing a trip round South East Asia, for example, you don't need to take as much as you would for South America, where temperatures are more extreme and nights at high altitude can be cold. Remember that you can always send stuff home along the way (cold-weather clothes you don't need any more, for instance).

CLOTHES

Take clothes that are quick and easy to wash and dry (and that won't look too awful creased). Natural fibres are usually best for comfort. Patterned clothes don't show up dirt and creases as much as plain ones. Dark clothes hide dirt, too, but they absorb heat, so light colours are better for hot climates.

Loose-fitting clothes are better for keeping you cool when it's hot, and can be layered on top of each other in cold climates. They also conceal the telltale bulge of your money belt. You should also wear loose-fitting clothes in countries where skin-tight items would offend local sensibilities. Clothes with pockets are extremely useful, especially if the pockets are zipped.

Your list of what to take should include the following:

* **Trousers.** Loose-fitting cotton are fave. Drawstring waists are good for coping with expanding or (more likely) shrinking waistlines. Sweat pants are good if it's going to get chilly. A pair of leggings can also come in handy. Jeans aren't very good for travelling as denim is heavy and takes ages to dry. Leave your

combats at home – foreign officials can be suspicious of military-style clothes.

* **Shorts.** Long and loose or cycling-style are both useful. Brief shorts may be OK on the beach or in western countries but are not the thing for more traditional societies.

* **Skirts.** Take a long one that reaches to at least mid-calf, for visiting temples. If you're in a situation where you have to go to the toilet in the open (by the side of the road on bus journeys, for example), it will also protect your modesty better than a pair of trousers.

* **Long-sleeved shirt.** For keeping warm, covering arms in temples, protecting them from the sun and avoiding mosquito bites.

* **Scarf.** To cover your head in temples, shield your scalp from the sun or, sprinkled with perfume and wrapped round your nose, to protect you from the stench of overused and undercleaned toilets. Also good as a dust mask.

* **T-shirts.** Pack three or four cotton ones. T-shirts with slogans (in English) are popular items for swapping and bartering with.

* **One warm jumper** or **fleece** (see Chapter 12). It can get chilly even in hot climates, and temperatures in desert areas can drop dramatically at night.

* **Sarong.** One of the most valuable items in your luggage, it can be anything you want it to be – skirt, towel, beach mat, sheet, scarf. Gives you instant modesty in temples and on beaches.

* **Walking boots** or **trainers** (see Chapter 12)

* **Sandals** or **flip-flops** (can be bought on arrival but you may have a problem finding large sizes in Asian countries)

* **Underwear** (thermal for cold climates)

* **Socks** (you won't need many for hot climates; more if you're doing lots of trekking)

* **Swimsuit**

* **Hat.** To shade you from the sun or keep you warm in the cold. Baseball caps are useful (and good for bartering, especially if they have logos or slogans on them). You can also get collapsible hats from Chinese stores that fold up flat to pack but open out into a wide-brimmed sunhat (they're usually quite a

hit, so you could take a couple of spares to give as presents).

Remember that you can buy clothes along the way. Cities like Bangkok and Hong Kong are great for stocking up on T-shirts, cotton tops and shorts, and sarongs. You can even have silk items made to measure – you can usually collect them the next day and they cost a fraction of the price you'd pay at home. If you're planning to work, remember to take some smart clothes with you. (It also helps to look as smart as possible when crossing borders, especially in places like Singapore and Russia where officials can be a bit fierce, so always try to keep at least one set of clean clothes to wear on such occasions.)

EQUIPMENT

See Chapter 12 for advice on choosing and buying equipment. A tent and sleeping bag are optional, depending on where you're going and what you'll be doing there. You'll need a mosquito net in malarial regions. The following items are essential wherever you're going:

* **Sheet sleeping bag**
* **Torch**
* **Money belt**
* **Padlock (for doors and rucksacks)**
* **Swiss Army knife** (make sure it's got a corkscrew and bottle opener)

A camera isn't essential but most people like to take one. Film is fairly widely available (though you should always check the expiry date). You can stock up in airports, or in major cities. Slide film is more difficult to find. Take a spare camera battery in case yours runs out; it can be hard to find the right sort while you're away.

TOILETRIES

A medical kit is a must for any traveller – see Chapter 8 for details of what to include.

* There's no need to load yourself down with enough suntan lotion, toothpaste, shampoo, soap and body lotion to last the whole trip. These are cheaper and easily available abroad, so just take enough to start you off. However, the choice of brands will probably be limited outside major cities so if you're fussy about your products, take your own supplies.

* Contact lens solutions, too, can usually be found in major cities so don't weigh yourself down by stocking up for the whole trip.

* Tampons are not always available so take enough to last you a while and remember to stock up in major cities. They can be very difficult to find in South America.

SUNDRIES

Some of the items we take for granted are expensive or difficult to find on the road. You might like to pack some or all of the following.

* Universal sink plug (about £3) – one of the YHA Adventure Shops' best-selling lines. Some travellers say a squash ball does the job just as well, and because it looks out of place in a bathroom, you're probably less likely to leave it behind when you leave a hotel.

* Earplugs. To help drown out the racket of busy streets, noisy neighbours, videos on buses, etc.

* Eyeshades. To help you sleep when it's light.

* Sunglasses (UV-protective)

* Travel alarm clock. How else will you wake up in time for those early-morning buses and trains?

* Towel. These take up a lot of room, so don't take a large one. On the beach, use a sarong instead – it's lighter, smaller and dries faster.

* Blow-up travel pillow (about £5). This can be a godsend on long journeys and makes the difference between some sleep and none at all.

* Mug or cup (tin or plastic). In countries like China and Russia trains have boiling water for passengers to make hot drinks as they travel.

* Mini sewing kit and safety pins

* Transparent plastic ziplock bags for keeping papers, books, passport, etc. dry. GO Travel Products do a pack of three PVC Pac-a-pouches in different sizes for £4.99.

* Toilet paper

* Nail brush. You'll be amazed at how dirty you and your clothes can get; a nail brush will help get things a bit cleaner.

* Books. Don't take too many as they're very heavy. You can swap with fellow travellers along the way (though you won't necessarily have the same taste in writers) or in hostel libraries or second-hand bookshops. A good guidebook is invaluable, but if you're only going to certain definite areas and don't mind mutilating it you can cut down the weight by ripping out and taking only the relevant pages.

* Diary or notebook and pens. To record your impressions.

* Telephone charge card and discount cards

* Sticky hooks. Useful for hanging up mosquito nets, or hanging clothes up in rooms with no hooks or rails.

* Walkman and tapes. Some will say this is a luxury, but in our book it's an essential and worth every ounce and square inch it takes up. It will get you through interminable delays, long journeys and help you tune out beach hawkers. And if you get a pair of mini speakers that plug into your headphone socket, you can have a party in your room. It helps if your travelling companion shares your taste in music. Check before you go what they're taking so that you don't duplicate tapes.

* Batteries for Walkman and torch, but don't go mad as they're heavy to carry and you can usually stock up en route. If you use an unusual size of battery, though, take enough to see you through.

* If you want to take presents for people, take something useful like pens (if you can get hold of them, BBC pens are highly appreciated around the world). Children everywhere, but especially in rural areas, love balloons. It's also nice to take photos or postcards of your home town to show people (inexplicably, postcards of the British royal family are said to go down a treat too). American cigarettes are well received just about everywhere, as is Johnnie Walker – with the obvious exception of 'dry' countries.

* In some countries the food can be relentlessly bland and boring so some travellers carry a bottle of soy or chilli sauce to add a bit of interest to their food.

DOCUMENTATION

Whatever you do, don't leave home without the following:

* **Passport and visas**

* **Tickets**

* **Money** (traveller's cheques, cash, credit cards)

* **Insurance documents**

* **Vaccination certificate** (keep it with your passport)

* **Photocopies of all the above**

* **Passport photographs** for any visas you're getting along the way. It can be difficult or expensive to get these done abroad.

* **Addresses**. Your friends and family will never forgive you if you don't send them cards.

* If you're planning to drive at all, a UK and/or International **Driving Licence**.

LUXURY ITEMS

* No, you won't need perfume, mascara or lipstick, but there may be times when you'll be really glad you have them and they don't take up much space, so allow yourself the odd luxury or two.

* Binoculars are expensive (especially if you go for the lightweight ones) but invaluable if you're planning any safari trips while you're away.

* Wet wipes. They're bulky to carry but there are times on a trip when the thing that makes you most happy is a clean, cool wet wipe!

* Playing cards and miniature travel games (e.g. dice, Pass the Pigs, roll-up backgammon) don't take up much room but can pass hours.

WHAT TO LEAVE AT HOME

Don't even think about taking a travel hairdryer or travel iron – you don't need them. Leave jewellery behind, too, especially if it has great sentimental or monetary value. It's safer and more fun to pick things up as you go along.

PACKING TIPS

Don't overdo it. The classic traveller's packing tip is to lay out on your bed everything you're planning to take with you, then halve the amount of clothes and double the money. Just because you have a certain amount of space doesn't mean you have to fill it, and anyway you need to leave room for all the things you'll doubtless end up acquiring along the way. So be ruthless about chucking things out – then ask for a second opinion.

Pack so that when the rucksack is on your back the heaviest items are nearest the top and close to your back. Make sure that anything you're going to want to get out is packed readily to hand, not right at the bottom. Items that you'll need frequently, such as lip salve, pen, sunblock and tissues, are best kept in a bumbag or daypack.

Use lots of plastic bags to keep things waterproof – either transparent ones so you can see what's in each, or different colours to distinguish them. Roll clothes rather than folding them to help prevent creasing.

If you're travelling with a friend (and don't anticipate splitting up with them before the end of the trip), you don't need one of everything each so sit down with a list and divide things up. You take the antiseptic cream if they carry the alarm clock, etc. If you're happy to share toiletries that will help too. You can also divide bits of a tent between you, one taking the tent itself while the other carries the poles and pegs.

Once you've filled your pack, pick it up and carry it round for a while. You might think it's not too bad at first but it doesn't take long for the true weight to tell. Remember that liquid is heavy – an empty water bottle won't make much difference to the weight of your pack, but a full one is a different story.

Put a note of your name and address inside the pack as well as on the outside, in case the outer label is ripped off and your baggage goes astray. Penknives are better packed in checked-in luggage as they may be confiscated from hand luggage. On some flights you also have to hand in any batteries at check-in (they're returned to you later on).

Avoid carrying anything in glass bottles, which may smash. Transfer the contents into plastic containers instead – available in chemists (or empty film containers are good). The exception is tablets or other medicines, which will look suspicious to customs and other officials if repackaged, so leave them in their original containers, with clear Sellotape wrapped round the labels so that they stay on and remain legible.

Make a note of everything you pack and when you return from a trip, check what you used or didn't use, and what you were missing. Next time you'll know...

'Packing for a three-month trip to South America, I didn't understand that it wasn't necessary to fill every inch of my rucksack. I could barely lift it up to get in the taxi to the airport. My friend advised me to unload a third of it, but I couldn't bear to leave anything behind. Two weeks into the trip I realized I couldn't buy any souvenirs because I had no means of carrying them. Also, my shoulders and back were starting to ache from carrying 18 kilos around every day. My friend went through everything ruthlessly and told me that I didn't need 12 T-shirts (she only had four), and I certainly didn't need perfume and matching body lotion (that went to a delighted cleaner at the hostel.) Also out went the nail varnish and remover, talcum powder, two skirts, a couple of sweaters, half of my airmail envelopes and writing paper (I only send postcards anyway), and many other things I thought I couldn't travel without. It did make life much easier and I'll definitely only half-fill my rucksack on my next trip.'

'Next time I go away I'll hardly take anything with me – much less than I took last time because I know now that you can just buy it along the way and get things made. We went shopping here before we left, buying T-shirts and whatever. Then you get out there and think what the hell did I buy this for? You can get all you want along the way, especially in Thailand. And I won't bother taking work things to wear in Australia because they don't look very good after they've spent seven months squashed in your rucksack. Better to just buy them there.'

CHAPTER 14

HOW TO BE A GOOD TRAVELLER

Take only photographs, leave only footprints, kill only time.

Tourism is the world's largest industry, affecting the lives of millions of people. Hundreds of millions of tourists travel abroad every year and the impact they make *en masse* on their destination countries is immense. Sometimes it can be for the good – they may encourage the preservation of native habitats and wildlife and may provide much needed cash for the local economy. But while the development of tourism brings rewards to some, the benefits are seldom spread evenly.

People living in many tourist destinations are now counting the cost of having an industry that often fails to put their interests and rights on a par with those of their visitors. Tourists use up precious reserves of water, electricity and food. Forests are felled to build new roads; villages bulldozed to make way for new hotels; tribes displaced, as in Kenya's Maasai Mara, which is now a National Park. Parts of Everest look little better than a rubbish dump since more and more climbers have been attempting the ascent. And as people venture ever further off the beaten track in search of deserted tropical beaches, some marine life breeding grounds are under threat.

The revenue generated from tourists often goes straight into the coffers of multinational companies or the hands of a few local bigwigs rather than benefiting the whole populace. Countries such as Myanmar (Burma) have even forced some of their people into virtual slavery to build roads, hotels and other facilities to attract the dollar-wielding tourist.

There are some simple steps you can take to help preserve the area you're visiting. If you're interested in finding out more about these and other travel-related issues, contact the organizations at the end of this chapter.

PROTECTING THE ENVIRONMENT

* To help limit deforestation, don't make open fires when camping or hiking. Where firewood is scarce, use as little as possible; it's better to take your own fuel supplies. Take great care when discarding matches and cigarettes.

* Always take all your litter away with you – not only is it unsightly, but it can be harmful to animals.

* Don't pollute streams and rivers by using detergents or other pollutants. Take with you only environmentally friendly, biodegradable shampoos and washing products.

* If there are no toilet facilities, bury or cover all waste, and make sure you are at least 30 metres away from water sources.

* Don't pick flowers or take cuttings from plants; in many areas, this is illegal as well as destructive to the environment.

* Don't buy animal or marine products, such as ivory, furs, feathers, butterflies, coral, tortoiseshell or turtle shells. You'd be endangering the natural environment and in many cases importing such articles into the UK is illegal.

* Treat coral with care – it is fragile and takes centuries to grow but you can damage it in an instant. Don't step on it, break it or anchor a boat to it.

* Stick to marked paths, whether on foot or in the car. Unsupervised off-road driving can damage soil and vegetation.

* Try to save water. For example, keep showers brief, and don't let the tap run when you clean your teeth. If you're staying somewhere upmarket, tell them you don't need clean towels every day: hotels could save millions of gallons if they washed guests' towels every other day, rather than every day.

* Before you go, remove all unnecessary packaging and wrapping from the products you're taking with you – the country you're going to may not have a waste disposal system that's up to dealing with the increased pressures of tourists.

* Switch off lights and air conditioning when you leave a room.

* On safari, keep your distance from animals – getting too close or making too much noise distresses them and can disrupt their

breeding and feeding cycles. In some cases, animals can contract human diseases to which they have no immunity.

* Don't encourage or take part in entertainments and events that cause suffering to animals such as bull-fighting, dancing bears, photographers' chimps, dolphinaria, etc.

RESPECTING LOCAL CULTURES

* Read up on the local culture before you go and make sure that you respect all local customs.

* In Muslim countries, use only your right hand for eating and greeting, never your left.

* Respect other people's privacy when taking photographs. Always ask permission first.

* Show respect for holy places. Do not touch or remove any religious artefacts. Follow whatever rules are given, such as removing shoes or covering heads when visiting temples. Don't shout, run about or laugh excessively.

* How you deal with beggars is largely down to your personal moral code. However, many people who work in countries where begging is widespread advise that any money would be more constructively spent if it were donated to a health centre, school or aid project.

* In Thailand and other Buddhist countries it's rude to point your feet at someone or touch their head.

* If you visit someone in their home, watch how they behave and copy them (taking off shoes before entering, for example).

* Don't touch other people. Handshakes are not appropriate in many cultures, especially between men and women.

* Avoid public displays of affection with your partner – public kissing and even hand-holding are unacceptable in some countries.

* Always dress modestly. Loose-fitting clothes are less offensive than body-hugging, skimpy and revealing ones. Even bare arms can cause offence in some countries so make sure you're sensitive to the local dress code.

* Always pay a fair price for what you buy. If you allow yourself to be overcharged, it makes it harder for those who come after you to avoid being overcharged, too. If you beat local prices

down too much, you are only getting your bargain at great expense to others who can ill afford it.

* Don't give money or sweets to children; pens, books or balloons are a better choice.

* Always be patient, friendly and sensitive. You are a guest in someone else's country.

* Buy locally produced foods and drinks rather than the imported versions, to help countries maintain their individual cultures and boost the local economy. And spend your money in locally owned shops, hotels and restaurants rather than in those owned by huge international companies.

* Buying quality arts and crafts will support local skills and help maintain the indigenous culture; buying mass-produced tourist tat will help kill it off.

* In areas with repressive governments, make sure that you don't unwittingly put anyone in danger by quizzing them about human rights abuses, for example, or asking awkward questions about politics and pro-democracy movements.

FURTHER INFORMATION

Once you return from your travels, you may find that your experiences while you're away inspire you to get involved with some sort of charity work or fundraising at home. There are many causes you could decide to support. Here are just a few contacts to start you off.

* Actionaid, Chataway House, Leach Road, Chard, Somerset TA20 1FA; 01460 62972. Works in poverty-stricken areas of Africa, Asia and Latin America.
www.actionaid.org

* The Cambodia Trust, 11 Friday Court, North Street, Thame, Oxfordshire OX9 3GA; 01993 811674. Non-governmental organization which works for the rehabilitation of amputees and other victims of war in Cambodia.
www.cambodiatrust.org.uk

* CERT (Campaign for Environmentally Responsible Tourism), Indabe House, 1 Hydeway, Thundersley, Essex SS7 3BE; 020 8761 1910. Aims to put resources into practical measures to help protect and look after the world's natural heritage.

* Children of the Andes, 4 Bath Place, Rivington Street, London

EC2A 3DR; 020 7739 1328. Helps street children in Colombia. www.children-of-the-andes.org

* Christina Noble Children's Foundation, Ground Floor, 10 Semley Place, Belgravia, London SW1W 9QJ; 020 7233 1413. Campaigns to house, educate and provide medical facilities for the street children of Vietnam. Have also set up a similar operation in Mongolia.
www.cncf.org

* Coalition on Child Prostitution and Tourism, Anti-Slavery International, Thomas Clarkson House, The Stableyard, Broomgrove Road, London SW9 9TL; 020 7501 8920. Seeks an end to child sex tourism in all tourist-destination countries of Asia, Africa, Europe and Latin America.
www.antislavery.org

* Population Concern, 3–5 Highgate Studios, 53–79 Highgate Road, London NW5 1TL; 020 7241 8500. Runs sexual and reproductive health programmes overseas, providing information and services, increasingly focused on young people.
www.populationconcern.org.uk

* Sight Savers International, 13 Cheap Street, Frome, Somerset BA11 1BN; 01373 452272. In countries such as India, Pakistan, Bangladesh and Sri Lanka, where up to one in 100 people are blind, four out of five of them needlessly so, SSI works to restore sight where possible, or to give incurably blind people the training required to make a living and support themselves.
www.sightsavers.org.uk

* Survival International, 11–15 Emerald Street, London WC1N 3QL; 020 7242 1441. A worldwide organization supporting tribal peoples in their efforts to protect their lives, lands and human rights.
www.survival-international.org

* Tourism Concern, Stapleton House, 277–281 Holloway Road, London N7 8HN; 020 7753 3330. Campaigns on behalf of people displaced by the travel industry and works to make tourism more responsible, sensitive and just. Membership (£20 waged, £12 unwaged) includes a subscription to *In Focus*, a quarterly magazine that looks at various tourism-related topics.
www.tourismconcern.org.uk

* Water Aid, Prince Consort House, 27–29 Albert Embankment, London SE1 7UB; 020 7793 4500. Works with communities in

Africa and Asia to improve and maintain water and sanitation services.
www.wateraid.org.uk

* World Wide Fund for Nature, Panda House, Weyside Park, Godalming, Surrey GU7 1XR; 01483 426444. Has a Buyer Beware! campaign against illegal imports of wildlife souvenirs by tourists.
www.wwf-uk.org

CHAPTER 15

READ ALL ABOUT IT

Finding out as much as you can about the places you'll be visiting adds greatly to the enjoyment of a country. Part of the fun of preparing for your trip is reading books about your destination, watching films set there, going to relevant exhibitions and museums, poring over maps and listening to music from the countries (Rough Guides have a great series of world music CDs and tapes, available in record shops or by mail order on 020 7498 5252). You'll find a list of bookshops at the end of this chapter.

GUIDEBOOKS

There are some who prefer to travel without guidebooks, complaining that they turn people into sheep, all herding towards the same few hostels and restaurants. But most of us feel happier with an authoritative guide in our hands, and, if it's your first time, it can be particularly reassuring to be pointed towards places where you're likely to meet other travellers.

That said, don't be ruled by them completely or you'll be missing out. If you go somewhere that a book recommends and it looks grotty to you, leave. Similarly, if you find somewhere great but it's not in the book, don't reject it on those grounds. It's exciting to discover your own new places – and you'll probably find them in the next edition.

Don't weigh yourself down with too many guides before you go – they're very heavy, and you can always pick them up as you go along, either buying them in second-hand bookshops or swapping them with backpackers heading in the opposite direction to you.

As the travel market has boomed, so the number of guidebooks has expanded enormously and any good bookshop will stock a wide selection. Faced with so many, it can be confusing deciding which to go for, but the acknowledged leaders in the backpacker market are Lonely Planet guides (their *South East Asia on a Shoestring* is clutched by every backpacker making the trip from Bangkok to Bali) and the Rough Guide series. Between them, they cover the globe and are generally very reliable, although prices may be out-of-date, especially in countries just opening up to tourists. Always check the date of publication, because a very out-of-date guidebook can be far more frustrating than no guidebook at all. Footprint (formerly Trade & Travel) Handbooks, although expensive, are also very good and are updated annually. Their award-winning *South American Handbook* is the acknowledged bible for that area.

Let's Go guides are aimed specifically at the budget traveller and are updated every year. Other guides are also worth reading for background information. In particular, Cadogan books are intelligent and well-written (but rather heavy to carry round) while Blue Guides can be a bit dry but tell you all you want to know about the cultural aspects of a country. Insight Guides have lots of glossy pictures that are great to look at both before you go and when you come back. The Culture Shock! series (published by Kuperard) gives a good general introduction to the culture and customs of a country – particularly useful if you're planning to live abroad. Other books aimed at the independent traveller include Bradt and Moon Handbooks.

MAPS

If you're planning to do any trekking, buy good maps in the UK as they're difficult to find abroad. It's a good idea to try out your orienteering skills before you leave, too, practising with a map and compass in countryside near your home. (You can break-in your hiking boots and get used to carrying a full rucksack at the same time.)

FICTION AND TRAVELOGUES

Guidebooks will give you the hard facts, but for a more personal flavour of the country check out works of fiction and travellers' accounts. The following list starts off with general, worldwide books, then goes into an alphabetical list of countries and continents. If you can't find anything for the country you're going to, look under the relevant continent. For example, if you're going to Laos, check out Asia (general) as well as Laos itself.

GENERAL/WORLDWIDE

A Thousand Miles from Nowhere Graham Coster (Penguin)

Around the World in Eighty Days Jules Verne (Alan Sutton)

Around the World in Eighty Days Michael Palin (BBC)

The Blessings of a Good Thick Skirt Mary Russell (Flamingo)

Brief Encounters ed. Michelle de Kretser (Lonely Planet)

Danziger's Travels Nick Danziger (Flamingo)

Full Tilt Dervla Murphy (Flamingo)

Great Journeys (BBC)

The Great Railway Bazaar Paul Theroux (Penguin)

Heroes John Pilger (Pan)

Holidays in Hell P. J. O'Rourke (Picador)

Last Chance to See Douglas Adams (Pan)

Letters Home Robert Byron (John Murray)

Lost Cowboys: From Patagonia to the Alamo Hank Wangford (Victor Gollancz)

Love Among the Butterflies Margaret Fountaine (Virago)

More Women Travel (Rough Guides)

Our Man in…Heaven and Hell Clive Anderson (BBC)

The Picador Book of the Beach ed. Robert Drewe (Picador)

Pole to Pole Michael Palin (BBC)

Spinsters Abroad: Victorian Lady Explorers Dea Birkett (Gollancz)

Travels Michael Crichton (Pan)

Unsuitable for Ladies: An Anthology of Women Travellers selected by Jane Robinson (Oxford)

Video Night in Kathmandu Pico Iyer (Transworld)

The Virago Book of Women Travellers ed. Mary Morris with Larry O'Connor (Virago)

The Wind in my Wheels Josie Dew (Warner)

Worst Journeys: The Picador Book of Travel ed. Keath Fraser (Picador)

AFRICA (GENERAL)

(see also individual countries)

A Cure for Serpents The Duke of Pirajno (Eland)

A Good Man in Africa William Boyd (Penguin)

African Silences Peter Matthiessen (Harvill)

Aspects of Africa David Robbins (Penguin)

Black Mischief Evelyn Waugh (Penguin)

Blood on the Tracks Miles Bredin (Picador)

Cause Celeb Helen Fielding (Picador)

The Coup John Updike (Penguin)

The Electronic Elephant Dan Jacobson (Penguin)

The English Patient Michael Ondaatje (Picador)

Heart of Darkness Joseph Conrad (Penguin)

The Heart of the Matter Graham Greene (Penguin)

Isabelle Annette Kobak (Virago)

Journey to the Vanished City Tudor Parfitt (Phoenix)

Malaria Dreams Stuart Stevens (Abacus)

Men at Arms Evelyn Waugh (Penguin)

The Music Programme Paul Micou (Black Swan)

Nomad Mary Anne Fitzgerald (Picador)

North of South: An African Journey Shiva Naipaul (Penguin)

On Foot Through Africa Ffyona Campbell (Orion)

Running with the Moon: A Boy's Own Adventure Jonny Bealby (William Heinemann)

Scoop Evelyn Waugh (Penguin)

She H. Rider Haggard (Oxford)

Tales from the Dark Continent Charles Allen (Abacus)

Travels in the Interior of Africa Mungo Park (Eland)

Travels in West Africa Mary Kingsley (Everyman)

Travels With Myself and Another Martha Gellhorn (Eland)

Travels With Pegasus: A Microlight Journey Across West Africa Christina Dodwell (Sceptre)

The Ukimwi Road Dervla Murphy (Flamingo)

Under African Skies ed. Charles Larson (Payback Press)

Venture to the Interior Sir Laurens van der Post (Penguin)

The Weather in Africa Martha Gellhorn (Eland)

The White Nile Alan Moorehead (Penguin)

ALBANIA

The File on H Ismail Kadare (Harvill)

ALGERIA

Desperate Spring Fettouma Touati (The Women's Press)
Exile and the Kingdom Albert Camus (Penguin)
The Magician's Wife Brian Moore (Flamingo)
The Outsider Albert Camus (Penguin)
The Plague Albert Camus (Penguin)

ANTARCTICA

Antarctic Oasis Tim and Pauline Carr (Norton)
Below the Convergence Alan Gurney (Pimlico)
The Birthday Boys Beryl Bainbridge (Penguin)
South Ernest Shackleton (Constable Robinson)
Terra Incognita Sara Wheeler (Vintage)
The Worst Journey in the World Apsley Cherry-Garrard
   (Picador Travel Classics)

ARCTIC

The Voyage of the Narwhal Andrea Barrett (Flamingo)

ARGENTINA

Bad Times in Buenos Aires Miranda France (Weidenfeld)
The Book of Imaginary Beings Jorge Luis Borges (Penguin)
The Drunken Forest Gerald Durrell (Penguin)
Far Away and Long Ago W. M. Hudson (Eland)
The Honorary Consul Graham Greene (Penguin)
Kiss of the Spider Woman Manuel Puig (Vintage)
Santa Evita Tomás Eloy Martínez (Anchor)
The Story of the Night Colm Tóibín (Picador)
The Whispering Land Gerald Durrell (Penguin)

ARMENIA

Armenia Christopher Walker (Routledge)

ASIA (GENERAL)
(see also individual countries)

Explorers of South-East Asia ed. Victor T. King (Oxford)

In Search of Conrad Gavin Young (Penguin)

In Xanadu William Dalrymple (Flamingo)

The Lands of Charm and Cruelty Stan Stesser (Picador)

The Lost Heart of Asia Colin Thubron (Penguin)

The Missionary and the Libertine Ian Buruma (Faber & Faber)

On the Road Again Simon Dring (BBC)

Tales from the South China Seas ed. Charles Allen (Abacus Travel)

The Travels Marco Polo (Penguin)

AUSTRALIA

A River Town Thomas Keneally (Sceptre)

A Secret Country John Pilger (Vintage)

Ancestors Robyn Davidson (Vintage)

Australiaville Andy Soutter (Abacus)

Blue Meridian – the Search for the Great White Shark
  Peter Matthiessen (Harvill)

Bobin Up Dorothy Hewett (Virago)

The Chant of Jimmie Blacksmith Thomas Keneally (Penguin)

Cloudstreet Tim Winton (Picador)

Daddy, We Hardly Knew You Germaine Greer (Penguin)

The Dead Heart Douglas Kennedy (Abacus)

Flight of the Kingfisher Monica Furlong (HarperCollins)

Girls' Night Out Kathy Lette (Picador)

The Great World David Malouf (Picador)

Homebush Boy Thomas Keneally (Sceptre)

Illywhacker Peter Carey (Faber & Faber)

In the Land of Oz Howard Jacobson (Penguin)

Kangaroo D. H. Lawrence (Penguin)

Mutant Message Down Under Marlo Morgan (Thorsons)

My Brilliant Career Miles Franklin (Virago)

No Worries Mark McCrum (Sinclair-Stevenson)

Oscar and Lucinda Peter Carey (Faber & Faber)

Oyster Jeanette Turner Hospital (Virago)

Picnic at Hanging Rock Joan Lindsay (Penguin)

Sean and David's Long Drive Sean Condon (Lonely Planet)

The Songlines Bruce Chatwin (Picador)

Sydney Jan Morris (Penguin)

The Thorn Birds Colleen McCullough (Warner)

Tracks Robyn Davidson (Vintage)

True North Jill Ker Conway (Vintage)

Voss Patrick White (Penguin)

Walkabout James Vance Marshall (Puffin)

AUSTRIA

The Third Man Graham Greene (Penguin)

BALI: see Indonesia

BANGLADESH

Lajja/Shame Taslima Nasreen (Penguin)

Songs at the River's Edge: Stories from a Bangladeshi Village
  Katy Gardner (Virago)

BELGIUM

The Folding Star Alan Hollinghurst (Vintage)

The Sorrow of Belgium Hugo Claus (Penguin)

Villette Charlotte Brontë (Oxford)

Tall Men in a Low Land Harry Pearson, Little, Brown

Xenophobe's Guide to the Belgians Antony Mason
  (Ravette Publishing)

BENIN

The Viceroy of Ouidah Bruce Chatwin (Picador)

BHUTAN

Bhutan: Mountain Fortress of the Gods (Serindia Publications)

Dreams of the Peaceful Dragon: Journey into Bhutan
  Katie Hickman (Coronet)

BOLIVIA

Before the Rainy Season Gert Hoffman (Minerva)

Digging up Butch and Sundance Anne Meadows
  (University of Nebraska Press)

The General in his Labyrinth Gabriel García Márquez (Penguin)

BORNEO

An Empire of the East Norman Lewis (Picador)

The Follow Linda Spalding (Bloomsbury)

Into the Heart of Borneo Redmond O'Hanlon (Penguin)

Kalimantan CS Godshalk (Abacus)

My Life in Sarawak Margaret Brooke, the Ranee of Sarawak (Oxford)

Queen of the Head-hunters Sylvia, Lady Brooke, the Ranee of Sarawak (Oxford)

Reflections of Eden Biruté M. F. Galdikas (Indigo)

The White Rajahs of Sarawak Robert Payne (Oxford)

BOSNIA

Bosnian Chronicle Ivo Andrić (Harvill)

The Bridge over the Drina Ivo Andrić (Harvill)

BOTSWANA

A Woman Alone Bessie Head (Heinemann)

The Cardinals Bessie Head (Heinemann)

Cry of the Kalahari Mark Owens and Delia Owens (HarperCollins)

Jamestown Blues Caitlin Davies (Penguin)

The Lost World of the Kalahari Laurens van der Post (Penguin)

The Missionary's Wife Tim Jeal (Warner)

Okavango – Jewel of the Kalahari Karen Ross (BBC)

Starlings Laughing June Vendall-Clark (Transworld)

BRAZIL

A Simple Brazilian Song James Woodall (Abacus Travel)

Blues for a Lost Childhood Antonio Torres (Readers International)

Brazilian Adventure Peter Fleming (Pimlico)

Dona Flor and Her Two Husbands Jorge Amado (Serpent's Tail)

The Land Antonio Torres (Readers International)

Mad White Giant: A Journey to the Heart of the Amazon Jungle Benedict Allen (Flamingo)

Rebellion in the Backlands Euclides da Cunha (Picador Travel Classics)

The Republic of Dreams Nelida Pinon (Picador)

The Snake Tree Uwe Timm (Picador)
Travellers' Tales: Brazil, True Stories of a Life on the Road
   ed. Annette Haddad and Scott Doggett (Haddad Doggett)
The Tribe that Hides from Man Adrian Cowell (Pimlico)
The War of the Saints Jorge Amado (Serpent's Tail)

BULGARIA

Rates of Exchange Malcolm Bradbury (Penguin)

BURMA: see Myanmar

CAMBODIA: see also Vietnam, Cambodia and Laos

Angkor George Coedès (Oxford)
Angkor and the Khmers Malcolm MacDonald (Oxford)
Distant Voices John Pilger (Vintage)
Gecko Tails Carol Livingston (Phoenix Press)
Surviving the Killing Fields Dr Haing Ngor (Macmillan)

CAMEROON

A Plague of Caterpillars Nigel Barley (Penguin)
A Zoo in My Luggage Gerald Durrell (Penguin)
Cameroon with Egbert Dervla Murphy (Flamingo)
Houseboy Ferdinand Oyono (Heinemann)
The Innocent Anthropologist Nigel Barley (Penguin)
Pieces of Light Adam Thorpe (Cape)
Talking Drums Shirley Deane (John Murray)

CANADA

A Jest of God Margaret Laurence (Vintage)
A Recipe for Bees Gail Anderson-Dargatz (Virago)
The Beggar Maid Alice Munro (Penguin)
Black Robe Brian Moore (Flamingo)
Cat's Eye Margaret Atwood (Virago)
'The Deptford Trilogy' Robertson Davies (Penguin)
The Museum Guard Howard Norman (Picador)
The Progress of Love Alice Munro (Flamingo)

St Urbain's Horseman Mordecai Richler (Vintage)

'The Salterton Trilogy' Robertson Davies (Penguin)

Shadows on the Rock Willa Cather (Virago)

The Shipping News E. Annie Proulx (Fourth Estate)

Solomon Gursky Was Here Mordecai Richler (Vintage)

The Stone Diaries Carol Shields (Fourth Estate)

Surfacing Margaret Atwood (Virago)

Winter Hunger Ann Tracy (Virago)

CARIBBEAN

A High Wind in Jamaica Richard Hughes (Panther)

A House for Mr Biswas V. S. Naipaul (Penguin)

A Small Place Jamaica Kincaid (Virago)

A View from the Mangrove Antonio Benitez-Rojo (Faber & Faber)

Caribbean: Sea of Lentils Antonio Benitez-Rojo (Faber & Faber)

The Crown of Columbus Michael Dorris and Louise Erdrich (Flamingo)

The Dragon Can't Dance Earl Lovelace (Longman)

Indigo Marina Warner (Vintage)

The Middle Passage V. S. Naipaul (Picador Travel Classics)

Omeros Derek Walcott (Faber & Faber)

Solibo Magnificent Patrick Chamoiseau (Granta)

Tar Baby Toni Morrison (Picador)

The Traveller's Tree Patrick Leigh Fermor (Penguin)

The Violins of Saint-Jacques Patrick Leigh Fermor (Oxford)

The Weather Prophet: A Caribbean Journey Lucretia Stewart (Vintage)

Wide Sargasso Sea Jean Rhys (Penguin)

Windward Heights Maryse Conde (Faber & Faber)

CENTRAL AFRICAN REPUBLIC

Song from the Forest Louis Sarne (Corgi)

CENTRAL AMERICA (GENERAL)
(see also individual countries)

Green Dreams: Travels in Central America Steve Benz
(Lonely Planet)

Nothing to Declare: Memoirs of a Woman Travelling Alone
Mary Morris (Penguin)

The Old Patagonian Express Paul Theroux (Penguin)

Reality Is the Bug That Bit Me in the Galapagos Charlotte du Cann and Mark Watson (Flamingo)

So Far From God: A Journey to Central America Patrick Marnham (Penguin)

Time Among the Maya Ronald Wright (Penguin)

CHILE

The Captain's Verses Pablo Neruda (Penguin)

Eva Luna Isabel Allende (Penguin)

Full Circle: A South American Journey Luis Sepúlveda (Lonely Planet)

House of the Spirits Isabel Allende (Black Swan)

Memoirs Pablo Neruda (Penguin)

Of Love and Shadows Isabel Allende (Black Swan)

Selected Poems Pablo Neruda (Penguin)

The Stories of Eva Luna Isabel Allende (Penguin)

Travels in a Thin Country Sara Wheeler (Abacus)

CHINA

A Bend in the Yellow River Justin Hill (Phoenix)

Behind the Wall: A Journey Through China Colin Thubron (Penguin)

China to Me Emily Hahn (Virago)

Chinese Take-Away Linda Stevens (Blink Publishing)

The Conquerors André Malraux (University of Chicago Press)

The Dream of the Red Chamber Cao Xueqin (Penguin)

Empire of the Sun J. G. Ballard (Flamingo)

Falling Leaves Adeline Yen Mah (Penguin)

Farewell to my Concubine Lilian Lee (Penguin)

From Emperor to Citizen: The Autobiography of Pu Yi, The Last Emperor of China (Oxford)

Frontier of Heaven Stanley Stewart (Flamingo)

The Garlic Ballads Mo Yan (Penguin)

The Ginger Tree Oswald Wynd (Eland)

The Good Earth Pearl S. Buck (Mandarin)

Grass Soup Zhiang Xianliang (Minerva)

Half of Man is Woman Zhang Xianliang (Penguin)

I Sailed with Chinese Pirates Aleko Lilius (Oxford)

The Joy Luck Club Amy Tan (Minerva)

The Kitchen God's Wife Amy Tan (Flamingo)

Leaden Wings Zhang Jie (Virago)

Life and Death in Shanghai Nien Cheng (Flamingo)

Peking Anthony Grey (Pan)

Picador Book of Contemporary Chinese Fiction ed. Carolyn Choa (Picador)

Raise the Red Lantern Su Tong (Touchstone/Simon & Schuster)

Red Azalea An Chi Minh (Victor Gollancz)

Red China Blues Jan Wong (Bantam)

Red Sorghum Mo Yan (Minerva)

Red Star Over China Edgar Snow (Penguin)

The Remote Country of Women Bai Hua
   (University of Hawaii Press)

Rice Su Tong (Touchstone/Simon & Schuster)

Riding the Iron Rooster Paul Theroux (Penguin)

The River at the Centre of the World Simon Winchester (Penguin)

Shanghai Harriet Sergeant (John Murray)

Shanghai '37 Vicki Baum (Oxford)

The Tribulations of a Chinese Gentleman Jules Verne (Oxford)

Wild Swans Jung Chang (Flamingo)

The Woman Warrior Maxine Hong Kingston (Picador)

The Yangtze and Beyond Isabella Bird (Virago)

COLOMBIA

Condor and Humming-bird Charlotte Mendez
   (The Women's Press)

The Fruit Palace Charles Nicholl (Vintage)

The General in his Labyrinth Gabriel García Márquez (Penguin)

Love in the Time of Cholera Gabriel García Márquez (Penguin)

Of Love and Other Demons Gabriel García Márquez (Penguin)

One Hundred Years of Solitude Gabriel García Márquez (Picador)

Señor Vivo and the Coca Lord Louis de Bernières (Minerva)

Whitewash Pablo Escobar (Pan)

CONGO

A Burnt-Out Case Graham Greene (Penguin)
Brazzaville Beach William Boyd (Penguin)
The Catastrophist Ronan Bennett (Review)
Congo Journey Redmond O'Hanlon (Penguin)
In Search of a Character Graham Greene (Penguin)
The Poisonwood Bible Barbara Kingsolver (Faber & Faber)

CORSICA

Granite Island Dorothy Carrington (Penguin)

COSTA RICA

Jurassic Park Michael Crichton (Arrow)

CUBA

Cuba: A Journey Jacobo Timerman (Picador)
Cuba Libre Elmore Leonard (Viking)
Dreaming in Cuban Cristina Garcia (Flamingo)
Driving Through Cuba: An East-West Journey Carlo Gébler (Abacus)
Islands in the Stream Ernest Hemingway (Flamingo)
The Land of Miracles Stephen Smith (Abacus Travel)
Los Gusanos John Sayles (Penguin)
The Mambo Kings Play Songs of Love Oscar Hijuelos (Penguin)
Our Man in Havana Graham Greene (Penguin)

CYPRUS

Bitter Lemons of Cyprus Lawrence Durrell (Faber & Faber)
Journey into Cyprus Colin Thubron (Penguin)

CZECH REPUBLIC

A Stricken Field Martha Gellhorn (Virago)
The Book of Laughter and Forgetting Milan Kundera
   (Faber & Faber)
Dracula Bram Stoker (Penguin)
The Engineer of Human Souls Josef Skvorecky (Vintage)
The Good Soldier Svejk Jaroslav Hašek (Penguin)

Judge on Trial Ivan Klima (Vintage)

Letters to Olga Vaclav Havel (Faber & Faber)

Magic Prague Angelo Maria Ripellino (Picador)

The Piper on the Mountain Ellis Peters (Headline)

The Republic of Whores Josef Skvorecky (Faber & Faber)

Saxophone Dreams Nicholas Royle (Penguin)

Too Loud a Solitude Bohumil Hrabil (Abacus)

The Trial Franz Kafka (Minerva)

The Unbearable Lightness of Being Milan Kundera (Faber & Faber)

Utz Bruce Chatwin (Picador)

DENMARK

Classic Fairy Tales Hans Christian Andersen (Gollancz)

The History of Danish Dreams Peter Høeg (Harvill)

Miss Smilla's Feeling for Snow Peter Høeg (Harvill)

Music and Silence Rose Tremain (Chatto & Windus)

Winter's Tales Isak Dinesen (Karen Blixen) (Penguin)

DOMINICAN REPUBLIC

Drown Junot Diaz (Faber & Faber)

ECUADOR

Nostromo Joseph Conrad (Penguin)

The Origin of Species Charles Darwin (Penguin)

Voyage of the Beagle Charles Darwin (Penguin)

EGYPT

'The Alexandria Quartet' Lawrence Durrell (Faber & Faber)

An Egyptian Journal William Golding (Faber & Faber)

'The Balkan Trilogy' (final two books: *The Spoilt City* and *Friends and Heroes*) Olivia Manning (Mandarin)

Beyond the Pyramids: Travels in Egypt Douglas Kennedy (Abacus)

'The Cairo Trilogy' (*Palace Walk, Palace of Desire* and *Sugar Street*) Naguib Mahfouz (Black Swan)

Cleopatra Lucy Hughes-Hallett (Pimlico)

Flaubert in Egypt Gustave Flaubert (Penguin)

God Dies by the Nile Nawal El Saadawi (Zed Books)

Harem Years: The Memoirs of an Egyptian Feminist Huda Sha'rawi
(Virago)

The Hidden Face of Eve Nawal El Saadawi (Zed Press)

In an Antique Land Amitav Ghosh (Granta Books)

The Innocents Abroad Mark Twain (Penguin)

Letters from Egypt Lucie Duff Gordon (Virago)

'The Levant Trilogy' Olivia Manning (Penguin)

The Map of Love Ahdaf Soueif (Bloomsbury)

Moon Tiger Penelope Lively (Penguin)

Old Serpent Nile Stanley Stewart (Flamingo)

Out of Egypt Andre Aciman (Panther)

The Photographer's Wife Robert Solé (Harvill)

Woman at Point Zero Nawal El Saadawi (Zed Books)

EL SALVADOR

Bitter Grounds Sandra Benitez (Sceptre)

ERITREA

Towards Asmara Thomas Keneally (Sceptre)

ESTONIA

The Christening Denise Neuhaus (Faber & Faber)

The Revolution in the Baltics Anatol Lieven (Yale University Press)

ETHIOPIA

Cry Wolf Wilbur Smith (Mandarin)

The Danakil Diary Wilfred Thesiger (Flamingo)

In Ethiopia with a Mule Dervla Murphy (Flamingo)

Waugh in Abyssinia Evelyn Waugh (Penguin)

EUROPE (GENERAL) (see also individual countries)

A Time of Gifts Patrick Leigh Fermor (Penguin)

Between the Woods and the Water Patrick Leigh Fermor (Penguin)

Clear Waters Rising Nick Crane (Penguin)

Don't Mention the War: A Shameful European Adventure
Stewart Ferris and Paul Bassett (Summersdale)

Exit Into History: a Journey Through Eastern Europe Eva Hoffman (Minerva)

Greenmantle John Buchan (Penguin)

Neither Here Nor There: Travels in Europe Bill Bryson (Minerva)

On the Shores of the Mediterranean Eric Newby (Picador)

The Pillars of Hercules Paul Theroux (Hamish Hamilton)

Stalin's Nose: Across the Face of Europe Rory MacLean (Flamingo)

States of Change: A Central European Diary Lynne Jones
  (Merlin Press)

FINLAND

The Downfall of Gerdt Bladh Christer Kilman (Peter Owen)

The Kanteletar Elias Lonnrot (OUP)

One Night Stand Rosa Liksom (Serpent's Tail)

FRANCE

Any 19th-century French novel: (Balzac (e.g. *Father Goriot*), Zola (e.g. *L'Assommoir, Nana, Germinal*), Hugo (e.g. *Les Misérables*), Flaubert (e.g. *Sentimental Education, Madame Bovary*), Stendhal (e.g. *Scarlet and Black*)

A Motor-Flight through France Edith Wharton
  (Picador Travel Classics)

A Moveable Feast Ernest Hemingway (Arrow)

A Tale of Two Cities Charles Dickens (Penguin)

A Year in Provence Peter Mayle (Pan)

Across the Channel Julian Barnes (Cape)

The Autobiography of Alice B. Toklas Gertrude Stein (Penguin)

'The Avignon Quintet' Lawrence Durrell (Faber & Faber)

Birdsong Sebastian Faulks (Vintage)

The Blessing Nancy Mitford (Penguin)

Bonjour Tristesse Françoise Sagan (Penguin)

Chocolat Joanne Harris (Black Swan)

The Collected Stories of Colette Colette (Penguin)

Cross Channel Julian Barnes (Picador)

Daughters of the House Michèle Roberts (Virago)

Don't Tell Alfred Nancy Mitford (Penguin)

Down and Out in Paris and London George Orwell (Penguin)

The Dud Avocado Elaine Dundy (Virago)

Flaubert's Parrot Julian Barnes (Picador)

Foreign Parts Janice Galloway (Vintage)

France and the French John Ardagh (Penguin)

French Leave P. G. Wodehouse (Penguin)

The Frontenac Mystery François Mauriac (Penguin)

The Girl at the Lion d'Or Sebastian Faulks (Vintage)

Granite Island Dorothy Carrington (Penguin)

The Horseman on the Roof Jean Giono (Harvill)

Hotel Pastis Peter Mayle (Penguin)

Incidents in the Rue Laugier Anita Brookner (Penguin)

Jericho Dirk Bogarde (Penguin)

Jigsaw Sybille Bedford (Penguin)

Le Grand Meaulnes Alain-Fournier (Penguin)

Letters from My Windmill Alphonse Daudet (Penguin)

Long Ago in France M. F. K. Fisher (Flamingo)

Perfume Patrick Suskind (Penguin)

Quartet Jean Rhys (Penguin)

Scum of the Earth Arthur Koestler (Eland)

Selected Short Stories Guy de Maupassant (Penguin)

The Swimming Pool Season Rose Tremain (Sceptre)

Tender is the Night F. Scott Fitzgerald (Penguin)

The Tenth Man Graham Greene (Penguin)

The Time Out Book of Paris Short Stories (Penguin)

To Noto, or London to Sicily in a Ford Duncan Fallowell (Bloomsbury)

Toujours Provence Peter Mayle (Pan)

Travels with a Donkey in the Cévennes Robert Louis Stevenson (Everyman)

The Water of the Hills: Jean de Florette and *Manon of the Springs* Marcel Pagnol (Picador)

GABON

One Dry Season Caroline Alexander (Phoenix)

The Rainbird Jan Brokken (Lonely Planet)

Travels in West Africa Mary Kingsley (Everyman)

GERMANY

A Patriot in Berlin Piers Paul Read (Phoenix)

All Quiet on the Western Front Erich Maria Remarque (Penguin)

Berlin Noir Philip Kerr (Penguin)
The Berlin Novels Christopher Isherwood (Minerva)
The Blue Flower Penelope Fitzgerald (Flamingo)
Buddenbrooks Thomas Mann (Penguin)
Fatherland Robert Harris (Arrow)
Germany and the Germans John Ardagh (Penguin)
The Glass Bead Game Hermann Hesse (Penguin)
Hopeful Monsters Nicholas Moseley (Minerva)
The Innocent Ian McEwan (Picador)
The Tin Drum Günter Grass (Picador)

GHANA

All God's Children Need Travelling Shoes Maya Angelou (Virago)
The Seasons of Beento Blackbird Akosua Busia (Hutchinson)

GOA: see India

GREECE

The Alexander Trilogy Mary Renault (Penguin)
An Island Apart Sara Wheeler (Abacus)
The Balkan Trilogy Olivia Manning (Mandarin)
Captain Corelli's Mandolin Louis de Bernières (Minerva)
The Dancing Floor John Buchan (OUP)
The Double Tongue William Golding (Faber & Faber)
Father Dancing Nick Papandreou (Penguin)
Freedom and Death Nikos Kazantzakis (Faber & Faber)
Fugitive Pieces Anne Michaels (Bloomsbury)
The Greek Myths Robert Graves (Penguin)
The Iliad Homer (Penguin)
The Magus John Fowles (Picador)
Mani Patrick Leigh Fermor (Penguin)
My Family and Other Animals Gerald Durrell (Penguin)
The Odyssey Homer (Penguin)
The Olive Grove: Travels in Greece Katherine Kizilos (Lonely Planet)
Pascali's Island Barry Unsworth (Penguin)
Roumeli Patrick Leigh Fermor (Penguin)

The Two Faces of January Patricia Highsmith (Penguin)
The Unwritten Places Tim Salmon (Lycabettus Press)
Zorba the Greek Nikos Kazantzakis (Faber & Faber)

GREENLAND

Miss Smilla's Feeling for Snow Peter Høeg (Harvill)

GUADELOUPE

Between Two Worlds Simone Schwarz-Bart (Heinemann)

GUATEMALA

Rites: A Guatemalan Boyhood Victor Perera (Flamingo)
Up Above the World Paul Bowles (Paul Owens)

GULF STATES

Arabia Through the Looking Glass Jonathan Raban (Picador)
Arabian Sands Wilfred Thesiger (Penguin)
Seven Pillars of Wisdom T. E. Lawrence (Penguin)

GUYANA

The Counting House David Dabydeen (Vintage)
Ninety-Two Days Evelyn Waugh (Penguin)
Palace of the Peacock Wilson Harris (Faber & Faber)
The Ventriloquist's Tale Pauline Melville (Minerva)
Buxton Spice Oonya Kempadoo (Phoenix House)

HAITI

Bonjour Blanc: A Journey Through Haiti Ian Thomson (Penguin)
Breath, Eyes, Memory Edwidge Danticat (Abacus)
The Comedians Graham Greene (Penguin)
The Kingdom of This World Alejo Carpentier (Deutsch)

HONDURAS

The Mosquito Coast Paul Theroux (Penguin)

HONG KONG

A Many Splendoured Thing Han Suyin (Arrow)

An Insular Possession Timothy Mo (Picador)

Hong Kong Jan Morris (Penguin)

The Honourable Schoolboy John Le Carré (Hodder)

I Sailed with Chinese Pirates Aleko E. Lilius (Oxford)

The Monkey King Timothy Mo (Vintage)

Noble House James Clavell (Coronet)

The Painted Veil W. Somerset Maugham (Mandarin)

Tai-Pan James Clavell (Coronet)

HUNGARY

Between the Woods and the Water Patrick Leigh Fermor (Penguin)

Under the Frog Tibor Fischer (Penguin)

ICELAND

Independent People Halldor Laxness (Harvill)

Journey to the Centre of the Earth Jules Verne

Letters from High Altitudes Lord Dufferin (The Merlin Press)

Letters from Iceland W. H. Auden and Louis MacNeice
    (Faber & Faber)

Moon Country Simon Armitage and Glyn Maxwell (Faber & Faber)

The Swan Gudberger Bergsson (Shad Thames)

INDIA

A Backward Place Ruth Prawer Jhabvala (Penguin)

A Fine Balance Rohinton Mistry (Faber & Faber)

A Goddess in the Stones Norman Lewis
    (in the *Norman Lewis Omnibus*) (Picador)

A House in Pondicherry Lee Langley (Minerva)

A Journey in Ladakh Andrew Harvey (Picador)

A Malgudi Omnibus R. K. Narayan (Vintage)

A Passage to India E. M. Forster (Penguin)

A Son of the Circus John Irving (Black Swan)

A Suitable Boy Vikram Seth (Phoenix)

Abdul's Taxi to Kalighat Joe Roberts (Profile Books)

The Age of Kali William Dalrymple (Flamingo)

An Area of Darkness V. S. Naipaul (Picador Travel Classics)

Ancient Futures: Learning from Ladakh
  Helena Norberg-Hodge (Rider)

Are You Experienced? William Sutcliffe (Penguin)

Baumgartner's Bombay Anita Desai (Penguin)

Bhowani Junction John Masters (Ulverscroft)

Bullet up the Grand Trunk Road Jonathan Gregson
  (Sinclair-Stevenson)

Chasing the Monsoon Alexander Frater (Penguin)

City of Djinns William Dalrymple (Flamingo)

City of Joy Dominique Lapierre (Arrow)

Clear Light of Day Anita Desai (Penguin)

The Far Pavilions M. M. Kaye (Penguin)

Funny Boy Shyam Selvadvrai (Vintage)

The God of Small Things Arundhati Roy (Flamingo)

Grandmother's Footsteps Imogen Lycett Green (Pan)

The Heart of India Mark Tully (Viking)

Heat and Dust Ruth Prawer Jhabvala (Penguin)

Hullabaloo in the Guava Orchard Kiran Desai (Faber & Faber)

In Rajasthan Royina Grewal (Lonely Planet)

India V. S. Naipaul (Minerva)

Indian Balm Paul Hyland (Flamingo)

Journey to Ithaca Anita Desai (Vintage)

The Jungle Book Rudyard Kipling (Penguin)

Karma Cola Gita Mehta (Minerva)

Letters of an Indian Judge to an English Gentlewoman Anon.
  (Mandarin)

The Life of Mahatma Gandhi Louis Fischer (HarperCollins)

Love and Longing in Bombay Vikram Chandra (Faber & Faber)

Lovely Frank Ronan (Sceptre)

Malgudi Days R. K. Narayan (Penguin)

*May You Be the Mother of a Hundred Sons: A Journey Among the Women of
  India* Elisabeth Bumiller (Random House)

Midnight's Children Salman Rushdie (Vintage)

More Tales From Malgudi R K Narayan (Minerva)

No Full Stops in India Mark Tully (Penguin)

On a Shoestring to Coorg Dervla Murphy (Flamingo)

Plain Tales from the Hills Rudyard Kipling (Penguin)

Plain Tales from the Raj Charles Allen (Abacus)

Raj Gita Mehta (Minerva)

The Raj Quartet The Jewel in the Crown, The Day of the Scorpion, The Towers of Silence and *A Division of the Spoils* Paul Scott (Pan)

The Ramayana R. K. Narayan (Penguin)

Red Earth and Pouring Rain Vikram Chandra (Faber & Faber)

Rumer Godden: A Storyteller's Life Anne Chisholm (Macmillan)

Shopping for Buddhas Jeff Greenwald (Lonely Planet)

The Siege of Krishnapur J. G. Farrell (Phoenix)

Staying On Paul Scott (Mandarin)

Stones of Empire Jan Morris (Penguin)

Third-Class Ticket Heather Wood (Penguin)

Three-Quarters of a Footprint Joe Roberts (Black Swan)

Travels Through Sacred India Roger Housden (Thorsons)

Up the Country: Letters from India Emily Eden (Virago)

The Vendor of Sweets R. K. Narayan (Penguin)

Where the Indus is Young Dervla Murphy (Flamingo)

INDONESIA: see also Borneo

A Tale from Bali Vicki Baum (Oxford)

An Empire of the East Norman Lewis (Picador)

The Buru Quartet (*This Earth of Mankind, Child of All Nations, Footsteps* and *House of Glass*) Pramoedya Ananta Toer (Penguin)

Distant Voices John Pilger (Vintage)

Diverse Lives: Contemporary Short Stories from Indonesia (Oxford)

Hunting the Gugin Benedict Allen (Paladin)

In Search of Conrad Gavin Young (Penguin)

The Last Paradise Hickman Powell (Oxford)

Lord Jim Joseph Conrad (Penguin)

Not a Hazardous Sport Nigel Barley (Penguin)

Six Moons in Sulawesi Harry Wilcox (Oxford)

Skulduggery Mark Shand (Penguin)

Victory Joseph Conrad (Penguin)

The Year of Living Dangerously Christopher Koch (Minerva)

IRAN

An Iranian Odyssey Gohar Kordi (Serpent's Tail)

The Blindfold Horse Shusha Guppy (Minerva)

Daughter of Persia Sattareh Farman Farmaian with Dona Munker (Corgi)

In the Eye of the Storm ed. Mahnaz Afkhami and Erika Friedl (IB Tauris)

Javady Alley Manny Sharazi (The Women's Press)

Nine Parts of Desire (The Hidden World of Islamic Women) Geraldine Brooks (Hamish Hamilton)

The Road to Oxiana Robert Byron (Penguin)

The Ruba'iyat of Omar Khayyam Edward Fitzgerald (Penguin Classics)

Siege of Azadi Square Manny Shirazi (The Women's Press)

The Valleys of the Assassins Freya Stark (Arrow)

Whirlwind James Clavell (Coronet)

IRAQ

A Reed Shaken by the Wind Gavin Maxwell (Eland)

Ancient Iraq Georges Roux (Penguin)

Arabian Sands Wilfred Thesiger (Penguin)

Baghdad Sketches Freya Stark (The Marlboro Press)

Desert, Marsh and Mountain Wilfred Thesiger (Flamingo)

The Marsh Arabs Wilfred Thesiger (Penguin)

Mothballs Alia Mamdosh (Garnet)

Myths from Mesopotamia translated by Stephanie Dalley (Oxford)

Return to the Marshes Gavin Young (Penguin)

Shadow over Babylon David Mason (Signet)

ISRAEL

A Perfect Peace Amos Oz (Vintage)

Jerusalem Colin Thubron (Penguin)

Jerusalem: City of Mirrors Amos Elon (Flamingo)

The Mandelbaum Gate Muriel Spark (Penguin)

Quarantine Jim Crace (Penguin)

Roots Schmoots Howard Jacobson (Penguin)

This Year in Jerusalem Mordecai Richler (Vintage)

The Yellow Wind David Grossman (Picador)

Where the Jackals Howl Amos Oz (Vintage)

ITALY

A Farewell to Arms Ernest Hemingway (Arrow)

A Rich Full Death Michael Dibdin (Faber & Faber)

A Room with a View E. M. Forster (Penguin)

A Small Place in Italy Eric Newby (Picador)

A Tuscan Childhood Kinta Beevor (Penguin)

A Valley in Italy Lisa St Aubin de Terán (Penguin)

The Aeneid Virgil (Penguin)

After Hannibal Barry Unsworth (Penguin)

The Agony and the Ecstasy Irving Stone (Mandarin)

An Italian Education Tim Parks (Minerva)

The Aspern Papers Henry James (Penguin)

The Betrothed Alessandro Manzoni (Penguin)

Cara Massimina Tim Parks (Minerva)

The Charterhouse of Parma Stendhal (Penguin)

Christ Stopped at Eboli Carlo Levi (Penguin)

Death at La Fenice Donna Leon (Pan)

Death in Venice and Other Stories Thomas Mann (Minerva)

The Death of Faith Donna Leon (Pan)

The Decameron Boccaccio (Penguin)

The Divine Comedy Dante (Penguin)

Don't Look Now and Other Stories Daphne Du Maurier (Penguin)

The Enchanted April Elizabeth von Arnin (Virago)

The English Patient Michael Ondaatje (Picador)

Europa Tim Parks (Vintage)

The Godfather Mario Puzo (Mandarin)

The Golden Honeycomb: A Sicilian Quest Vincent Cronin (Harvill)

The Hotel Elizabeth Bowen (Penguin)

I, Claudius and *Claudius the God* Robert Graves (Penguin)

In the Valley of the Fireflies Peter Hobday (Michael Joseph)

Innocence Penelope Fitzgerald (Flamingo)

Inspector Zen series: *Dead Lagoon; Vendetta; Così Fan Tutti; Cabal; Ratking* Michael Dibdin (Faber & Faber)

Isolina Dacia Maraini (The Women's Press)

The Italian Anne Radcliffe (Oxford)

Italian Folktales Italo Calvino (Penguin)

The Italian Girl Iris Murdoch (Penguin)

Italian Neighbours Tim Parks (Minerva)

Journeys to the Underworld Fiona Pitt-Kethley (Chatto & Windus)

The Judas Cloth Julia O'Faolain (Minerva)

The Last Father Marina Warner (Vintage)

The Leopard Giuseppe di Lampedusa (Harvill Press)

Lives of the Artists Giorgio Vasari (Penguin)

Love and War in the Apennines Eric Newby (Picador)

Marcovaldo Italo Calvino (Minerva)

Mimi's Ghost Tim Parks (Minerva)

The Name of the Rose Umberto Eco (Minerva)

Nocturne Lisa St Aubin de Terán (Penguin)

Old Calabria Norman Douglas (Picador Travel Classics)

Orlando Furioso Ludovico Ariosto (Penguin)

The Passion Jeanette Winterson (Penguin)

Portofino Frank Schaeffer (Black Swan)

Sea and Sardinia D. H. Lawrence (Olive Press)

The Shrine Cristina Odone (Phoenix)

The Slow Train to Milan Lisa St Aubin de Terán (Penguin)

Stone Virgin Barry Unsworth (Penguin)

The Story of San Michele Axel Munthe (Flamingo)

Summer's Lease John Mortimer (Penguin)

To Noto, or London to Sicily in a Ford Duncan Fallowell (Bloomsbury)

Two Lives William Trevor (Penguin)

Under the Tuscan Sun Frances Mayes (Bantam)

Venice Jan Morris (Faber & Faber)

Venus in Copper, The Iron Hand of Mars, Last Act in Palmyra, Poseidon's Gold, Time to Depart, A Dying Light in Corduba and *The Course of Honour* Lindsey Davies (Arrow)

Volcanic Airs Elizabeth Pewsey (Sceptre)

Watermark Joseph Brodsky (Hamish Hamilton)

Where Angels Fear to Tread E. M. Forster (Penguin)

The Wings of the Dove Henry James (Mandarin)

JAPAN

A Japanese Mirror Ian Buruma (Vintage)

A Pale View of Hills Kazuo Ishiguro (Faber & Faber)

A Personal Matter Kenzaburo Oë (Picador)

A Quiet Life Kenzaburo Oë (Picador)

An Artist of the Floating World Kazuo Ishiguro (Faber & Faber)

Death in Midsummer and Other Stories Yukio Mishima (Penguin)

Forbidden Colours Yukio Mishima (Penguin)

Gai-Jin James Clavell (Coronet)

The Hard Boiled Wonderland and the End of the World
  Haruki Murakami (Penguin)

Inspector Otani series James Melville (Secker)

The Japanese Chronicles Nicholas Bouvier (Polygon)

The Lady and the Monk Pico Iyer (Black Swan)

Lizard Banana Yoshimoto (Faber & Faber)

Lost Japan Alex Kerr (Lonely Planet)

The Makioka Sisters Junichiro Tanizaki (Vintage Classic)

On the Narrow Road to the Deep North Lesley Downer (Sceptre)

Pictures from the Water Trade John David Morley (Abacus)

The Pillow Boy of the Lady Onogoro Alison Fell (Serpent's Tail)

The Roads to Sata Alan Booth (Penguin)

Sailor Who Fell From Grace Yukio Mishima (Penguin)

Shogun James Clavell (Coronet)

The Shooting Gallery and Other Stories Yuko Tsushima
  (The Women's Press)

Silence Shusako Endo (Penguin)

Sir Phoebus's Ma Zoë Teale (Phoenix House)

Snow Country and Thousand Cranes Yasunari Kawabata (Penguin)

Thirst for Love Yukio Mishima (Penguin)

Unbeaten Tracks in Japan Isabella Bird (Virago)

JORDAN

Kingdom of the Film Stars Annie Caulfield (Lonely Planet)

Pillars of Salt Fadia Faqir (Quartet Books)

KAZAKHSTAN

The Lost Heart of Asia Colin Thubron (Penguin)

KENYA

A Small Town in Africa Daisy Waugh (Large Print Books)
African Nights Kuki Gallmann (Penguin)
An Ice-Cream War William Boyd (Penguin)
The Book of Secrets M. G. Vassanji (Picador)
Devil on the Cross Ngugi wa Thiong'o (Heinemann)
Elephant Memories Cynthia Moss (Fontana/Collins)
The Flame Trees of Thika Elspeth Huxley (Penguin)
I Dreamed of Africa Kuki Gallmann (Penguin)
The Jacaranda Flower Toril Brekke (Methuen)
The Lives of Beryl Markham Errol Trzebinski (Mandarin)
My Kenya Days Wilfred Thesiger (Flamingo)
No Man's Land George Monbiot (Picador)
On the Edge of the Great Rift Paul Theroux (Penguin)
Out of Africa Karen Blixen (Isak Dinesen) (Penguin)
Ripples in the Pool Rebeka Njau (Heinemann)
Shadows on the Grass Karen Blixen (Isak Dinesen) (Penguin)
The Weather in Africa Martha Gellhorn (Eland)
West With the Night Beryl Markham (Virago)
White Mischief James Fox (Vintage)

KOREA

I am the Clay Chaim Potok (Penguin)
One Thousand Chestnut Trees Mira Stout (Flamingo)

KYRGYSTAN

The Lost Heart of Asia Colin Thubron (Penguin)

LAOS: see also Vietnam, Cambodia and Laos

One Foot in Laos Dervla Murphy (John Murray)
Stalking the Elephant Kings Christopher Kremmer
  (Allen & Unwin)

LATVIA

The Revolution in the Baltics Anatol Lieven (Yale University Press)

LEBANON

An Evil Cradling Brian Keenan (Vintage)
Beirut Blues Hanan Al-Shaykh (Vintage)
Blueprint for a Prophet Carl Gibeily (Black Swan)
The Hills of Adonis Colin Thubron (Penguin)
Pity the Nation – Lebanon at War Robert Fisk (Oxford)
The Rock of Tanios Amin Maalouf (Abacus)
The Story of Zahra Hanan Al-Shaykh (Quartet Books)

LIBERIA

Journey Without Maps Graham Greene (Penguin)

LIBYA

Libyan Sands R. A. Bagnold (Picador)

LITHUANIA

The Revolution in the Baltics Anatol Lieven (Yale University Press)

MACAU

A Macao Narrative Austin Coates (Oxford)
I Sailed with Chinese Pirates Aleko E. Lilius (Oxford)

MADAGASCAR

Madagascar Travels Christina Dodwell (Hodder & Stoughton)
Muddling Through in Madagascar Dervla Murphy (Flamingo)

MALAWI

On the Edge of the Great Rift Paul Theroux (Penguin)

MALAYSIA AND SINGAPORE: see also Borneo

A Gentle Occupation Dirk Bogarde (Penguin)
The Borneo Stories W. Somerset Maugham (Mandarin)
The Chersonese with the Gilding Off Emily Innes (Oxford)

Collected Short Stories (vol 4) W. Somerset Maugham (Mandarin)

Far Eastern Tales W. Somerset Maugham (Mandarin)

Foreign Bodies Hwee Hwee Tan (Michael Joseph)

The Golden Chersonese Isabella Bird (Oxford)

King Rat James Clavell (Coronet)

Lord Jim Joseph Conrad (Penguin)

'The Malayan Trilogy' Anthony Burgess (Penguin)

Saint Jack Paul Theroux (Penguin)

The Shadow Line Joseph Conrad (Penguin)

The Singapore Grip J. G. Farrell (Phoenix)

The Soul of Malaya Henri Fauconnier (Oxford)

The Teardrop Story Woman Catherine Lin (Orion)

Turtle Beach Blanche d'Alpuget (Penguin)

Under the Durian Tree Fergus Linehan (Mandarin)

Victory Joseph Conrad (Penguin)

MALTA

The Jukebox Queen of Malta Nicholas Rinaldi (Black Swan)

MAURITIUS

The Book of Colour Julia Blackburn (Vintage)

Isabelle Marcelle Lagesse (Quartet)

MEXICO

A Trip to the Light Fantastic: Travels with a Mexican Circus
Katie Hickman (Flamingo)

A Visit to Don Otavio Sybille Bedford (Picador Travel Classics)

Air and Fire Rupert Thomson (Penguin)

Beyond the Mexique Bay Aldous Huxley (Flamingo)

Like Water for Chocolate Laura Esquivel (Black Swan)

Mornings in Mexico D. H. Lawrence (Penguin)

Nostromo Joseph Conrad (Picador Classics)

On Mexican Time Tony Cohan (Bloomsbury)

The Plumed Serpent D. H. Lawrence (Penguin)

The Power and the Glory Graham Greene (Penguin)

Under the Volcano Malcolm Lowry (Picador)

Viva Mexico! Charles Flandrau (Eland)

Year of the Jaguar James May (Sceptre)

MIDDLE EAST

Among the Believers V. S. Naipaul (Penguin)

Coming Up Roses Michael Carson (Black Swan)

The Crossing Place: A Journey Among the Armenians
   Philip Marsden (Flamingo)

Eothen: Traces of Travel Brought Home from the East
   Alistair Kinglake (Picador Travel Classics)

From the Holy Mountain: A Journey in the Shadow of Byzantium William
   Dalrymple (Penguin)

'The Levant Trilogy' Olivia Manning (Penguin)

The Price of Honour Jan Goodwin (Warner Books)

The Seven Pillars of Wisdom T. E. Lawrence (Penguin)

MONGOLIA

In Xanadu William Dalrymple (Flamingo)

The Last Disco in Outer Mongolia Nick Middleton (Phoenix)

On the Edge of Blue Heaven Benedict Allen (BBC)

Storm from the East Robert Marshall (Penguin)

The Travels Marco Polo (Penguin)

MOROCCO

Abdullah's Feet Hafid Bouazza (Review)

A Woman of my Age Nina Bawden (Virago)

By Bus to the Sahara Gordon West (Black Swan)

The Game of Forgetting Mohamed Berrada (Quartet)

The Harem Within Fatima Mernissi (Bantam)

Hideous Kinky Esther Freud (Penguin)

See Ouarzazate and Die: Travels Through Morocco Sylvia Kennedy (Abacus)

The Sheltering Sky Paul Bowles (Flamingo)

The Spider's House Paul Bowles (Abacus)

Tangier Iain Finlayson (Flamingo)

The Tangier Diaries John Hopkins (Arcadia Books)

MOZAMBIQUE

Kalashnikovs and Zombie Cucumbers Nick Middleton (Phoenix)

MYANMAR (Burma)

A Burmese Legacy Sue Arnold (Sceptre)
Burmese Days George Orwell (Penguin)
Freedom from Fear Aung San Suu Kyi (Penguin)
Golden Earth Norman Lewis (Eland)
Kim Rudyard Kipling (Penguin)
The Lacquer Lady F. Tennyson Jesse (Virago)
Letters from Burma Aung San Suu Kyi (Penguin)
Under the Dragon: Travels in a Betrayed Land Rory MacLean
   (HarperCollins)

NAMIBIA

The Burning Shore Wilbur Smith (Pan)
The Lost World of the Kalahari Laurens van der Post (Penguin)
The Skeleton Coast Benedict Allen (BBC)

NEPAL

Against a Peacock Sky Monica Connell (Penguin)
Shopping for Buddhas Jeff Greenwald (Lonely Planet)
The Snow Leopard Peter Matthiessen (Vintage)
The Waiting Land Dervla Murphy (Arrow)

NETHERLANDS

The Diary of a Young Girl Anne Frank (Penguin)
Nicolas Freeling's Van der Valk detective novels (Penguin)
Tulip Fever Deborah Moggach (Vintage)

NEW GUINEA: see also Papua New Guinea

Islands in the Clouds Isabella Tree (Lonely Planet)
Skulduggery Mark Shand (Penguin)
Under the Mountain Wall Peter Matthiessen (Harvill)

NEW ZEALAND

The Bone People Keri Hulme (Pan)

Collected Stories Katherine Mansfield (Penguin)

Crime Story Maurice Gee (Faber & Faber)

Dunedin Shena Mackay (Penguin)

Going West Maurice Gee (Faber & Faber)

Living in the Manioto Janet Frame (The Women's Press)

Once Were Warriors Alan Duff (Vintage)

Owls Do Cry Janet Frame (The Women's Press)

Oxford Book of New Zealand Short Stories ed. Vincent O'Sullivan (Oxford)

The Picador Book of Contemporary New Zealand Fiction ed. Fergus Barrowman (Picador)

River Lines Elspeth Sandys (Sceptre)

Scented Gardens for the Blind Janet Frame (The Women's Press)

Tapu Judy Corbalis (Vintage)

NICARAGUA

Desperadoes Joseph O'Connor (Flamingo)

The Jaguar Smile: A Nicaraguan Journey Salman Rushdie (Picador)

Wild Shore: Life and Death with Nicaragua's Last Shark Hunters Edward Marriott (Picador)

NIGERIA

A Month and a Day Ken Saro-Wiwa (Penguin)

Anthills of the Savannah Chinua Achebe (Picador)

Dangerous Love Ben Okri (Phoenix)

The Famished Road Ben Okri (Vintage)

Incidents at the Shrine Ben Okri (Vintage)

The Interpreter Wole Soyinka (Heinemann)

Lemona's Tale Ken Saro-Wiwa (Penguin)

No Longer at Ease Chinua Achebe (Heinemann)

Sozaboy Ken Saro-Wiwa (Longman)

Stars of the New Curfew Ben Okri (Penguin)

NORWAY

A Doll's House and Other Plays Ibsen (Penguin)

Dina's Book Herbjorg Wassmo (Black Swan)

The Wanderer Knut Hamsun (Souvenir)

PACIFIC BASIN

The Happy Isles of Oceania Paul Theroux (Penguin)

In Search of Tusitala: Travels in the Pacific After Robert Louis Stevenson
Gavin Bell (Picador)

The Island of the Colour Blind and Cycad Island Oliver Sacks (Picador)

Island of Dreams Tony Williams (Signet)

Paradise News David Lodge (Penguin)

Slow Boats Home Gavin Young (Penguin)

Tales of the Pacific Jack London (Penguin)

Transit of Venus: Travels in the Pacific Julian Evans (Minerva)

Typee Herman Melville (Oxford)

PAKISTAN

Daughter of the East Benazir Bhutto (Mandarin)

The Golden Horde Sheila Paine (Penguin)

The Golden Peak: Travels in Northern Pakistan Kathleen Jamie (Virago)

My Feudal Lord Tehmina Durrani (Corgi)

So That You Can Know Me eds. Yasmin Hameed and Asif Aslam Farrukhi
(Garnet)

To the Frontier Geoffrey Moorhouse (Phoenix)

Where the Indus is Young Dervla Murphy (Flamingo)

PANAMA

Getting to Know the General Graham Greene (Penguin)

The Tailor of Panama John Le Carré (Sceptre)

PAPUA NEW GUINEA: see also New Guinea

A Papua New Guinea Sojourn E. A. Markham (Carcanet)

Into the Crocodile Nest Benedict Allen (Flamingo)

The Lost Tribe Edward Marriott (Picador)

The Proving Grounds Benedict Allen (Flamingo)

Under the Mountain Wall Peter Matthiessen (Harvill)

PARAGUAY

The Drunken Forest Gerald Durrell (Penguin)

PERU

Alive Piers Paul Read (Mandarin)
Amazon Dream Roberta Allen (City Lights)
Aunt Julia and the Scriptwriter Mario Vargas Llosa (Faber & Faber)
Eight Feet in the Andes Dervla Murphy (Flamingo)
Inca-Kola: A Traveller's Tale of Peru Matthew Parris (Phoenix)
The Notebooks of Don Rigoberto Mario Vargas Llosa (Faber & Faber)
Overthrown by Strangers Ronan Bennett (Penguin)
Three Letters from the Andes Patrick Leigh Fermor (Penguin)
Touching the Void Joe Simpson (Vintage)
The Vision of Elena Silves Nicholas Shakespeare (Picador)

PHILIPPINES

The Blue Afternoon William Boyd (Penguin)
Ghosts of Manila James Hamilton-Paterson (Vintage)
The Last Time I Saw Mother Arlene J. Chai (Review)

PITCAIRN ISLANDS

Serpent in Paradise Dea Birkett (Picador)

POLAND

If Not Now, When? Primo Levi (Abacus)
In the Memory of the Forest Charles T. Powers (Anchor)
Schindler's List (originally called *Schindler's Ark*) Thomas Keneally (Sceptre)
Scum Isaac Bashevis Singer (Penguin)
Slaughterhouse 5 Kurt Vonnegut (Vintage)
Wartime Lies Louis Begley (Picador)
Winter in the Morning Janina Bauman (Virago)

PORTUGAL

Backwards out of the Big World Paul Hyland (Flamingo)
The History of the Siege of Lisbon José Saramago (Harvill)

The Last Guests of the Season Sue Gee (Arrow)

Lucio's Confession Mário de Sá Carneiro (Dedalus)

Passport to Portugal Mike Gerrard and Thomas McCarthy (Serpent's Tail)

The Relic Eça de Queiroz (Dedalus European Classics)

ROMANIA

Looking for George: Love and Death in Romania Helena Drysdale (Picador)

Out of Romania Dan Antal (Faber & Faber)

Saxophone Dreams Nicholas Royle (Penguin)

RUSSIA

A Dry Ship to the Mountains: Down the Volga and Across the Caucasus in My Father's Footsteps Daniel Farson (Penguin)

A Month in the Country I. S. Turgenev (Penguin)

Among the Russians Colin Thubron (Picador Travel Classics)

Anna Karenina Leo Tolstoy (Penguin)

Beyond Siberia Christina Dodwell (Sceptre)

The Big Red Train Ride Eric Newby (Picador)

Crime and Punishment Fyodor Dostoyevsky (Penguin)

Dr Zhivago Boris Pasternak (Harvill)

First Russia, Then Tibet Robert Byron (Penguin)

Gorky Park Martin Cruz Smith (Pan)

The Gulag Archipelago Aleksandr Solzhenitsyn (Harvill)

Immortal Love Ludmilla Petrushevskaya (Virago)

Journey into the Mind's Eye Lesley Blanch (Pimlico)

Journey into Russia Laurens van der Post (Penguin)

Little Vera Maria Khmelik (Bloomsbury)

Moscow Mule James Young (Arrow)

Oblomov Ivan Goncharov (Penguin)

On the Golden Porch and Other Stories Tatyana Tolstaya (Penguin)

One Day in the Life of Ivan Denisovich Aleksandr Solzhenitsyn (Penguin)

The Penguin Book of New Russian Writing ed. Victor Erofeyev (Penguin)

The Portable Chekhov (Penguin)

Pushkin House Andrei Bitov (Collins Harvill)

Rancid Aluminium James Hawes (Vintage)

The Russian Album Michael Ignatieff (Penguin)

The Time: Night Ludmilla Petrushevskaya (Virago)

Volga, Volga: A Voyage Down the Great River Lesley Chamberlain (Picador)

War and Peace Leo Tolstoy (Penguin)

The Wild East (Granta)

RWANDA

Gorillas in the Mist Dian Fossey (Penguin)

Rules of the Wild Francesca Marciano (Jonathan Cape)

Season of Blood Fergal Keane (Penguin)

SAMOA

Rain W. Somerset Maugham (in *Short Stories*) (Minerva)

Rascals in Paradise James Michener and Arthur Grove Day (Mandarin)

Return to Paradise James Michener (Mandarin)

Tales of the South Pacific James Michener (Corgi)

SAUDI ARABIA

Eight Months on Ghazzah Street Hilary Mantel (Penguin)

The Southern Gates of Arabia Freya Stark (John Murray)

SERBIA

Merry Christmas Mr Larry Larry Hollingworth (Mandarin)

SIERRA LEONE

Our Grandmother's Drums Mark Hudson (Mandarin)

SINGAPORE: see also Malaysia

The Bond Maid Catherine Lim (Orion)

SOLOMON ISLANDS

Rascals in Paradise James Michener and Arthur Grove Day (Mandarin)

Tales of the South Pacific James Michener (Corgi)

SOMALIA

In the Name of our Fathers Abdirazak Y. Osman (HAAN Publishing)

Warriors Gerald Hanley (Eland)

SOUTH AFRICA

A Chain of Voices André Brink (Minerva)

A Dry White Season André Brink (Minerva)

A World of Strangers Nadine Gordimer (Penguin)

Age of Iron J. M. Coetzee (Penguin)

Ah, But Your Land is Beautiful Alan Paton (Penguin)

The Betrayal Gillian Slovo (Virago)

Buckingham Palace District Six Richard Rive (Heinemann)

The Conservationist Nadine Gordimer (Penguin)

Cry, the Beloved Country Alan Paton (Penguin)

Cry Freedom John Briley (Penguin)

Disgrace J.M. Coetzee (Secker & Warburg)

Dreambirds Rob Nixon (Doubleday)

Imaginings of Sand André Brink (Minerva)

Innocents in Africa Drury Pifer (Granta)

King Solomon's Mines H. Rider Haggard (Penguin)

The Life and Times of Michael K J. M. Coetzee (Penguin)

Long Walk to Freedom Nelson Mandela (Abacus)

Manly Pursuits Ann Harries (Bloomsbury Paperbacks)

Middlepost Antony Sher (Abacus)

My Traitor's Heart Rian Malan (Vintage)

None to Accompany Me Nadine Gordimer (Penguin)

The Penguin Book of Contemporary South African Short Stories (Penguin)

The Power of One Bryce Courtenay (Mandarin)

Prester John John Buchan (Penguin)

Selected Stories Nadine Gordimer (Penguin)

The Smell of Apples Mark Behr (Abacus)

Somewhere Over the Rainbow: Travels in South Africa Gavin Bell (Little, Brown)

The Sound of Thunder Wilbur Smith (Mandarin)

The Story of an African Farm Olive Schreiner (Oxford)

Where the Lion Feeds Wilbur Smith (Mandarin)

SOUTH AMERICA (GENERAL)
(see also individual countries)

The Beautiful Game Chris Taylor (Gollancz)

Between Extremes Brian Keenan and John McCarthy (Bantam Press)

The Cloud Forest Peter Matthiessen (Harvill)

Dream Catching: On the Road Reluctantly Dyan Sheldon (Little, Brown)

In Patagonia Bruce Chatwin (Picador)

The Motorcycle Diaries: A Journey Around South America Ernesto Che Guevara (Fourth Estate)

Saddled with Darwin Toby Green (Weidenfeld)

Señor Vivo and the Coca Lord Louis de Bernières (Minerva)

Tarantulas and Marmosets: An Amazon Diary Nick Gordon (Metro)

Through Jaguar Eyes Benedict Allen (Flamingo)

The Tiger Lisa St Aubin de Terán (Penguin)

The Troublesome Offspring of Cardinal Guzman Louise de Bernières (Minerva)

The War of Don Emmanuel's Nether Parts Louis de Bernières (Minerva)

SPAIN

A Rose for Winter Laurie Lee (Penguin)

A Woman Unknown Lucia Graves (Virago)

The Angst-Ridden Executive Manuel Vazquez Montalban (Serpent's Tail)

As I Walked Out One Midsummer Morning Laurie Lee (Penguin)

Between Hopes and Memories: A Spanish Journey Michael Jacobs (Picador)

Death in the Afternoon Ernest Hemingway (Arrow)

Desperately Seeking Julio Maruja Torres (Fourth Estate)

Don Quixote Miguel de Cervantes (Penguin)

Driving Over Lemons Chris Stewart (Sort of Books)

The Face of Spain Gerald Brenan (Penguin)

Fiesta/The Sun Also Rises Ernest Hemingway (Arrow)

For Whom the Bell Tolls Ernest Hemingway (Arrow)

Here We Go: A Summer on the Costa del Sol Harry Ritchie (Penguin)

Homage to Barcelona Colm Tóibín (Penguin)

Homage to Catalonia George Orwell (Penguin)

Leo the African Amin Maalouf (Abacus)

Life with Picasso Françoise Gilot and Carlton Lake (Virago)

The Lonely Hearts Club Raul Nunez (Serpent's Tail)

Monsignor Quixote Graham Greene (Penguin)

The South Colm Tóibín (Picador)

South from Granada Gerald Brenan (Penguin)
Spain Jan Morris (Penguin)
Voices of the Old Sea Norman Lewis (Picador)
The Windfall Prue Carmichael (Warner Books)
The Year of the Flood Eduardo Mendoza (Panther)

SRI LANKA

Cinnamon Gardens Shyam Selvadurai (Anchor)
Facing Out to Sea Peter Adamson (Sceptre)
The Flower Boy Karen Roberts (Phoenix)
Monkfish Moon Romesh Gunesekera (Granta/Penguin)
Reef Romesh Gunesekera (Granta/Penguin)
Running in the Family Michael Ondaatje (Pan)

SUDAN

African Comedy David Hopkins (Flamingo)

SWEDEN

Blackwater Kerstin Ekman (Vintage)
My Life as a Dog Reidar Jönsson (Farrer, Straus & Giroux)

SWITZERLAND

Belle du Seigneur Albert Cohen (Penguin)
Dr Fischer of Geneva or The Bomb Party Graham Greene (Penguin)
Hotel du Lac Anita Brookner (Penguin)
Mer de Glace Alison Fell (Serpent's Tail)

SYRIA

Cleopatra's Wedding Present: Travels Through Syria Robert Tewdwr Moss
(Duckworth)
The Gates of Damascus Lieve Joris (Lonely Planet)
Mirror to Damascus Colin Thubron (Penguin)

TAIWAN

Death in a Cornfield Ching Hsi Pserng and Chiu-Kuei Wang (OUP)

TAJIKISTAN

The Lost Heart of Asia Colin Thubron (Penguin)

TANZANIA

An Ice-Cream War William Boyd (Penguin)
The Book of Secrets M. G. Vassanji (Picador)
No Man's Land George Monbiot (Picador)

THAILAND

An English Governess at the Court of Siam Anna Leonowens (Oxford)
The Beach Alex Garland (Penguin)
Borderlines Charles Nicholl (Picador)
Bridge on the River Kwai Pierre Boulle (Mandarin)
Descriptions of Old Siam comp. Michael Smithies (Oxford)
Year of the Roasted Ear Donna Carrère (Summersdale)

TIBET

First Russia, Then Tibet Robert Byron (Penguin)
From Heaven Lake Vikram Seth (Phoenix)
Journey to Lhasa: The Personal Story of the Only White Woman Who Succeeded in Entering the Forbidden City Alexandra David-Neel (Virago)
Naked Spirits Adrian Abbotts (Canongate)
Running a Hotel on the Roof of the World: Five Years in Tibet Alec de Sueur (Summersdale)
Seven Years in Tibet Heinrich Harrer (Flamingo)
Tibetan Foothold Dervla Murphy (Flamingo)

TUNISIA

Behind Closed Doors Monia Hejaiej (Quartet)

TURKEY

A Fez of the Heart Jeremy Seal (Picador)
A Proper Holiday Ann Oakley (Flamingo)
Dervish Tim Kelsey (Hamish Hamilton)
Istanbul: The Imperial City John Freely (Penguin)
Memed, my Hawk Yashar Kemal (Panther)

Mooncranker's Gift Barry Unsworth (Penguin)
Portrait of a Turkish Family Irfan Orga (Eland)
Stamboul Train Graham Greene (Penguin)
The Towers of Trebizond Rose Macaulay (Flamingo)
The Turkish Labyrinth James Pettifer (Penguin)
The Undying Grass Yashar Kemal (Harvill)
The White Castle Orhan Pamuk (Faber & Faber)

TURKMENISTAN

The Lost Heart of Asia Colin Thubron (Penguin)

UGANDA

The Last King of Scotland Giles Foden (Faber & Faber)
On the Edge of the Great Rift Paul Theroux (Penguin)

UKRAINE

Borderland Anna Reed (Wiedenfeld & Nicholson)

USA

American novels are too numerous to list. Take your pick from the big
name classic writers – Edith Wharton, Henry James, John Steinbeck,
Dorothy Parker, F. Scott Fitzgerald, Carson McCullers, Mark Twain and
Jack London. Or try crime, from vintage writers like Dashiel Hammett
and Raymond Chandler or contemporary writers such as Sara Paretsky
and Elmore Leonard. There's a rich vein of black writing from the likes
of Maya Angelou, Toni Morrison, James Baldwin, Alice Walker and
Terry Macmillan. And you can't go far wrong with anything by Alice
Hoffman, Alison Lurie, John Irving and Anne Tyler.

So we've restricted ourselves to listing a selection of travel writing,
plus some fiction particularly relevant to travelling or to specific areas.

General

America Observed Alistair Cooke (Penguin)
American Heartbeat Mick Brown (Penguin)
Bury My Heart at Wounded Knee Dee Brown (Vintage)
Dances with Wolves Michael Blake (Penguin)
Drive Thru America Sean Condon (Lonely Planet)
From Sea to Shining Sea Gavin Young (Penguin)

The Great American Bus Ride Irma Kurtz (Fourth Estate)
Into the Badlands John Williams (Flamingo)
The Kinky Friedman Crime Club Kinky Friedman (Faber & Faber)
The Lost Continent Bill Bryson (Abacus)
Old Glory Jonathan Raban (Picador)
On the Road Jack Kerouac (Penguin)
The Oxford Book of American Short Stories ed. Joyce Carol Oates (Oxford)
Travels in a Strange State Josie Dew (Warner)
USA John Dos Passos (Penguin)
Where I'm Calling From Raymond Carver (Harvill)

Deep South and Florida

A Confederacy of Dunces John Kennedy Toole (Penguin)
Accordion Crimes E. Annie Proulx (Fourth Estate)
As I Lay Dying William Faulkner (Vintage)
Beloved Toni Morrison (Picador)
Cold Mountain Charles Frazier (Vintage)
The Color Purple Alice Walker (The Women's Press)
Divine Secrets of the Ya Ya Sisterhood Rebecca Wells (Pan)
Double Whammy Carl Hiaasen (Pan)
Gone With the Wind Margaret Mitchell (Pan)
In God's Country: Travels in the Bible Belt, USA Douglas Kennedy
   (Abacus)
Miami Joan Didion (Flamingo)
Miami Blues Charles Willeford (No Exit Press)
Midnight in the Garden of Good and Evil John Berendt (Vintage)
Skin Tight Carl Hiaasen (Pan)
Sort of Rich James Wilcox (Fourth Estate)
Strip Tease Carl Hiaasen (Pan)
The Sound and the Fury William Faulkner (Vintage)
To Have and Have Not Ernest Hemingway (Arrow)
To Kill a Mockingbird Harper Lee (Mandarin)

New York and East Coast

A Tree Grows in Brooklyn Betty Smith (Mandarin)
A Walk in the Woods Bill Bryson (Doubleday)
Bonfire of the Vanities Tom Wolfe (Picador)

Bright Lights, Big City Jay McInerney (Flamingo)

The Catcher in the Rye J. D. Salinger (Penguin)

Flesh and Blood Michael Cunningham (Penguin)

The Heart of the World Nik Cohn (Vintage)

Jazz Toni Morrison (Picador)

The New York Trilogy Paul Auster (Faber & Faber)

The Novels of Old New York (*The Age of Innocence, The Custom of the Country* and *The House of Mirth*) Edith Wharton (Penguin)

Our Noise Jeff Gomez (Penguin)

The Secret History Donna Tartt (Penguin)

Slaves of New York Tama Janowitz (Picador)

Suffragette City Kate Muir (Macmillan)

West Coast and South-West

All the Pretty Horses Cormac McCarthy (Picador)

The Black Dahlia James Ellroy (Arrow)

Dead Man's Walk Larry McMurtry (Phoenix)

Double Indemnity James M. Cain (Hale)

Even Cowgirls Get the Blues Tom Robbins (Bantam)

Generation X Douglas Coupland (Penguin)

Get Shorty Elmore Leonard (Penguin)

The Journal of Antonia Montoya Rick Collignon (Fourth Estate)

The Joy Luck Club Amy Tan (Minerva)

Lonesome Dove Larry McMurtry (Phoenix)

Los Angeles Without a Map Richard Rayner (Flamingo)

The Loved One Evelyn Waugh (Penguin)

Mildred Pierce James M. Cain (Hale)

Motel Nirvana Melanie McGrath (Flamingo)

Pigs in Heaven Barbara Kingsolver (Faber & Faber)

The Postman Always Rings Twice James M. Cain (Chivers)

Snow Falling on Cedars David Guterson (Bloomsbury)

Tales of the City series Armistead Maupin (Black Swan)

Tortilla Curtain T. Coraghessan Boyle (Bloomsbury)

Mid-West

A Lady's Life in the Rocky Mountains Isabella Bird (Virago)

A Map of the World Jane Hamilton (Black Swan)

A Thousand Acres Jane Smiley (Flamingo)

The Beet Queen Louise Erdrich (Flamingo)

Lake Wobegon Days Garrison Keillor (Faber & Faber)

Moo Jane Smiley (Flamingo)

Who Will Run the Frog Hospital? Lorrie Moore (Faber & Faber)

Alaska

Kolymsky Heights Lionel Davidson (Mandarin)

Into the Wild Jon Krakauer (Pan)

UZBEKISTAN

The Lost Heart of Asia Colin Thubron (Penguin)

Samarkand Amin Maalouf (Abacus)

VENEZUELA

The Creature in the Map Charles Nicholl (Jonathan Cape)

The Hacienda, My Venezuelan Years Lisa St Aubin de Terán (Virago)

In Trouble Again (A Journey Between the Orinoco and the Amazon) Redmond O'Hanlon (Penguin)

VIETNAM, CAMBODIA AND LAOS

A Bright Shining Lie Neil Sheehan (Picador)

A Dragon Apparent Norman Lewis (Eland)

A Good Scent from a Strange Mountain Robert Olen Butler (Minerva)

A Phoenix Rising: Impressions of Vietnam Zoë Schramm-Evans (Flamingo)

A Wavering Grace: A Vietnamese Family in War and Peace Gavin Young (Penguin)

Bridge Across My Sorrows Christina Noble (Corgi)

The Deep Green Sea Robert Olen Butler (Secker & Warburg)

Derailed in Uncle Ho's Victory Garden Tim Page (Touchstone/ Simon & Schuster)

Dispatches Michael Herr (Pan)

Heroes John Pilger (Pan)

If I Die in a Combat Zone Tim O'Brien (Flamingo)

In Pharaoh's Army Tobias Wolff (Picador)

Lord Jim Joseph Conrad (Penguin)

The Lover Marguerite Duras (Fontana)

Novel Without a Name Duong Thu Huong (Picador)
The Quiet American Graham Greene (Penguin)
River of Time Jon Swain (Minerva)
Romancing Vietnam Justin Wintle (Penguin)
The Sorrow of War Bao Ninh (Minerva)
Swimming to Cambodia Spalding Grey (Picador)
Three Moons in Vietnam Maria Coffey (Abacus)
Tiger Balm Lucretia Stewart (Chatto & Windus)

YEMEN

The Southern Gates of Arabia Freya Stark (Large Print Books)
Yemen: Travels in Dictionary Land Tim Mackintosh-Smith (John Murray)

ZAIRE

The Forest People Colin Turnbull (Pimlico)

ZAMBIA

Survivor's Song Delia and Mark Owens (HarperCollins)

ZIMBABWE

A Time to Die Wilbur Smith (Pan)
African Laughter Doris Lessing (Flamingo)
The Grass is Singing Doris Lessing (Flamingo)
The Leopard Hunts in Darkness Wilbur Smith (Mandarin)
Mukiwa: A White Boy in Africa Peter Godwin (Picador)
Nervous Conditions Tsitsi Dangaremga (The Women's Press)
Songs to an African Sunset Sekai Nzenza-Shand (Lonely Planet)
Under my Skin Doris Lessing (HarperCollins)

TRAVEL MAGAZINES

Wanderlust, PO Box 1832, Windsor, Berkshire SL4 1YT (01753 620426). Bi-monthly, £2.95. Annual subscription: £16 (six issues).

Adventure Travel, PO Box 6254, Alcester, Warwickshire B49 6PS (01789 488166). Bi-monthly, £2.80. Annual subscription: £15 (six issues); £30 (12 issues and a free gift).

Business Traveller, Russell Square House, 10–12 Russell Square, London WC1B 5ED (020 7580 9898). Monthly, £2.90. Annual subscription: £42.95 (UK); £47.25 (Eire); £65.65 (Europe).

Condé Nast Traveller, Vogue House, Hanover Square, London W1R 0AD (020 7499 9080). Monthly, £3. Annual subscription: £34 (call 01858 438 819 or visit www.cntraveller.co.uk).

Food and Travel, Fox Publishing Ltd, 51a George Street, Richmond, Surrey TW9 1HJ (020 8332 9090). Monthly, £2.90. Annual subscription: £34.80 (UK); £40 (Europe); £55 (rest of the world). Call 01795 414 921.

Traveller. Published by WEXAS International, 45–49 Brompton Road, London SW3 1DE (020 7589 0500). Annual subscription: £43.98 (UK); £55.96 (overseas).

Planet Talk is a free quarterly newsletter produced by Lonely Planet, 10a Spring Place, London NWJ 3BH (020 7428 4800).

Rough News is a free quarterly newsletter produced by Rough Guides, 62–70 Shorts Gardens, London WC2H 9AB (020 7556 5001).

TNT Magazine, free every Monday (London and Edinburgh). They also produce **Independent Travellers Guides to Australia & New Zealand** and to **Southern Africa** every two months – you can pick them up free in London, at travel shows like Independent Travellers' World, via the ITG website (www.i-t-g.co.uk) or by calling 020 7373 3377. Other travellers' magazines, such as **Traveller Magazine** and **Southern Cross** also appear free in dispensing stands every week in London.

TRAVEL BOOKSHOPS

Most good bookshops now carry a range of guidebooks and travel literature but there are also several specialist travel bookshops around if you want a wider selection. All of the following shops carry guidebooks and maps and some have a mail order service:

Daunt Books
83 Marylebone High Street, London W1M 3DE
020 7224 2295

Stanfords
12–14 Long Acre, London WC2E 9LP
020 7836 1321
Also at British Airways (156 Regent Street, London W1R 5TA; 020 7434 4744) and Campus Travel (52 Grosvenor Gardens, London SW1W 0AG; 020 7730 1314), and at 29 Corn Street, Bristol BS1 1HT; 0117 929 9996.

The Travel Bookshop
13 Blenheim Crescent, London W11 2EE
020 7229 5260

Blackwell's Map & Travel Shop
53 Broad Street, Oxford OX1 3BQ
01865 792792

Heffers Map Shop
20 Trinity Street, Cambridge CB2 1TY
01223 568467
Mail order service but no catalogue.

The Map Shop
15 High Street, Upton-upon-Severn, Worcestershire WR8 0HJ
01684 593146
Has a mail order service.

CHAPTER 16

INFORMATION ON THE INTERNET

The Internet continues to boom as a source of travel information and advice. Bear in mind, though, that while some sites are useful, authoritative and well researched, others are more subjective. Many are just set up by individuals giving their own particular slant on things so don't take everything you read as gospel.

We give a listing of some websites here but they're increasing all the time, so if you come across a particularly good one, write and let us know. You'll find other sites listed in the relevant chapters of the book.

DESTINATION GUIDES

www.lonelyplanet.com
Selected text from Lonely Planet guides and updates of selected guidebooks, plus the useful Thorn Tree page, where travellers can exchange news and tips. Can also find their new monthly e-mail newsletter at www.lonelyplanet.com/comet

www.roughguides.com
Information on countries covered by Rough Guides and readers' comments. Can also find full text of some Rough Guide books at www.hotwired.com/rough/

www2.travelocity.com/destg/index.html
Destination guide to countries, including economic profile, environment, recommended reading, attractions, culture, weather, hotels, visas, etc.

www.timeout.co.uk
Guides and listings for cities featured in the *Time Out* series, including Amsterdam, New York, Sydney, San Francisco and Tokyo.

www.bootsnall.com
Loads of information on planning your trip, plus travel stories and a Discussion Board.

www.odci.gov/cia/publications/factbook/index.html
CIA World Factbook, full of factual info on every country, including statistics on everything from birth rates to religions to political parties to natural resources.

www.moon.com
Moon Travel Handbooks site includes Travel Matters, an online travel magazine.

www.the-planet.co.uk
Holiday reports from destinations around the world, plus anecdotes and experiences from the *Daily Telegraph* travel team.

www.wtgonline.com/
Columbus Travel Guide, including all the usual information plus frequencies for the BBC World Service.

www.arab.net
Information on over 20 Arab countries, with details of culture, business, geography, travel, etc.

www.gorp.com
Great Outdoor Recreation Pages, with reviews of outdoor adventure activities (mainly in the USA) and links to other information sites.

www.city.net
Has information on world cities.

www.caribbean-on-line.com
and
www.caribinfo.com
Both have information on the Caribbean islands.

TRAVEL AND TRANSPORT INFORMATION

www.usitcampus.co.uk
Information on branches, fares, visas, vaccinations, insurance, info sheets, books etc. – and noticeboard to look for travel advice, find companions, buy books, etc.

www.itn.net/aow
Airline information, timetables, etc.

www.all-destinations.com
Cheap flights and travel insurance.

www.cheapflights.com
A guide to agents and airlines with cheap air tickets from the UK to destinations around the world, plus links to other useful sites.

www.wexas.com
Info on Wexas services.

www.youra.com/ferry
Details of ferry timetables, fares and routes around the world.

www.gtpnet.com
Details of ferry services in Greece.

www.cis.ohio-state.edu/hypertext/faq/usenet/travel/air/ handbook/top.html
Air Traveler's Handbook with tips on fare types and classes, baggage limits, courier travel, etc.

ACCOMMODATION

www.iyhf.org/index.html
International YHA sites in 115 countries.

www.hotelstravel.com
Hotels and Travel on the Net: a directory of 100,000 hotels around the world, but also with useful links to other sites

www.hostels.com/hostels/
Information on hostelling worldwide.

HEALTH

www.masta.org
Up-to-date health information from MASTA.

www.shoreland.com
www.tripprep.com
Shoreland's Travel Health Online, with daily-updated information on travel health.

www.cdc.gov/travel
Health advice from the American Centers for Disease Control and Prevention.

www.tmvc.com.au
Health advice from the Australian Travellers Medical Vaccination Centre.

www.tmb.ie
Health information site from the Tropical Medical Bureau.

www.travelhealth.com
Travel Health Information Service.

SAFETY

www.fco.gov.uk/
Foreign & Commonwealth Office site; includes information on safety in over 130 countries and a guide to consular services worldwide.

www.travel.state.gov/travel_warnings.html
US State Department travel warnings and consular information sheets, including assessments of countries' medical facilities, crime rates, airline safety record, etc.

WEATHER

www.meto.govt.uk
UK Met Office site including 5-day forecasts for foreign travel (charged for).

www.intellicast.com/weather/intl/
Details of weather forecasts around the world for four days ahead.

www.weather.yahoo.com
Weather forecasts (five days ahead) and reports for cities worldwide.

www.weather.com/
US site with forecasts for American and international cities.

EQUIPMENT

www.cotswold-outdoor.co.uk
Pages on topics such as understanding water filters and gear for trekking, as well as links to other sites.

www.walkabouttravelgear.com/
Travel gear, tips, info.

www.explorers-online.com
The Explorer's Online Store for outdoor gear.

www.gearworld.com
Specialist clothing and equipment for anyone planning some wall-climbing, mountain biking, etc.

ON-LINE TRAVEL MAGAZINES

www.journeywoman.com
Journeywoman, on-line travel magazine for women. Can join to network connecting travelling women around the world

www.travelmag.co.uk/travelmag/index.html
On-line magazine sponsored by Wexas

www.bigworld.com
Information about independent traveller's magazine based in the UK, plus links to other backpacker-type sites

BOOKS AND MAPS

www.map-guides.com
UK-based site selling maps and guides.

www.mapquest.com
Interactive atlas, with maps of cities and countries worldwide.

www.metro.jussieu.fr:10001/bin/cities/english
Underground maps for 60+ cities

www.travelbookshop.com
World Traveller Books and Maps.

www.gorp.com/atbook.htm
Adventurous Traveller Bookstore.

www.stanfords.co.uk
Books, guides and maps covering the globe.

GENERAL

www.backpackers.com
Info, tales from travellers and free e-mail. UK-based.

www.travellerseye.com/
Advice, bulletins, and lots of links to other useful sites.

www.backpackers.com.au
Website for VIP Backpackers Resorts of Australia.

www.backpackers.net
Can get e-mail anywhere ($15 for three months; $50 for a year); also live chat and bulletin board.

www.yahoo.com/recreation/travel/backpacking
Links to e-mail providers, details of hostels, etc.

www.towd.com
Tourism Offices Worldwide Directory – gives locations of and links to official national tourist offices and convention and visitor bureaux around the world.

www.newsd.com
News Directory.com, with links to local newspapers around the world.

www.dmoz.org/recreation/travel/budget_travel/backpacking
Lots of links to useful backpacker sites.

www.hilink.com.au/times
Gives local times around the world.

www.samexplo.org
South American Explorers Club.

www.travel.epicurious.com
Includes travel advice, information on festivals around the world, back issues of Condé Nast *Traveler* and details of how to get into town from airports around the world.

www.visa.com or www.mastercard.com
Information on using your Visa or MasterCard worldwide, including locations of 24-hour ATMs in 120 countries.

www.holidayfestival.com
World Wide Holiday and Festival Page with details of national and religious holidays in more than 200 countries.

www.kropla.com
Steve Kropla's Help for World Travelers – one man's advice, including facts about electrical and telephonic systems around the world.

www.festivals.com and www.whatsonwhen.com
Festivals and events around the world.

www.travel-library.com/
Travel information and advice on RTW trips, with lots of tips from other travellers.

www.totallyfreestuff.com/email
Long list of free email suppliers.

CHAPTER 17

A–Z COUNTRY GUIDE

TOURIST INFORMATION OFFICES IN GREAT BRITAIN

Many countries, especially some of the smaller African states or Pacific islands, for example, don't have tourist information offices. If no tourism information contact is given for the country or countries you plan to visit, consult a good guidebook instead or try the embassy/consulate/high commission to see if they can help.

Many of the tourist offices are starting to introduce premium rate information lines for which you can usually expect to pay 50p–60p per minute.

EMBASSIES AND CONSULATES IN GREAT BRITAIN

The visa situation changes all the time. In many countries, UK citizens won't need a visa. In some, you may not need a visa for tourism but will if you intend to work or if you plan to spend longer than a certain amount of time (often three months). Other countries may at certain times refuse to issue visas at all. The best course is always to check with the relevant embassy or consulate. Many of the offices are only open during limited hours, so if at first you don't get an answer, keep trying. Where no embassy contact is given, visas are usually issued on arrival or at the embassies in neighbouring countries; enquire on the spot or call the MASTA Visa & Passport Information Line on 0906 5501 100 for up-to-date advice (calls cost £1 a minute).

WORLD WEATHER

We've given a very rough idea of the weather patterns in each country but for more detailed information, consult a goguidebook or call the Meteorological Office Overseas Enquiry Bureau on 01344 420242 and ask about the countries you're interested in. Calls are charged at premium rate (60p per minute).

AFGHANISTAN

Climate

Extreme climate, with hot, dry summers and cold winters with lots of snow.

Contacts

Afghan Embassy,
31 Prince's Gate,
London SW7 1QQ
020 7589 8891

ALBANIA

Climate

Mediterranean on the coast with warm, dry summers (May to September) and cool, damp winters. Most rain falls November to April. Sea breezes moderate temperatures in coastal areas. The climate in the mountains is harsher, with snow and rain in winter.

Contacts

Albanian Embassy,
4th Floor,
38 Grosvenor Gardens,
London SW1W 0EB
020 7730 5709

ALGERIA

Climate

Hot. Warm and temperate on the coast, with temperatures ranging from 12°C in winter to 25°C in summer. Temperatures inland are higher. Rainfall is erratic – desert regions have next to none but the northern mountains can get heavy rain. Most rain falls in winter.

Contacts

Algerian Consulate,
6 Hyde Park Gate,
London SW7 5EW
020 7589 6885

ANDORRA

Climate

Alpine, with warm, dry summers, mild, wet springs, and long winters with plenty of snow.

Contacts

Andorran Delegation and Tourist Office,
63 Westover Road,
London SW18 2RF
020 8874 4806

ANGOLA

Climate

Mix of temperate and tropical. Generally hot year-round with temperatures ranging from around 23°C in winter (June to September) to 30°C in summer. Rainy season runs from November to April. Desert climate in the south but hot, humid and equatorial in the north, which gets more rain. Cooler and drier on the coast.

Contacts

Angolan Embassy,
98 Park Lane,
London W1Y 3TA
020 7495 1752

ANGUILLA
(UK Dependent Territory)

Climate

Tropical and generally pleasant. Hot and humid much of the year, but trade winds relieve the humidity, especially from January to April. The rainiest months are usually May to November and it is wetter on the windward (north-east) sides of the island and in the interior. Hurricane season runs from June to November, with August and September the riskiest months.

Contacts

Anguilla Tourist Office,
7 Westwood Road,
London SW13 0LA
020 8876 9025

ANTIGUA & BARBUDA

Climate

Tropical and generally pleasant, with hot sunny winters and even hotter summers (August to October), though the trade winds and sea breezes provide relief, especially from January to April. Average temperatures year-round are around 27°C. Low rainfall, most of it in November; it is wetter on the windward (north-east) sides of the island and in the interior. Hurricane season runs from June to November, with July and August the riskiest months.

Contacts

Antigua & Barbuda Tourist Information,
Antigua House,
15 Thayer Street,
London W1M 5LD
020 7486 7073
www.antigua-barbuda.com
Antigua & Barbuda High Commission, as above.

ARGENTINA

Climate

Temperate, with mild winters and warm summers. Hot and subtropical in the north-east rainforests. Dry in the western lowlands. The central pampas plains are mild, with rain in summer. Buenos Aires has warm, sunny summers (it can be very hot and humid from December to February) and mild winters. The best time to visit is during the winter months (June to October). Tierra del Fuego, in the far south of the country, has a sub-arctic climate: cold, wet and stormy.

Contacts

Argentinian Embassy,
65 Brook Street,
London W1Y 1YE
020 7318 1300
www.argentine-embassy-uk.org

ARMENIA

Climate

Continental, with warm summers and very cold winters. Rain falls year-round but is heaviest in summer.

Contacts

Armenian Embassy,
25a Cheniston Gardens,
London W8 6TG
020 7938 5435

AUSTRALIA

Climate

In such a huge country, the climate varies from one area to the next, from cool temperate to tropical monsoon. In the southern half of the country, summer months (the best time to visit) are November to March; winter months (June to August) can be cold and wet. In the northern half, the climate is tropical and the seasons basically divide into wet (November to April) and dry (May to October). Places like Cairns and Darwin are pretty hot year-round (though nights in the desert are cold). Tropical cyclones with high winds and torrential rain are fairly frequent in the north-east and north-west. The western half of the country is mostly arid desert. Rain decreases from the coast inland. The north-east has the highest rainfall. If you want fine weather, aim to spend winter in the north and summer in the south.

Contacts

Australian Tourist Commission,
Gemini House,
10–18 Putney Hill,
London SW15 6AA
ATC Helpline: 09068 633 235
Brochure line: 09068 070707
www.australia.com
Australian High Commission,
Australia House,
Strand,
London WC2B 4LA
020 7379 4334
Visa Information Service: 09001 600 333;
0161 228 1344; 01233 211800; 01270 626 626
www.australia.org.uk

AUSTRIA

Climate

Climate is changeable and varies with the altitude but as a general rule summers are warm and sunny, springs are wet and winters are cold and snowy. Rain falls throughout the year (especially May to August) and snow falls from December to March.

Contacts

Austrian National Tourist Office,
14 Cork Street,
London W1X 1PF
020 7629 0461
www.austria-tourism.at/
Austrian Embassy,
18 Belgrave Mews West,
London SW1X 8HU
020 7235 3731
Visa Hotline (24hr): 0900 1 600 250
www.austria.org.uk

AZERBAIJAN

Climate

Continental, with warm summers and cold, dry winters. Low rainfall, mostly in summer. On the Black Sea coast, summers (June to September) are warm and humid. Temperatures are more extreme in the steppe regions – hotter in summer, colder in winter (November to April).

Contacts

Azerbaijan Embassy,
4 Kensington Court,
London W8 5DL
020 7938 3412

BAHAMAS

Climate

Subtropical, with hot summers, low humidity and mild (sometimes cool) winters. Plenty of rain, especially in summer. Hurricane season runs from July to December.

Contacts

Bahamas Tourist Office,
3 The Billings,
Walnut Tree Close,
Guildford,
Surrey GU1 4UL
01483 448900
Bahamas High Commission,
10 Chesterfield Street,
London W1X 8AH
020 7408 4488
www.bahamas.com

BAHRAIN

Climate

Very hot, humid summers (May to October), with daytime temperatures as high as 40°C or more. Mild winters (November to March) with warm days and cool nights. This is the best time to visit. Extremely low rainfall.

Contacts

Bahrain Embassy & Tourist Information,
98 Gloucester Road,
London SW7 4AU
020 7370 5132/3

BALI: see Indonesia

BANGLADESH

Climate

Hot and humid. Heavy monsoon rains in summer months frequently cause floods; cyclones are also possible at that time of year.

Contacts

Bangladesh High Commission and Tourist Information,
28 Queen's Gate,
London SW7 5JA
020 7584 0081

BARBADOS

Climate

Moderately tropical and generally pleasant. Warm and sunny year-round, with temperatures between 25°C and 28°C. Atlantic breezes have a cooling effect, especially from January to April. The driest months are December to June. Most rain falls from July to November, which is also hurricane season, though they usually miss the island.

Contacts

Barbados Tourism Authority,
263 Tottenham Court Road,
London W1P 0LA
020 7636 9448
www.barbados.org/uk
Barbados High Commission,
1 Great Russell Street,
London WC1B 3JY
020 7631 4975

BELARUS (Belorussia)

Climate

Continental, with warm, wet summers and long, cold, dry winters (December to April), with temperatures below freezing and lots of snow. The warmest month is July. Moderate rainfall; wettest months are June to August.

Contacts

Embassy of Belarus,
6 Kensington Court,
London W8 5DL
020 7937 3288

BELGIUM

Climate

Maritime, temperate and very changeable, but with no real extremes. Mild winters, cool to warm summers (June to September) and lots of rain, especially on the coast.

Contacts

Belgian Tourist Office,
225 Marsh Wall,
London E14 9FW
Brochure line: 0900 1887799
www.belgium-tourism.org
Belgian Embassy,
103 Eaton Square,
London SW1W 9AB
020 7470 3700
Visa info: 0900 1 600 255
www.belgium-embassy.co.uk

BELIZE

Climate

Most of the country is hot, humid and tropical throughout the year, with temperatures pretty consistent at about 23°C to 27°C. In the mountains, it can get cool at night. The rainforests of southern Belize are very humid because of the heavy rainfall. The dry season runs from November to May, which is the best time to travel round. Winter (mid-December to April) is a busy tourist season. The rainy season runs from May to October with July, September and October the wettest months and a risk of hurricanes from June to November.

Contacts

Belize High Commission and Tourist Information Office,
22 Harcourt House,
19 Cavendish Square,
London W1M 9AD
020 7499 9728
www.travelbelize.org

BENIN

Climate

Hot year-round. The south has two rainy seasons, April to mid-July (most rain falls in June) and mid-September to late October. In the north there is only one rainy season – June to late October. The climate in the north is tropical and temperatures can reach 46°C. In the south temperatures range from 18°C to 35°C. The hottest months are March to June. Dusty winds in the dry season (December to March).

Contacts

Benin Consulate,
Dolphin House,
16 The Broadway,
Stanmore,
Middlesex HA7 4DW
020 8954 8800

BERMUDA

(UK Dependent Territory)

Climate

Subtropical. Great climate with hot summers and warm winters. Rain falls year-round but less in summer.

Contacts

Bermuda Tourism,
1 Battersea Church Road,
London SW11 3LY;
020 7771 7001
www.bermudatourism.com

BHUTAN

Climate

Changes with the altitude: in the northern highlands it is always cold and harsh, the centre is temperate and the southern lowlands are sub-tropical. Warmer in the east than the west in the central valleys. Monsoon rains fall from June to August.

Contacts

No embassy or tourist information centre in the UK. Visas for travel to Bhutan can be issued in Calcutta.

BOLIVIA

Climate

High plateau has extreme tropical climate. Hot and humid in north and west. Wettest in the summer months, from November to February. La Paz gets rain daily and can get cold winds from the Altiplano. Snow in mountains. The winter months of April to October are drier and temperatures pleasant, though it can be cold at night. The western plains are arid in the south, humid and tropical in the north.

Contacts

Bolivian Embassy,
106 Eaton Square,
London SW1W 9AD
020 7235 4248/2257

BORNEO

Climate

Wettest months are October to December.

Contacts

See Malaysia, Indonesia or Brunei
(Borneo is divided into Kalimantan, a province of Indonesia; Sabah and Sarawak, which form Eastern Malaysia; and Brunei)

BOSNIA and HERZEGOVINA

Climate

Hot summers, very cold winters with snow, especially at altitude. Colder and rainier in the north, and in the mountains it can rain at any time.

Contacts

The Embassy of the Republic of Bosnia and Herzegovina,
Morley House,
320 Regent Street,

London W1R 5AB
020 7255 3758

BOTSWANA

Climate

Mostly dry. Rainfall is low and erratic but there is a wet season in the summer (November to March). These months are also very humid and hot, with daytime temperatures up to 40°C. Winter months (late May to August) are very dry and can be subject to droughts. Winter can be the best time to view wild animals as they cluster round the water holes. Winters are warm and sunny, with cool nights. Night-time temperatures in the Kalahari can be bitterly cold in June and July, with occasional frosts.

Contacts

Botswana High Commission and Tourist Information,
6 Stratford Place,
London W1N 9AE
020 7499 0031

BRAZIL

Climate

The Amazon basin is hot and humid year-round, with a rainy season from April to July. The south has hot summers and cool winters; wettest months are December to March. Rio is hot and tropical, with sunny summers and mild winters; the rainy season is November to April, when it's also hot and humid. Winter months are June to August when temperatures range from 13°C to 18°C. Summer months are December to February when temperatures can rise into the 30°s and 40°sC. It can be very humid in many places. In the north, winters are cooler, with rainfall in summer. The north-east can have droughts.

Contacts

Brazilian Embassy,
32 Green Street,
London W1Y 4AT
020 7499 0877
Brazilian Consulate General,
6 St Albans Street,
London SW1Y 4SQ
020 7930 9055
www.brazil.org.uk

BRITISH VIRGIN ISLANDS
(UK Dependent Territory)

Climate

Tropical and generally pleasant. Hot and humid much of the year but trade winds relieve the humidity, especially from January to April. It's wetter on the windward (north-east) sides of the islands and in the interior, with May to November seeing the highest rainfall. The hurricane season runs from June to November, with August and September the riskiest months.

Contacts

British Virgin Islands Tourist Board,
54 Baker Street,
London W1M 1DJ
020 7240 4259

BRUNEI

Climate

Tropical and humid. Temperatures are stable at between 26°C and 31°C all year. Heavy rainfall, especially during the north-east monsoon from September to January.

Contacts

Brunei High Commission,
19 Belgrave Square,
London SW1X 8PG
020 7581 0521
Visa Section,
19 Belgrave Mews West,
London SW1X 8HT
020 7581 0521

BULGARIA

Climate

Temperate, with cold, damp winters (when temperatures can fall to below freezing) and warm, dry summers. The mountains get most rain. In winter, snow is likely everywhere. Most rain falls in the summer months.

Contacts

Bulgarian Embassy,
186–188 Queen's Gate,
London SW7 5HL
020 7584 9400/9433
Bulgarian Tourist Office, as above.

BURKINA FASO

Climate

Tropical. Dry and cool from November to February; the hottest months are March to early June. Rainfall is erratic and the region is prone to droughts.

Contacts

Burkina Faso Embassy,
5 Cinnamon Row,
Plantation Wharf,
London SW11 3TW
020 7738 1800

BURMA: see Myanmar

BURUNDI

Climate

Temperate but very humid. Hottest and most humid in lowland regions, and near Lake Tanganyika, with temperatures around 30°C. In the northern highlands, temperatures are cooler. Plenty of rain, especially from October to May (with a brief dry period in December to January).

Contacts

No embassy or tourist information office in the UK.

CAMBODIA

Climate

Tropical. Hot year-round, with average temperatures over 25°C. Summer (May to October) is hot and humid, with temperatures around 33°C and humidity as high as 90 per cent; this is also the time of the heavy monsoon rains. Dry season is November to January; average temperatures around 27°C. From January to April temperatures and humidity rise.

Contacts

No embassy or tourist information centre in the UK. Visas for travel to Cambodia are issued in Saigon, Moscow or Bangkok.

CAMEROON

Climate

Rainfall varies from north to south. The south has an equatorial climate, with lots of rain. The rainy seasons are March/April and May to November. Floods are possible in July and August. There is less rain inland. In the north, the rainy season runs from June to September. The far north can have droughts.

Contacts

Cameroon High Commission and Tourist Information,
84 Holland Park,
London W11 3SB
020 7727 0771

CANADA

Climate

On the whole, the climate is continental – hot summers and harsh winters – but climate varies according to altitude, latitude and proximity to the sea. Winters and summers are both more extreme in the interior of the country. Temperatures on the Pacific coast are generally milder. Wettest months are November to January. Montreal has hot sunny summers and very cold winters with lots of snow and ice from December to March. Toronto is similar. Vancouver has a similar climate to the UK, with warm summers and mild, wet winters; it rains year-round but especially from November to February. Newfoundland has heavy fog and icebergs.

Contacts

Visit Canada
09068 715000
Canadian High Commission (visa section),
38 Grosvenor Street,
London W1X OAA
020 7258 6600
Immigration Visa Information Service:
0906 8616644

CANARY ISLANDS
(island province of Spain)

Climate

Dry, sunny summers. Can get hot, dusty winds from the Sahara. Mild winters, with the odd stormy day.

Contacts

See Spain

CAPE VERDE ISLANDS

Climate

Cooler than mainland west Africa. July to October are the hottest months, when temperatures go up to 27°C. It can get very cool from December to March. Rainfall is erratic; most occurs between late August and early October. The rest of the year is very dry and subject to long droughts and can be very windy, especially from December to February.

Contacts

No embassy or tourist information office in the UK.

CAYMAN ISLANDS
(UK Dependent Territory)

Climate

Pleasant year-round, with average temperatures of around 25°C. Most rain falls between May and October.

Contacts

Cayman Islands Government Office and Department of Tourism,
6 Arlington Street,
London SW1A 1RE
020 7491 7771

CENTRAL AFRICAN REPUBLIC

Climate

Hot and dry in the north (Sahara desert), where temperatures can go up to 40°C from February to May. Equatorial in the south, with fairly heavy rain year-round, especially from June to October. High humidity.

Contacts

French Consulate General,
21 Cromwell Road,
London SW7 2EN
020 7838 2000/2050
Visa Information Service:
0900 1887733

CHAD

Climate

Desert climate in the north, on the edge of the Sahara; tropical in the south; semi-arid in between. Hottest months are March to May, with daytime temperatures of 45°C and even higher. Milder from December to February, when nights can be chilly. Heavy rains in the south from June to September.

Contacts

No embassy or tourist information office in the UK.

CHILE

Climate

Generally temperate, with mild winters and warm summers, but there are great variations from top to bottom, and depending on the altitude. Generally hot and dry in the north. The far south is constantly cold and can be stormy and windy. Central regions have hot, dry summers and mild winters. Snow year-round on high mountain peaks. Wettest months are April, June and December. Santiago has a Mediterranean climate, with hot, sunny, dry summers and mild, temperate winters – average temperatures around 28°C in January; 10°C in July. Nights can be cold with bitter winds from the mountains. Rainy season is May to August. Most rain falls in the winter months, when there may also be frost and snow inland. Easter Island is hot and dry.

Contacts

Embassy of Chile and Tourist Information Office,
12 Devonshire Street,
London W1N 2DS
020 7580 6392

CHINA

Climate

Such a huge country obviously has very different weather conditions from one area to the next. The north has an extreme continental climate – winters (December to March) are harsh and very cold (temperatures can drop as low as -30°C) but dry and sunny. Summers (May to August) are hot (temperatures can go up to the high 30°sC) and rainy (most rain falls in July and August). North-western areas have hot, dry summers. Spring and autumn are the best times to visit, with temperatures between 20°C and 30°C though nights can be cold. Central regions have hot and humid summers (April to October); winters are cold and wet, with temperatures below freezing. In the south, summers (April to September) can be hot (temperatures up to 38°C), humid and wet. Typhoons are possible in coastal regions from July to September. The winter months are January to March. Autumn and spring are the best times to visit. Temperatures in the desert areas can be very high. In winter it is very cold with temperatures falling to -10°C.

Contacts

China National Tourist Office,
4 Glentworth Street,
London NW1 5PG
020 7935 9787
Information line:
0900 1600188
Chinese Embassy,
Visa Section,
31 Portland Place,
London W1N 3AG
020 7631 1430
Visa and General Information Service:
0900 1880808

COLOMBIA

Climate

Tropical, though temperatures vary with the altitude. Hot and wet on the coast; cooler in the highlands. Bogotá temperatures stay fairly constant (18° to 19°C) year-round. Warm and sunny days but the nights can be cool. Most rain falls from March to May and October to November.

Contacts

Colombian Embassy,
Flat 3a,
3 Hans Crescent,
London SW1X 0LN
020 7589 9177
Colombian Consulate,
15-19 Great Titchfield Street,
London W1P 7FB
020 7637 9893

COMOROS

Climate

Hot and humid year-round. Moderate rainfall, most of it in the summer months of November to April, which is also cyclone season. Temperatures at this time of year are around 35°C. It is cooler and drier from May to October, with south-east trade winds.

Contacts

No embassy or tourist information office in the UK but Sun International, on 01491 411 222, can give some information.

CONGO

Climate

Hot, tropical and humid year-round. The rainy season is October to November and February to April/May. Rainfall is especially heavy in the north of the country. Temperatures range from 21°C to 27°C. The best time to visit is from June to September, the driest months. Travel in the rainy season can be difficult.

Contacts

No embassy or tourist information office in the UK.

CONGO, DEMOCRATIC REPUBLIC OF (formerly Zaire)

Climate

Tropical and humid. North of the equator rain falls year-round. The east of the country has a Mediterranean climate, with two rainy seasons (March to May and mid-September to mid-December). In the rest of the country, the rainy season is from February to May, with a dry season from June to September. Travel in the rainy season can be very difficult.

Contacts

Embassy of the Democratic Republic of Congo,
26 Chesham Place,
London SW1X 8HG
020 7235 6137

COOK ISLANDS

Climate

December to April are the rainiest and hottest months. It is coldest from June to September. The hurricane season runs from November to March. The best time to visit is between May and October but the climate is pleasant year-round, with no real extremes of temperature.

Contacts

South Pacific Tourism Organisation (SPTO)
203 Sheen Lane
London SW14 8LE
020 8876 1938
www.tcsp.com

COSTA RICA

Climate

Temperatures are affected by altitude. Hot, humid and tropical along the coast; more temperate in the highlands. The dry season runs from late December to April. The rest of the year is wet, with the Caribbean region wetter than the rest of the country. The dry season is particularly dry in the highlands and on much of the Pacific coast, with neglible rainfall. On the southern Pacific coast there is rain year-round. The Caribbean coast is particularly hot.

Contacts

Costa Rica Embassy and Tourist Information Office,
Flat 1,
14 Lancaster Gate,
London W2 3LH
020 7706 8844

CROATIA

Climate

The Adriatic coast has a Mediterranean

climate, with hot, dry summers and mild, rainy winters. Sea breezes moderate temperatures along the coast in spring and summer. Spring and autumn are the best times to visit. The interior has a temperate continental climate, with cold winters and warm summers.

Contacts

Croatia National Tourist Office,
2 The Lanchesters,
162–164 Fulham Palace Road,
London W6 9ER
020 8563 7979
Embassy of the Republic of Croatia,
21 Conway Street,
London W1P 5HL
020 7387 1144

CUBA

Climate

Subtropical – hot and sunny year-round. The coolest months are December to March, with average temperatures of 26°C. In the hottest months (July and August) average temperatures rise to 32°C. Most rain falls between May and October, especially in September and October, when humidity is also high. Hurricanes are rare but possible in autumn (August to November).

Contacts

Cuban Embassy,
167 High Holborn,
London WC1V 6PA
020 7240 2488
Cuban Consulate Visa, Tourism and General Information Service:
0900 1880820
Tourist Office
154 Shaftesbury Avenue,
London WC2H 4JT
020 7240 6655

CYPRUS

Climate

Mediterranean, with hot, dry, sunny summers (May to September) and mild winters, with snow in the mountains. Most rain falls in the winter.

Contacts

Cyprus Tourist Office,
17 Hanover Street,
London W1R 0AA
020 7569 8800

Cyprus Consulate,
93 Park Street,
London W1Y 4ET
020 7629 5350

CYPRUS, NORTHERN: see Northern Cyprus

CZECH REPUBLIC

Climate

Mix of temperate and continental. Winters are cool to cold; temperatures can go below freezing and thick fogs are likely. Summers are warm (this is also when most of the rain falls). Prague has changeable weather, with cold, icy winters and mild, sunny summers.

Contacts

Embassy of the Czech Republic,
28 Kensington Palace Gardens,
London W8 4QY
020 7243 1115
Information Service (including visa enquiries):
0900 1171267
Czech Centre,
95 Great Portland Street,
London W1N 5RA
Tourism enquiries: 020 7291 9920

DENMARK

Climate

Cool and temperate, very like the British climate, with no real extremes. It's mild, equable and changeable. Mild summers; cold, wet winters; moderate rainfall year-round, especially in summer and autumn.

Contacts

Danish Embassy,
55 Sloane Street,
London SW1X 9SR
020 7235 1255 or 333 0200
Danish Tourist Board,
55 Sloane Street,
London SW1X 9SY
020 7259 5959
Information Line: 0900 1600109

DJIBOUTI

Climate

Hot and dry year-round and very hot in June to August. Temperatures range from 25°C to 35°C. Coolest months are October to April when there may also be a little rain.

Contacts

French Consulate General,
21 Cromwell Road,
London SW7 2EN
020 7838 2000/2050
Visa Information Service:
0900 1887733

DOMINICA

Climate

Tropical and generally pleasant, with average temperatures over 25°C. It is hot and humid much of the year, but trade winds relieve the humidity, especially from January to April. The rainiest months are usually May to November and it is wetter on the windward (north-east) sides of the island and in the interior. The hurricane season runs from June to November, with August and September the riskiest months.

Contacts

Dominica Tourist Office,
Mitre House,
66 Abbey Road,
Bush Hill Park,
Enfield EN1 2QE
020 8350 1000
www.mki.ltd.uk
Dominica High Commission,
1 Collingham Gardens,
Earls Court,
London SW5 0HW
020 7370 5194

DOMINICAN REPUBLIC

Climate

Hot, humid and tropical around the coast; cooler in the highlands. Plenty of rain (especially in the north-east).

Contacts

Dominican Republic Embassy and Consulate,
139 Inverness Terrace,
London W2 6JF
020 7727 6214/6285
Tourist Board:
18-22 Hand Court,
High Holborn,
London WC1V 6JT
020 7242 7778
Tourist Info Line: 0900 1600 305

DUBAI

Climate

Warm and hot year-round. Very low rainfall, mostly from December to February. High humidity.

Contacts

Dubai Tourism Promotion Board,
125 Pall Mall,
London SW1Y 5EA
020 7839 0580
UAE Embassy, Visa Section,
30 Prince's Gate,
London SW7 1PJ
020 7581 1281

EASTER ISLAND: see Chile

EASTERN CARIBBEAN
(St Kitts & Nevis; St Lucia;
St Vincent & the Grenadines)

Climate

Tropical and generally pleasant, with temperatures between 16°C and 33°C. It is hot and humid much of the year but trade winds relieve the humidity, especially from January to April. There is lots of rain year-round, especially from May to November; it is wetter on the windward (north-east) sides of the island and in the interior. Spring is the driest time. The hurricane season runs from June to November, with August and September the riskiest months.

Contacts

Eastern Caribbean High Commission,
10 Kensington Court,
London W8 5DL
020 7937 9522
Tourist offices for St Kitts & Nevis
(020 7376 0881) and
St Vincent & the Grenadines (020 7937 6570)
are also at this address.
www.interknowledge.com/stkitts-nevis
www.vincy.com

ECUADOR

Climate

Tropical, hot and humid on the coast; cooler in the mountains. The wettest months are January to May. Very changeable weather. The Galapagos and coastal areas are hot and rainy from January to April. The Amazon area is constantly rainy and also hot. The highlands have a dry season from June to September and December, and cooler temperatures. Can get landslides on mountain roads in the wet season.

Contacts

Embassy of Ecuador,
Flat 3b,
3 Hans Crescent,
London SW1X OLS
020 7584 2648

EGYPT

Climate

Generally has hot summers (June to September) and mild winters. In the south, it's hot year-round but cooler at nights. Hot Saharan winds can blow between March and June. The best time to visit is May or October to November. Little rain apart from in the coastal region. Cairo is hot and sunny year-round – it has a desert climate, with next to no rain.

Contacts

Egyptian Tourist Office,
Egyptian House,
170 Piccadilly,
London W1V 9DD
020 7493 5282
Brochure Service:
0900 1600299
Egyptian Consulate General,
2 Lowndes Street,
London SW1X 9ET
020 7235 9719
Visa Information Service:
0900 1887777
Egyptian Embassy,
75 South Audley Street,
London W1Y 5FF
020 7499 2401

EL SALVADOR

Climate

Tropical and hot, with temperatures fairly constant, from 30°C to 34°C. The coastal plain is hotter than the rest of the country. Highland regions are cooler and more temperate. Winter (May to October) is the wet season but it may only rain for about an hour a day; summer (November to April) is dry and can be dusty.

Contacts

Embassy of El Salvador,
Tennyson House,
159 Great Portland Street,
London W1N 5FD
020 7436 8282

EQUATORIAL GUINEA

Climate

Hot, wet and humid year-round, with heavy rainfall. The rainy season runs from July to January and is especially wet from July to October. The mainland is slightly drier and cooler than Bioko Island, with most of its rain in April to May and October to December.

Contacts

No embassy or tourist information office in the UK.

ERITREA

Climate

Hot in the desert; warm in the mountains. The coast is hot but temperatures are lower inland. Erratic rainfall and subject to droughts.

Contacts

Eritrean Consulate,
96 White Lion Street,
London N1 9PF
020 7713 0096

ESTONIA

Climate

Temperate, with very cold winters (November to February), warm summers (May to September), and steady rain throughout the year. Hottest and wettest months are July and August. Snow is likely from December to March.

Contacts

Estonian Embassy and Tourist Information,
16 Hyde Park Gate,
London SW7 5DG
020 7589 3428

ETHIOPIA

Climate

The east of the country is mostly arid plateaux, hot and dry, with serious droughts. The highlands are warm and usually get good rains in summer (June to September), though subject to occasional droughts. Can get snow on the mountains. Best time to visit is October to April.

Contacts

Ethiopian Embassy,
17 Prince's Gate,
London SW7 1PZ
020 7589 7212

FALKLAND ISLANDS
(UK Crown Colony)

Climate

Temperate and can be windy. Temperatures rarely reach the mid-20°sC. In the winter months of December and January it is wet and cold.

Contacts

Falkland Islands Government Office (including tourist information),
Falkland House,
14 Broadway,
London SW1H 0BH
020 7222 2542

FAROE ISLANDS
(Self-governing island region of Denmark)

Climate

Stormy, wet and changeable but mild temperatures year-round.

Contacts

See Denmark

FIJI

Climate

Tropical. High temperatures all year. Rain falls year-round but the wettest months are November to December and March to April, which are also hot and humid. It's cooler and drier between May and October, and also better on the coast because of the sea breezes. Sunny year-round with fairly constant temperatures between 20°C in July to August and 29°C from November to April.

Contacts

Fijian Embassy,
34 Hyde Park Gate,
London SW7 5DN
020 7584 3661
South Pacific Tourism Organisation (SPTO),
203 Sheen Lane,
London SW14 8LE
020 8876 1938
www.tcsp.com

FINLAND

Climate

Long and very cold winters, with lots of snow. Short, warmer and sunny summers (with lots of mosquitoes). The north has a particularly harsh climate with very little sunlight in winter. Low rainfall, especially in the north.

Contacts

Embassy of Finland,
38 Chesham Place,
London SW1X 8HW
020 7235 9531/838 6200
Finnish Tourist Board,
30–35 Pall Mall,
London SW1Y 5LP
020 7839 4048
www.mek.fi

FRANCE

Climate

The north is temperate, damp and changeable – summers quite warm and sunny, winters cold and frosty (most rain falls in summer). The south has a Mediterranean climate: hot, sunny summers with very little rain, and mild winters with some rain.

Contacts

French Consulate General,
21 Cromwell Road,
London SW7 2EN
020 7838 2000/2050
Visa Information Service:
0900 1887733
French Embassy,
58 Knightsbridge,
London SW1X 7JT
020 7201 1000
www.ambafrance.org.uk
French Tourist Office,
178 Piccadilly,
London W1V 0AL
0906 8244123
www.franceguide.com

FRENCH GUIANA
(Overseas Department of France)

Climate

Tropical, hot, wet and humid in the lowlands, with cooling breezes on the coast. Cooler in the highlands. The rainy season runs from December to June, with especially heavy rainfall in May.

Contacts

French Consulate General,
21 Cromwell Road,
London SW7 2EN
020 7838 2000/2050
Visa Information Service:
0900 1887733

FRENCH POLYNESIA (including Tahiti)
(Overseas Territory of France)

Climate

Hot and can be humid. Sunny all year and fairly constant temperatures, between 20°C and 32°C. Rain falls year-round, especially from November to April. It's drier and cooler from May to October, with average temperatures of around 25°C.

Contacts

French Consulate General,
21 Cromwell Road,
London SW7 2EN
020 7838 2000/2050
Visa Information Service:
0900 1887733

GABON

Climate

Hot and tropical year-round, with temperatures around 30°C. High humidity. Cooler on the coast. Heavy rain most of the year with a rainy season from January to May. The driest months are June to September.

Contacts

Gabonese Embassy,
27 Elvaston Place,
London SW7 5NL
020 7823 9986

GALAPAGOS ISLANDS: see Ecuador

THE GAMBIA

Climate

Hot and tropical with temperatures usually around 30°C. The wettest months are between July and September, when it rains most days and humidity is high. The hottest months are October to November and mid-February to late June. In between these two hot periods, the weather is dry and pleasantly warm. Coastal areas are generally cooler than inland.

Contacts

Gambia High Commission,
57 Kensington Court,
London W8 5DG
020 7937 6316
Gambia Tourist Information Office,
address as above
020 7376 0093
www.thegambia-touristoff.co.uk

GEORGIA

Climate

Generally warm though colder at altitude. The west gets the most rain. Subtropical on the coast.

Contacts

Georgian Embassy,
3 Horton Place,
London W8 4LZ
020 7937 8233

GERMANY

Climate

Temperate in north and central areas; more extreme in the south. The east is colder. Frankfurt and Munich have mild, warm summers and chilly winters. Rains year-round, especially in summer.

Contacts

German National Tourist Office,
Nightingale House,
65 Curzon Street,
London W1Y 8NE
0900 1600100
German Embassy, Visa Section,
23 Belgrave Square,
London SW1X 8PZ
020 7824 1300
Visa Information Service:
0906 8331166
www.german-embassy.org.uk

GHANA

Climate

Tropical, with temperatures from 21°C to 32°C year-round. Rainfall is heaviest in the rainforests; the north and coastal regions are drier. The north has one wet season from May to September.

Contacts

Ghana High Commission,
Visa Information and Tourist Office,
104 Highgate Hill,
London N6 5HE
020 7201 5900

GREECE

Climate

Mainly Mediterranean, with hot, dry summers (with winds in the islands) and mild, wet winters. Alpine in northern mountain areas, which can get snow. Low rainfall, mostly between November and January.

Contacts

National Tourist Organisation of Greece,
4 Conduit Street,
London W1R ODJ
020 7734 5997
Greek Embassy,
1a Holland Park,
London W11 3TP
020 7221 6467
Greek General Consulate Visa
Information Service:
0900 1171202

GREENLAND
(Self-governing island region of Denmark)

Climate

Unpredictable Arctic climate. Often windy but the coldest winter days are often clear and calm. In summer, fog is common on the coast, especially in the far south. Average summer temperatures are 10° to 20°C in the south, 5 to 10C in the north. In winter they can go as low as -20°C in the south, -50°C in the north.

Contacts

See Denmark

GRENADA

Climate

Tropical and generally pleasant. It is hot and humid much of the year, but trade winds relieve the humidity, especially from January to April. There is plenty of rain, mostly in the summer months (July to November), and it is wetter on the windward (north-east) sides of the island and in the interior. Hurricane season runs from June to November, with August and September the riskiest months.

Contacts

Grenada Board of Tourism,
1 Collingham Gardens,
Earls Court,
London SW5 0HW
020 7370 5164
Grenada High Commission, address as above;
020 7373 7809

GUADELOUPE
(Overseas Department of France)

Climate

Tropical and generally pleasant. It is hot and humid much of the year, but trade winds relieve the humidity, especially from January to April. The rainiest months are usually May to November and it is wetter on the windward (north-east) sides of the island and in the interior. Hurricane season runs from June to November, with August and September the riskiest months.

Contacts

See France

GUAM
(External territory of USA)

Climate

Tropical oceanic climate. Warm and humid year-round, with temperatures ranging from around 21°C to 32°C (average daily temperature is 27°C). The best time to visit is between December and March, the driest, least humid and coolest months. Typhoons are possible between August and December.

Contacts

See USA

GUATEMALA

Climate

The dry season runs from October to May, when the climate is warm and pleasant in the central highlands. On both Pacific and Caribbean coasts and in the northern lowland, the climate is tropical, hot (temperatures can go up to 38°C), humid and rainy. Most rain falls in the summer.

Contacts

Embassy of Guatemala and Tourist Information,
13 Fawcett Street,
London SW10 9HN
020 7351 3042
www.travel-guatemala.org.gt

GUINEA

Climate

Tropical, with heavy annual rainfall on the coast, especially in July and August. The central mountains are drier, with rainfall between May and October. Hot Sahara winds blow in the dry season.

Contacts

Republic of Guinea Consulate,
20 Upper Grosvenor Street,
London W1X 9PB
020 7333 0044

GUINEA-BISSAU

Climate

Tropical, with a rainy season from late May to early November. The coast is much wetter than the interior. It is humid almost year-round, especially just before the rainy season. December to April are dry, with hot winds. The best time to visit is between November and February.

Contacts

Guinea-Bissau Consulate,
32 Abbots House
St Mary Abbots
London W14 8NU
020 7603 9016

GUYANA

Climate

Tropical, hot, wet and humid in the lowlands, with cooling breezes on the coast. Cooler in the highlands. There are two rainy seasons, from April to August and from November to late January.

Contacts

Guyana High Commission,
3 Palace Court,
Bayswater Road,
London W2 4LP
020 7229 7684

HAITI

Climate

Tropical. Hot and humid on the coast; more temperate in highland regions. Rainy year-round.

Contacts

No embassy or tourist information office in the UK.

HAWAII
(State of USA)

Climate

Tropical; warm year-round. Constant temperatures between 20°C and 28°C. Can be wet in the mountains but drier on the coast. The wettest months are December and January.

Contacts

See USA

HONDURAS

Climate

Tropical, hot and humid in coastal regions. The Caribbean coast gets rain year-round, especially from September to January and February. In these months there are sometimes floods in the north. In the rest of the country, the summer rainy season runs from May to October. It's relatively dry from November to April. Cooler, drier and more temperate inland in the mountains. Coolest months are December and January.

Contacts

Honduras Embassy,
115 Gloucester Place,
London W1H 3PJ
020 7486 4880

HONG KONG

Climate

Sub-tropical, with hot, humid, wet summers and cool but usually dry winters. Most rain falls May to September. Typhoon season is July to August. The best time to visit is between October and February – temperatures and humidity fall and there are lots of clear sunny days.

Contacts

Hong Kong Tourist Association,
6 Grafton Street,
London W1X 3LB
020 7533 7100
Hong Kong Embassy, address as above;
020 7499 9821

HUNGARY

Climate

Temperate continental climate. Winters are very cold, with snow. Warm summers from June to August. Rain year-round but especially in May to June and November. The west is wetter than the east.

Contacts

Hungarian National Tourist Office,
PO Box 4336,
London SW18 4XE
020 7823 1032
www.hungarytourism.hu
Hungarian Embassy,
35b Eaton Place,
London SW1X 8BY
020 7235 2664/5218

ICELAND

Climate

Changeable and moderate, with cold winters and cool, short summers. Wettest times of year are autumn and winter.

Contacts

Iceland Tourist Information,
Icelandair,
3rd Floor,
172 Tottenham Court Road,
London W1P OLY
020 8874 1000
Brochure Line:
020 7286 8008
Embassy of Iceland,
1 Eaton Terrace,
London SW1W 8EY
020 7590 1100

INDIA

Climate

Varies hugely, but on the whole tropical with monsoons in summer. The south-west monsoon brings the rainy season to most of India starting in the south-west and spreading north and east from mid-May through to early July. The best time to visit is generally between November and April (although early June is the best time for trekking in the northern regions). From February to the start of the south-west monsoon in May, the northern Indian plains are very hot but northern hill stations are cooler (they usually have a severe winter). The pre-monsoon season is extremely hot – temperatures in central India can reach 45°C. Most of the country has three seasons: hot, wet and cool. Winter temperatures in the far south are pleasantly warm, but it can get chilly at night in Delhi and in the north, especially in December and January.

Contacts

India Tourist Office,
7 Cork Street,
London W1X 2LN
020 7437 3677
www.indiatouristoffice.org
Indian High Commission,
India House,
Aldwych,
London WC2B 4NA
020 7836 8484

INDONESIA

Climate

Varies slightly across the islands but is generally hot and humid, with tropical monsoons bringing wet seasons from October to March/April. The dry season (which is cooler) is usually May to June to August to September (the best time to visit). The nearer you get to Australia, the longer the dry season lasts. Travel can be difficult in the rainy months. The hottest months are February to March. Temperatures are fairly constant, ranging from 23°C to 31°C, though hilly areas are cooler. Typhoons are possible, though rare, in Timor.

Contacts

Indonesian Tourist Office,
Whitehall House,
41 Whitehall,
London SW1A 2BY
020 7423 9456
Indonesian Embassy,
38 Grosvenor Square,
London W1X 9AD
020 7499 7661

IRAN

Climate

Harsh, desert climate, with extremes – very hot summers and very cold winters. Temperatures range from -20°C to 50°C. More temperate around the Caspian Sea. Low humidity and little rain (most of it in winter, between December and April). The coast is humid but relieved by sea breezes. Hot, dry, dusty desert winds blow at the start and end of the summer.

Contacts

Iranian Consulate,
50 Kensington Court,
London W8 5DB
020 7937 5225
www.iran-embassy.org.uk

IRAQ

Climate

Very hot, dry summers and mild winters, with some rain, in the south. Dry summers and harsh winters in the north. Low rainfall.

Contacts

Iraqi Embassy,
21 Queen's Gate,
London SW7 5GJ
020 7584 7141

ISRAEL

Climate

Mostly Mediterranean, with warm, sunny summers (which can get very humid) and mild, wet winters. The hottest months are July and August. Rain falls mostly in winter, especially between December and February. The Negev Desert in the south is very hot and dry.

Contacts

Israel Tourist Office,
180 Oxford Street,
London W1N 9DG
020 7299 1111
www.infotour.co.il
Embassy of Israel,
2 Palace Green,
London W8 4QB
020 7957 9500
www.israel-embassy.org.uk

ITALY

Climate

Mostly Mediterranean, with warm summers and mild winters, with some rain. Extremes in the north and mountains. Milan has hot summers and very cold winters, with snow and frost; most rain falls in late spring and October to November. Rome has a Mediterranean climate, with hot, sunny, mostly dry summers and mild winters; there's little rain, most of it between October and January.

Contacts

Italian State Tourist Office,
1 Princes Street,
London W1R 8AY
020 7408 1254
Brochure Line: 0900 1600 280
www.italiantourism.com
Italian Consulate General Visa Section,
38 Eaton Place,
London SW1X 8AN
020 7235 9371
Visa Information Service:
0900 1600340
www.embitaly.org.uk

IVORY COAST

Climate

Hot year-round. In the south, there is heavy rain from May to October. The north is drier, with a shorter rainy season from June to September. Humidity in the south is high but temperatures rarely go over 32°C. Dusty desert winds can blow from the Sahara in the northern mountains from early December to February.

Contacts

Ivory Coast Embassy,
2 Upper Belgrave Street,
London SW1X 8BJ
020 7235 6991

JAMAICA

Climate

Tropical, hot and humid around the coast but more temperate inland. Hurricane season is from June to November. Wetter in the mountains. In the south of the island rains fall mostly in May and October. Temperatures are fairly constant, around 30°C.

Contacts

Jamaica Tourist Board,
1–2 Prince Consort Road,
London SW7 2BZ
020 7224 0505
Jamaica High Commission,
Address as above
www.jamaicatravel.com

JAPAN

Climate

Temperate oceanic, with warm, sunny springs; hot, humid summers with rain. Winters are generally mild though in the north it can be very cold, with heavy snow. Rain falls year-round but especially in June, September and October. Japan is subject to frequent earthquakes, monsoons, typhoons and tidal waves. Except for Hokkaido, the large cities are very hot in summer. The best times to visit are spring and autumn.

Contacts

Japan National Tourist Organisation,
20 Savile Row,
London W1X 1AE
020 7734 9638
www.jnto.go.jp
Japanese Embassy,
101 Piccadilly,
London W1V 9FN
020 7465 6500
www.embjapan.org.uk

JORDAN

Climate

The eastern valleys are hot and dry, with average temperatures above 36°C (they can go up to 49°C) and little rain. West and east of the valleys, the climate is milder and wetter but summer temperatures are still around 30°C to 35°C; the short winters in this area can be cool and wet. Below sea level it's especially hot in summer and warm in winter. Desert areas have very high temperatures in summer, very cold winters and little rain. The best times to visit are spring and autumn.

Contacts

Jordan Tourism Board,
Representation House,
Unit 11,
121 Blades Court,
Deodar Road,
London SW15 2NV
020 8877 4524
www.tourism.com.jo
Jordanian Embassy,
6 Upper Phillimore Gardens,
London W8 7HB
020 7937 3685

KAZAKHSTAN

Climate

Dry continental, with hot summers and very cold winters. Summers are hottest in the desert south; winters coldest in the northern steppes.

Contacts

Kazakhstan Embassy and Consulate,
33 Thurloe Square,
London SW7 2SD
020 7581 4646
Visa Information Service:
0900 1600207
www.kazakhstan-embassy.org

KENYA

Climate

Hot, humid and tropical year-round on the coast, though sea breezes provide relief. Temperatures are consistent, at between 22°C and 30°C. The central plateau is temperate. North of the equator, much of the land is arid semi-desert, with temperatures ranging from 20°C to 40°C. Hot summers from December to March. Mild winters but chilly at nights. In the central highlands and Rift Valley, the climate is temperate and pleasant. Two rainy seasons: March to May ('the long rains') are hot and wet; October to December ('the short rains') are warm and wet. Generally, January and February are hot and dry; from June to October it is warm and dry. Rain can fall any time at high altitude.

Contacts

Kenya Tourist Office,
25 Brooks Mews,
London W1Y 1LF
020 7355 3144
Kenya High Commission,
45 Portland Place,
London W1N 4AS
020 7636 2371/5

KIRIBATI

Climate

Central islands have a maritime equatorial climate. Northern and southern islands are tropical, with constant high temperatures. Low rainfall.

Contacts

Kiribati Honorary Consulate,
7 Tufton Street,
London SW1P 3QN
020 7222 6952
South Pacific Tourism Organisation (SPTO),
203 Sheen Lane,
London SW14 8LE
020 8876 1938
www.tcsp.com

KOREA: see North Korea and South Korea

KUWAIT

Climate

Desert climate, with very hot, dry summers (April to September) when temperatures can reach 52°C. Rainfall is negligible. Cooler, mild winters, with some rain and maybe even frost. Can be very humid, especially near the coast. Sand-storms year-round, especially in spring.

Contacts

Kuwait Information Centre,
Hyde Park House,
60/60A Knightsbridge,
London SW1X 7JU
020 7235 1787
Kuwait Embassy,
2 Albert Gate,
London SW1X 7JU
020 7589 4533

KYRGYZSTAN (Kirghizia)

Climate

Hostile, with hot, dry summers and very cold but quite short winters. Rainfall is low. Low regions have a hot desert climate. Cooler in the mountains, which also have year-round snow in the highest parts.

Contacts

Embassy of the Russian Federation,
5 Kensington Palace Gardens,
London W8 4QS
020 7229 8027
Russian Consular Information Service:
0900 1171 271

LAOS

Climate

Hot. Monsoon rains from May to October, when temperatures are in the 30°sC. The best time to visit is during the winter months (November to April) , which are cool and dry, with temperatures of around 15°C, but rising towards the monsoon. Temperatures in the highland areas are lower and can drop to freezing in December and January.

Contacts

No embassy or tourist information office in the UK. Visas can be issued in Bangkok.

LATVIA

Climate

Very cold winters (November to February), warm summers (May to September), steady rain. The hottest and wettest months are July and August. Snow is likely from December to March.

Contacts

Embassy of Latvia,
45 Nottingham Place,
London W1M 3FE
020 7312 0040

LEBANON

Climate

Hot, dry summers (May to October); humid on the coast. Sometimes gets hot desert winds in early/late summer. Mild winters, though it can get cool and may rain.

Contacts

Lebanon Tourist Office,
90 Piccadilly,
London W1V 9HB
020 7409 2031
www.lebanon-tourism.gov.lb
Lebanese Embassy,
15 Palace Garden Mews, Kensington,
London W8 4RA
020 7229 7265

LESOTHO

Climate

Temperate, warm and pleasant. Hot and wet in summer, when temperatures can be in the 30°sC. Cold winters with frosts and snow on the mountains in winter. Rainy season runs from October to April.

Contacts

Lesotho High Commission,
7 Chesham Place,
Belgravia,
London SW1X 8HN
020 7235 5686

LIBERIA

Climate

Average daily temperatures are over 25°C year-round and can rise to 33°C. There is lots of rain: the wet season runs from May to October, and June and July are especially wet. Coastal regions are much wetter than the interior. The dry season, from November to April, is the best time to visit.

Contacts

Embassy of Liberia,
2 Pembridge Place,
London W2 4XB
020 7221 1036

LIBYA

Climate

Hot and dry year-round. In the south, temperatures can get as high as 45°C. On the coast the climate is more temperate – summer temperatures are around 30°C and it may be humid; winters are mild and damp. Spring and autumn are pleasant but dusty desert winds can blow at this time.

Contacts

Libyan Interests Section,
119 Harley Street,
London W1N 1DH
020 7486 8387

LIECHTENSTEIN

Climate

Temperate, with warm, dry summers and cold winters with snow from December to March.

Contacts

Switzerland Tourism,
10th Floor,

Swiss Centre, Swiss Court,
London W1V 8EE
020 7734 1921
www.switzerlandvacation.ch
Swiss Embassy,
16 Montagu Place,
London W1H 2BQ
020 7616 6000

LITHUANIA

Climate

Temperate, with cold winters, cool summers and steady rain.

Contacts

Lithuanian Embassy,
84 Gloucester Place,
London W1H 3HN
020 7486 6401

LUXEMBOURG

Climate

Temperate, with warm summers and cold winters. Heavy snow in highland areas in winter.

Contacts

Luxembourg Tourist Office,
122 Regent Street,
London W1R 5FE
020 7434 2800
Luxembourg Embassy,
27 Wilton Crescent,
London SW1X 8SD
020 7235 6961
www.luxembourg.co.uk

MACAU
(Handed back from Portugal to China in 1999)

Climate

Subtropical, with hot, humid, wet summers and cool but usually dry winters. The typhoon season is July to August. Late September to early December is the best time to visit – temperatures and humidity have fallen and there are lots of clear sunny days.

Contacts

Macau Tourist Office,
1 Battersea Church Road,
London SW11 3LY
020 7771 7006
www.macau.gov.mo

MACEDONIA

Climate

Wet springs, dry autumns, hot, dry summers and very cold winters, with snow in the mountains.

Contacts

Macedonian Embassy,
19a Cavendish Square,
London W1M 9AD
020 7499 5152

MADAGASCAR

Climate

Tropical. Generally, there is a wet season from October to April but it varies according to latitude and altitude. The wettest months are December to February and March, which is also cyclone season in the east and north. Parts of the south have very little rain; rainfall is heavier in the north. In the mountains, winter temperatures can drop to -15°C and snow may fall.

Contacts

Madagascar Consulate,
16 Lanark Mansions,
Pennard Road,
London W12 8DT
020 8746 0133

MALAWI

Climate

Subtropical: hot and humid in the south; cooler in the highlands. Rainfall varies. The dry season runs from May to October. The rainy season runs from October to April, with December to February the wettest months.

Contacts

Malawi High Commission,
33 Grosvenor Street,
London W1X 0DE
020 7491 4172

MALAYSIA

Climate

Tropical: hot, sunny and very humid year-round, with temperatures rarely dropping below 22°C. On the east coast of peninsular Malaysia and in Sabah and Sarawak, October to January and February is the wettest period. The west coast gets more rain from September to November and December. However, rain can fall year-round. Typhoons can occur in East Malaysia but are very rare.

Contacts

Tourism Malaysia,
57 Trafalgar Square,
London WC2N 5DU
020 7930 7932
www.tourism.gov.my
Malaysian High Commission,
45 Belgrave Square,
London SW1X 8QT
020 7235 8033
Visa Line: 0900 1887700

MALDIVES

Climate

Tropical, hot and humid year-round.
Temperatures range from 24°C to 33°C but are
moderated by sea breezes. Rains year-round
but especially during the south-west monsoon
(April to November) when there can be violent
storms. The sunniest months are October to
April and May, which is high season.

Contacts

High Commission of the Maldives,
22 Nottingham Place,
London W1M 3FB
020 7224 2135

MALI

Climate

Hot year-round, especially from March to May.
Average temperatures are around 30°C but can
rise to 40°C. There is virtually no rain in the north
(over half the country is arid desert) but rain falls
in the south in summer (June to September). The
region has droughts and dry desert winds blow
from December to February. October and
November are the best months to visit.

Contacts

No embassy or tourist information office in the
UK.

MALTA

Climate

Mediterranean, with hot, dry, sunny summers,
little rain and mild winters. Cooling sea breezes.
Spring and autumn can get siroccos (hot winds).

Contacts

Malta High Commission and Tourist Office,
Malta House,
36–38 Piccadilly,
London W1V 0PQ
020 7292 4800
www.tourism.org.mt

MARSHALL ISLANDS

Climate

Tropical oceanic: warm and humid year-
round, but cooled by trade winds.
Temperatures range from around 21°C to 32°C
(average daily temperature is 27°C). The best
time to visit is between January and March, the
driest, coolest and least humid months. The
northern islands are quite dry; the southern
islands get more rain. The wettest months are
August to November and typhoons, though
rare, are also possible at that time.

Contacts

No tourist office or consulate in the UK; visas
are issued on arrival.

MARTINIQUE
(Overseas Department of France)

Climate

Tropical and generally pleasant. It is hot and
humid much of the year, but trade winds relieve
the humidity, especially from January to April.
The rainiest months are usually May to
November and it is wetter on the windward
(north-east) sides of the island and in the
interior. The hurricane season runs from June to
November, with August and September the
riskiest months.

Contacts

See France

MAURITANIA

Climate

The weather is generally hot and dry, with
dusty winds and sometimes droughts. Rainfall
is sporadic; there is very little in the north but
the south has a short rainy season from July to
September. Summers (April to October) are
very hot, winters are mild. Coastal regions are
cooled by sea breezes. December to March are
the most pleasant months.

Contacts

Honorary Consulate of Mauritania,
140 Bow Common Lane,
London E3 4BH
020 8980 4382

MAURITIUS

Climate

Tropical climate, with hot, sunny days and
warm nights. Sea breezes help temper the
humidity. Rain falls year-round but especially

from December to April, when there may be cyclones and the weather is very hot and humid. The winter months (July to September) are drier and less humid, with temperatures around 24°C.

Contacts

Mauritius High Commission,
Passport Section,
32–33 Elvaston Place,
London SW7 5NW
020 7581 0294
Mauritius Tourist Office, address as above;
020 7584 3666
www.mauritius.net

MEXICO

Climate

The north and north-west are dry; the tropical far south has heavy rainfall. On the west coast the climate is tropical. The wettest months are July to September, when it can also be very humid. It is warm and sunny most of the year. The central plateau is mild and temperate. The coastal plain is hot and humid. The best time to visit is the winter dry season (October to March). The mountains and plains on the Caribbean side get plenty of rain year-round, especially from September to February. The mountains and plains on the Pacific side get little rain from December to April. The central and northern regions have a longer dry season and even in the wet season, rain is limited. Temperatures are affected by altitude – the high heat and humidity at the peak of the wet season is uncomfortable at lower altitudes.

Contacts

Mexican Tourist Office,
60–61 Trafalgar Square,
London WC2N 5DS
020 7488 9392
www.mexico-travel.com
Mexican Consulate,
8 Halkin Street,
London SW1X 7DW
020 7235 6393
Mexican Embassy,
42 Hertford Street,
London W1Y 7TF
020 7499 8586
Visa Line: 0900 1 600125
www.demon.co.uk/mexuk

MOLDAVIA (Moldova)

Climate

Warm summers, mildish winters; moderate rainfall.

Contacts

Embassy of the Russian Federation,
5 Kensington Palace Gardens,
London W8 4QS
020 7229 8027
Russian Consular Information Service:
0900 1171 271

MONACO

Climate

Mediterranean: hot, dry summers; mild, sunny winters.

Contacts

Monaco Tourist Office,
The Chambers,
Chelsea Harbour,
London SW10 0FE
020 7352 9962 or 0500 006114
www.monaco-congres.com
Consulate of Monaco,
4 Cromwell Place,
London SW7 2JE
020 7225 2679

MONGOLIA

Climate

Continental. Summers (June to August) are mild and can have thunderstorms. Spring and autumn are cool. Winters are long, dry and very cold, with lots of snow.

Contacts

Mongolian Embassy,
7 Kensington Court,
London W8 5DL
020 7937 0150

MONTSERRAT
(UK Crown Colony)

Climate

Tropical and generally pleasant. It is hot and humid much of the year, but trade winds relieve the humidity, especially from January to April. The rainiest months are usually May to November and it is wetter on the windward (north-east) sides of the island and in the interior. The hurricane season runs from June to November, with August and September the riskiest months.

Contacts

Monserrat Tourist Board,
Fourth Floor,
High Holborn House,
52–54 High Holborn,
London WC1V 6RB

020 7242 3131
www.mrat.com

MOROCCO

Climate

Variable. Coastal areas have a temperate, Mediterranean climate, with mild winters and hot, sunny summers. Much of the country is dry and arid. Can get low temperatures and snow in the mountains. Summers can get very hot. Temperatures are most extreme in the Sahara, where they can rise to 50°C in summer and fall to 3°C in winter. Freezing nights can follow extremely hot days. The lowlands are warm to hot in winter (around 30°C) though temperatures drop at night. In summer it is very hot in the day and still around 23°C at night. Rainfall is light; most of it is in winter, between November and April.

Contacts

Moroccan Tourist Office,
205 Regent Street,
London W1R 7DE
020 7437 0073
www.tourism-in-morocco.com
Moroccan Embassy,
49 Queen's Gate Gardens, London SW7 5NE
020 7581 5001

MOZAMBIQUE

Climate

Tropical. The dry season runs from April to September. The wet months (October to March) are hot and humid, with temperatures rising to 29°C on the coast. Inland areas are cooler.

Contacts

Mozambique Embassy,
21 Fitzroy Square,
London W1P 5HJ
020 7383 3800

MYANMAR (Burma)

Climate

Tropical monsoon. The coast and lowland regions are hot and tropical year-round. The coast is also very humid. The monsoon season runs from May to October. In central regions, the wettest months are August to September and October, when floods are possible. Most rain falls in the mountains in the north and east. November to February are the best months to visit because they're cool and dry. Temperatures rise from February onwards. The hottest months are March to May, when temperatures can reach 40°C. In highland regions, they can fall below freezing in December and January.

Contacts

Myanmar Embassy,
19a Charles Street,
London W1X 8ER
020 7629 6966

NAMIBIA

Climate

Sunny pretty well year-round throughout the country. The most pleasant time to visit is in winter (May to September). It can get extremely hot between December and March, when it is probably best avoided. The country is generally arid, especially in the central Namib, but there are two rainy seasons: the 'little' rains from October to December and the 'big' rains from January to March and April. In these months, roads in the Caprivi Strip can become impassable owing to floods. The coast gets very foggy.

Contacts

Namibia High Commission,
6 Chandos Street,
London W1M 0LQ
020 7636 6244
Namibia Tourism, address as above;
020 7636 2924
www.iwwn.com.na/namtour

NAURU

Climate

Tropical, equatorial climate – hot year-round. Sometimes get droughts. Best time to visit is November to March.

Contacts

No embassy or tourist information office in the UK.

NEPAL

Climate

Warm monsoon climate from July to October. Dry, sunny and mild the rest of the year. The best time to go trekking is October to November, just after the monsoon, but February to April is also good. The wettest months are June to August. Subtropical on the plain; arctic on the peaks. March is pleasant (rhododendrons in bloom).

Contacts

Nepalese Embassy,
Visa Section,

12a Kensington Palace Gardens,
London W8 4QU
020 7229 6231/1594

THE NETHERLANDS

Climate

Mild, maritime climate, similar to that of the UK. Winters are mild and rainy, summers cool. North Sea gales in autumn/winter.

Contacts

The Netherlands Board of Tourism,
18 Buckingham Gate,
London SW1E 6LB
020 7931 0661
www.holland.com
Royal Netherlands Embassy,
38 Hyde Park Gate,
London SW7 5DP
020 7590 3200

NEW CALEDONIA
(Overseas Territory of France)

Climate

Temperate year-round, with an average annual temperature of 23°C. Warm and humid from November to February; the coolest time of the year is July and August. Humidity is pretty high most of the year, especially between February and April, which are the wettest months. May is the driest month but there is no dry season as such – heavy downpours can happen at any time of year. The west coast is drier than the east.

Contacts

See France
South Pacific Tourism Organisation (SPTO),
203 Sheen Lane,
London SW14 8LE
020 8876 1938
www.tcsp.com

NEW ZEALAND

Climate

Temperate and damp. The far north is almost subtropical, with mild winters and warm, humid summers. South Island has cooler winters and upland snow. The weather is changeable, rather like the British climate, but there's plenty of sun. The best time to visit is probably in the late spring/summer months of November to March. May to October is the ski season (there are year-round snowfields in the south). The best time to swim with the dolphins is October to April. The wettest months are May to August; the west coast is much wetter than the east. North Island is temperate.

Contacts

New Zealand Tourism Board,
New Zealand House,
80 Haymarket,
London SW1Y 4TQ
020 7930 1662
www.purenz.com
New Zealand High Commission, address as above;
020 7930 8422
New Zealand Visa and Immigration Service:
09069 100 100
www.immigration.govt.nz
Brochures and General Information:
09063 640 650

NICARAGUA

Climate

Varies according to altitude. The Pacific lowlands are hot and tropical. May to November are the rainiest months, and also very humid. The dry season runs from December to April; March and April can be particularly hot. The Caribbean lowlands are hot and wet, with heavy annual rainfall. There is a brief dry season from March to May, but even then there can be heavy rain. In the mountains, the weather is much cooler.

Contacts

Nicaraguan Consulate,
58–60 Kensington Church Street,
London W8 4DB
020 7938 2373

NIGER

Climate

Hot year-round. March to June are the hottest months, especially April, when temperatures can go up to 45°C. The coolest months are December to February, when temperatures in the desert can drop to freezing. The south gets some rain in late May but the country as a whole is extremely dry, especially in the Sahara regions of the north.

Contacts

No embassy or tourist information office in the UK.

NIGERIA

Climate

Tropical, with temperatures high and fairly even year-round. The north is hot and dry, with one wet season from May to September. From March to May, temperatures can rise to 45°C. The south is slightly cooler, but humidity is high and rainfall heavier. Rain in these areas falls mainly from April to July and from September to October.

Contacts

Nigeria High Commission,
9 Northumberland Avenue,
London WC2N 5BX
020 7839 1244

NIUE: see South Pacific

NORTHERN CYPRUS

Climate

Mediterranean: hot, dry, sunny summers (May to September); mild winters, with snow in the mountains. Most rain falls in the winter.

Contacts

North Cyprus Tourist Office,
29 Bedford Square,
London WC1B 3EG
020 7631 1930
www.northcyprus.co.uk
Embassy of Turkish Republic of Northern Cyprus, address as above;
020 7631 1930

NORTH KOREA

Climate

Continental: warm summers and cold winters; snow in the north. Temperatures vary from -10°C in winter to 30°C in summer. Most rain falls during the summer months.

Contacts

No embassy or tourist information office in the UK. Visas can be obtained in Macau or China.

NORWAY

Climate

Mild on the coast; more extreme inland. Warm summers and cold, snowy winters. Warmer summers and colder winters inland. Rain throughout the year but heaviest from June to October. Coast modified by the North Atlantic Drift. Lots of rain in the northern mountains.

Contacts

Norwegian Tourist Board, Charles House,
5–11 Lower Regent Street,
London SW1Y 4LR
020 7839 6255
Norwegian Embassy,
25 Belgrave Square,
London SW1X 8QD;
020 7591 5500
www.norway.org.uk

OMAN

Climate

Very hot in the north, especially in summer. Monsoon rains fall in the southern uplands from June to September. Hot and mostly dry; the coast is more humid than the interior. October to February and March is the best time to visit.

Contacts

Omani Embassy,
167 Queen's Gate,
London SW7 5HE
020 7225 0001

PAKISTAN

Climate

Temperatures are generally warm year-round and can be very high in the south and west, very low in the Hindu Kush. The wettest months are between June and August. December to February see warm, sunny days with cooler nights, then it's very hot until the rainy season starts. Can be very humid from May to September. The west is semi-desert. Monsoon rains are especially heavy in the northern mountains.

Contacts

Pakistan High Commission,
36 Lowndes Square,
London SW1X 9JN
020 7664 9200

PALAU

Climate

Tropical oceanic climate. Warm and humid year-round, with average daily temperatures around 30°C. The dry season is February to April, which is also the best time to visit. The wettest months are June to August, with lots of thunderstorms in June.

Contacts

No tourist office or consulate in the UK. Visas are issued on arrival.

PANAMA

Climate

There are two main seasons: the dry season runs from January to mid-April, the rainy season from May to December (the summer months) – but heavy rain is possible at any time of year. Rainfall is lightest on the Pacific coast. It is generally hot and humid in the lowlands (with temperatures fairly constant around 32°C) and cooler in highland areas.

Contacts

Panamanian Consulate,
40 Hertford Street,
London W1Y 7TG
020 7409 2255
www.segumar.com

PAPUA NEW GUINEA

Climate

Tropical. Pretty hot and humid year-round in
the coastal lowlands. Cooler in the highlands,
which can have snow. The dry season runs
from May to December. Lots of rain, especially
between December and March.

Contacts

Papua New Guinea High Commission,
14 Waterloo Place,
London SW1Y 4AR
020 7930 0922/4
South Pacific Tourism Organisation (SPTO),
203 Sheen Lane,
London SW14 8LE
020 8876 1938
www.tcsp.com

PARAGUAY

Climate

Subtropical. Temperatures range from 22°C to
35°C. Rain is fairly constant throughout the
year. Hot, rainy, humid summers from
December to March. Mild winters. Hotter and
drier in the north-west, where rainfall is more
erratic. The best time to visit is between May
and October, when it's relatively dry.

Contacts

Paraguayan Embassy,
Braemar Lodge,
Cornwall Gardens,
London SW7 4AQ
020 7937 1253/6629

PERU

Climate

Coastal plains have a desert climate: they're hot
and dry from January to March; their coldest
months are June to November, with little rain
but high humidity and fog. Lima, in the centre
of this area, has hot summers and warm winters.
In the interior plateau, there's a wide range of
temperatures: the lower mountain slopes are
temperate, higher up they're covered in snow.
The Andes have a dry season from May to
September when days are warm and sunny but
it can be very cold at night; what little rain there
is in the mountains falls mainly from December

to May, when travel on mountain roads can be
difficult. In the eastern lowlands, the climate is
hot, humid and wet year-round, but especially
rainy from November to February.

Contacts

Embassy of Peru,
52 Sloane Street,
London SW1X 9SP
020 7235 1917
www.peruembassy-uk.com

PHILIPPINES

Climate

Tropical but with a maritime tempering
influence – mostly warm and humid. Hot,
sunny and very humid in the rainy season (May
to October), when the islands can also get
torrential rains and typhoons, especially in the
north. Southern islands are less affected by the
monsoon and heavy showers are interspersed
with long sunny periods. The best time to visit
is October to February, when it is mostly cool
and dry. March to May is usually very hot.

Contacts

Philippine Embassy,
9a Palace Green,
London W8 4QE
020 7937 1600
www.philemb.demon.co.uk
Department of Tourism,
146 Cromwell Road,
London SW7 4EF
020 7835 1100
www.tourism.gov.ph

POLAND

Climate

Continental. Cold winters (December to
March), especially in the mountains. There
may be snow but the Carpathian mountains
are sunny. Hot summers (June to August),
especially on the coast. Summer/autumn is
also when most of the rain falls. In spring the
days are warm but the nights can be cool.

Contacts

Polish National Tourist Office,
1st Floor, Remo House,
310–312 Regent Street,
London W1R 5AJ
020 7580 8811
Polish Consulate General,
73 New Cavendish Street,
London W1M 8LS
020 7580 0476

PORTUGAL

Climate

Cooler in the north; warmer in the south, with mild, dry winters. Lisbon has a sunny, temperate climate, with hot, sunny summers and mild winters. Some rain, mainly in December, January and March.

Contacts

Portuguese Tourist Office,
2nd Floor,
22–25a Sackville Street,
London W1X 2LY
020 7494 1441
Portuguese Embassy,
11 Belgrave Square,
London SW1X 8PP
020 7235 5331
Brochure Line: 0900 1600370

PUERTO RICO
(Self-governing Commonwealth of USA)

Climate

Warm, sunny winters; hot, sunny summers; rain throughout the year.

Contacts

Puerto Rico Tourist Office,
c/o Cerrano,
2–2 Izda,
28001 Madrid,
Spain;
0800 898920 (toll free number)
See also US Embassy

QATAR

Climate

Desert climate. Very hot summers (May to September), with average temperatures 37°C and sometimes as high as 50°C. Summers are also very humid. Winters are milder but still warm, though cool in the evenings. Limited rainfall in winter but rain is generally low. Sandstorms can occur year-round, especially in spring. The best time to visit is November or late February to early March.

Contacts

Qatar Embassy,
1 South Audley Street,
London W1Y 5DQ
020 7493 2200
Visa Information Line:
09068 633 233

RÉUNION
(Overseas Department of France)

Climate

The hot, wet summer months (October to March) are prone to cyclones. Winter (April to September) is cool and dry. The east coast is wetter than the west. On the coast, summer temperatures average 28°C. Mountain areas are cooler, and cold in winter.

Contacts
See France

ROMANIA

Climate

Continental, with hot, humid summers, though it can be cold in the mountains. The Black Sea coast has particularly warm summers, though temperatures are modified by breezes. The winters (December to March) are very cold and snowy, especially in the mountains. Rainy in spring.

Contacts

Romanian Tourist Office,
83a Marylebone High Street,
London W1M 3DE
020 7224 3692
Romanian Embassy,
4 Palace Green,
London W8 4QD
020 7937 9666
Visa Information Service: 020 7376 0683

RUSSIAN FEDERATION (Russia)

Climate

This huge country has big variations from sub-arctic to Mediterranean to desert. Moscow has warm summers and very cold winters with snow and ice; coldest months are November to March; warmest, wettest months are July and August. St Petersburg is changeable, with mild, sunny summers and icy cold winters, with snow and frost. The country has rain year-round, especially late summer and autumn. In Siberia, winter is very harsh (temperatures can fall to -25°C in January) but dry and sunny. Summers (July/August) can be warm with temperatures going up to 30°C. Autumn (September and October) is changeable. Snow falls December and January. East of Lake Baikal there is year-round permafrost. The Black Sea coast has milder winters and warm, humid summers (June to September). November to May are the rainiest months. The Volga region has a continental climate: temperatures can range from -10°C to -15°C in winter (January) to 20°C to 25°C in summer (July). Low humidity. May to September are the best months to visit.

Contacts

Embassy of the Russian Federation,
5 Kensington Palace Gardens,
London W8 4QS
020 7229 8027
Russian Consular Information Service:
0900 1171271

RWANDA

Climate

Tropical and warm year-round, with average temperatures ranging from 30°C to 34°C, though highland regions are cooler. Dry seasons run from May to October and December to March. Rainy seasons run from March to May and October to December.

Contacts

No embassy or tourist information office in the UK.

ST KITTS & NEVIS: see Eastern Caribbean

ST LUCIA

Climate

See Eastern Caribbean

Contacts

St Lucia Tourist Board,
421a Finchley Road,
London NW3 6HJ
020 7431 3675
www.stlucia.org
Eastern Caribbean High Commission,
10 Kensington Court,
London W8 5DL
020 7937 9522

ST VINCENT & THE GRENADINES: see Eastern Caribbean

SAMOA

Climate

Hot and humid year-round, but tempered from April to October by trade winds. Hottest months are December to April, which is also cyclone season. The driest months are May to September, which is a good time to visit. Average temperatures are between 21°C and 32°C.

Contacts

No embassy or tourist information office in the UK.

SÃO TOMÉ & PRÍNCIPE

Climate

Hot and humid, with lots of rain. The dry season is July to August. Consistent temperatures up to 30°C year-round.

Contacts

No embassy or tourist information office in the UK.

SAUDI ARABIA

Climate

Extremely hot in summer (April to October), when temperatures can reach 45°C. Winters are warm. Humidity is generally low but can be high in coastal regions in summer. The coast gets regular rain but rainfall is generally low. The best time to visit is November to February.

Contacts

Royal Embassy of Saudi Arabia,
Consular Section,
30 Charles Street,
London W1X 8LP
020 7917 3000

SENEGAL

Climate

Tropical, with temperatures generally ranging from 22°C to 28°C. It is hot and humid in the rainy season. In the far south, this runs from May to October; in the rest of the country it is shorter, from July to September. From November to March the weather is cool and dry – this is a good time to visit. The coast gets cool winds. Dry dusty winds blow from the Sahara from December.

Contacts

Senegalese Embassy,
39 Marloes Road,
London W8 6LA
020 7938 4048

SEYCHELLES

Climate

Tropical: hot, sunny and humid. Rains all year round but especially from November to April. January is the wettest month; Mahé is the rainiest island. The driest months are July and August. Temperatures are pretty constant year-round, between 24°C and 30°C.

Contacts

Seychelles Tourist Office,
2nd Floor, Eros House,
111 Baker Street,
London W1M 1FE

020 7224 1670
Seychelles High Commission,
address as above
020 7224 1660
www.seychelles.uk.com

SIERRA LEONE

Climate

Hot and tropical year-round, with high rainfall. The rainy season runs from May to early November; it's especially wet and humid from July to September. The dry season runs from November to April but dry winds blow dust from the Sahara from December onwards. November, after the rains and before the dusty winds, is a good time to visit. The weather is cooler in December and January.

Contacts

Sierra Leone High Commission,
Oxford Circus House,
245 Oxford Street,
London W1L 1LF
020 7287 9884

SINGAPORE

Climate

Equatorial – hot, sunny and humid year-round. Temperatures range from 20°C to 30°C. Rain falls year-round: the wettest months are October and November to January; the driest months are May to July.

Contacts

Singapore Tourist Promotion Board,
126-130 Regent Street,
London W1R 5FE
020 7437 0033
www.newasia/singapore.com
Singapore High Commission,
Consular Dept,
9 Wilton Crescent,
London SW1X 8SA
020 7245 0273

SLOVAKIA REPUBLIC (Slovakia)

Climate

Continental, with warm to hot summers; steady rain; and cold winters with snow. The Danube lowland has the most attractive climate. The high Tatra mountains have extremes of climate and are the rainiest part of the country.

Contacts

Slovak Embassy,
25 Kensington Palace Gardens,
London W8 4QY

020 7243 0803
Information service:
0900 1600360

SLOVENIA

Climate

Continental, with warm summers and cold winters (with snow in the mountains). Mediterranean on coast; more extreme in the mountains inland. The best time to visit is late spring to autumn (April to September).

Contacts

Slovenian Tourist Office,
49 Conduit Street,
London W1R 9FB
020 7287 7133
www.tourist-board.si
Slovenian Embassy,
Cavendish Court,
11–15 Wigmore Street, London W1H 9LA
020 7495 7775
www.embassy-slovenia.org.uk

SOLOMON ISLANDS

Climate

Tropical. The summer season (November to April) is hot, humid and wet, especially from January. This is also cyclone season. The best time to go is in the winter months (May to December), when temperatures are in the mid-20°sC, with light rainfall, though there may sometimes be high winds bringing heavy rain at this time of year. The northern islands are hot and humid year-round.

Contacts

South Pacific Tourism Organisation (SPTO),
203 Sheen Lane,
London SW14 8LE
020 8876 1938
www.tcsp.com

SOMALIA

Climate

Hot and humid on the north coast; otherwise very dry. The Indian coast gets moderate rainfall.

Contacts

No embassy or tourist information office in the UK.

SOUTH AFRICA

Climate

The coast round Cape Town has a temperate Mediterranean climate: wet and cold in winter

(May to August); hot, sunny and often windy in summer (October to March). January and February can be very hot; the coolest months are June and July. The flowers of the Cape are best in September. Johannesburg has dry, sunny, mild winters and warm, sunny summers, with most rain falling in the summer; humidity is low. Summer in the Transkei and Natal can be very hot and humid but highland areas are pleasant. On the east coast, the climate becomes more tropical the further north you go.

Contacts

South African Tourism Board,
5–6 Alt Grove,
Wimbledon,
London SW19 4DZ
020 8944 8080
Brochure Line: 0541 55 00 44
Information Line: 0906 3 640 640
South African High Commission,
Trafalgar Square,
London WC2N 5DP
020 7930 4488/451 7229
South African Consulate General Information Service: 020 7925 8900

SOUTH KOREA

Climate

Winters are dry, sunny and very cold; summers are hot, wet and humid. The rainy season is July to August, when over half of the annual rain falls and it can be very hot and humid. Most snow falls from November to March. Can get typhoons in summer. The best times to visit are spring and autumn. September to early November have warm, sunny days and cool evenings. It can be windy in spring.

Contacts

South Korean Tourist Board,
8th Floor,
New Zealand House,
Haymarket,
London SW1Y 4TQ
020 7321 2535
www.knto.org.kr
Korean Embassy,
60 Buckingham Gate,
London SW1E 6AJ
020 7227 5500

SOUTH PACIFIC (Cook Islands, Fiji, Kiribati, New Caledonia, Niue, Papua New Guinea, Solomon Islands, Tahiti, Tonga, Tuvalu, Vanuatu, Western Samoa)

Climate

See individual entries

Contacts

South Pacific Tourism Organisation (SPTO),
203 Sheen Lane,
London SW14 8LE
020 8876 1938
www.tcsp.com
Also see individual entries

SPAIN

Climate

Temperate maritime in the north; hotter and drier in the south. Extremes on the central plateau. Hot summers, cold winters, very little rain. Can get hot winds and dust.

Contacts

Spanish Tourist Office,
22-23 Manchester Square,
London W1M 5AP
020 7486 8077
Brochure request line:
0900 1669920
www.tourspain.co.uk
Spanish Embassy,
Consular Section,
20 Draycott Place,
London SW3 2RZ
020 7589 8989
Spanish Consulate Visa Information Service:
0900 1600123

SRI LANKA

Climate

Tropical and equatorial with hot summers, warm winters and rain year-round. High humidity. Breezes on the coast; cooler in the highlands. The north-east of the island is hotter and drier than the south and west. Very hot in the north (temperatures over 38°C); cooler in the south. The south-west monsoon brings rain from May to August in Colombo and the south-west. North-east monsoon affects the north-east from November to February. The best time to visit is our winter time.

Contacts

Sri Lanka Tourist Board,
22 Regent Street,
London SW1Y 4QD
020 7930 2627
Sri Lanka High Commission,
13 Hyde Park Gardens,
London W2 2LU
020 7262 1841

SUDAN

Climate

Much of the country, particularly the north and west, is hot, arid desert. The south is humid, tropical and equatorial, and usually has rain from April to November. The hottest months in the south are February and March, when temperatures can reach 40°C. Dust storms can occur in summer.

Contacts

Sudan Embassy,
3 Cleveland Row, St James,
London SW1A 1DD
020 7839 8080

SURINAME

Climate

Tropical, hot and humid with lots of rain (particularly from April to July and from December to January), especially inland.

Contacts

No embassy or tourist information office in the UK.

SWAZILAND

Climate

Hot and dry in the east; cooler and wetter in the high veld. Warm, wet season from October to March; drier and cooler from May to December.

Contacts

Swaziland High Commission,
20 Buckingham Gate,
London SW1E 6LB
020 7630 6611

SWEDEN

Climate

Mild in the south. Stockholm has cold winters and warm summers. Plenty of rain falls year-round (though less in the east) and snow in winter. Long winters in the north and lots of snow.

Contacts

Swedish Tourist Office,
11 Montagu Place,
London W1H 2AL
020 7724 5868
Brochure Line:
01476 578811
www.visit-sweden.com
Embassy of Sweden,
11 Montagu Place,
London W1H 2AL
020 7724 2101
www.swedish-embassy.org.uk

SWITZERLAND

Climate

Seasons are the same as in the UK, though slightly warmer most of the year. Mild, warm summers (average July temperatures of 18°C to 19°C) and cold winters. Altitude means cold winters and snow. Rainy in the summer months (May to September), with snow on the mountains. The best months to visit are May to September (unless, of course, you plan to do some skiing) when most mountain passes are open. The alpine flowers are at their best in June and July. July and August can be crowded and expensive.

Contacts

Switzerland Tourism,
Swiss Centre,
Swiss Court,
London W1V 8EE
020 7734 1921
www.switzerlandtourism.ch
Swiss Embassy,
16 Montagu Place,
London W1H 2BQ
020 7616 6000

SYRIA

Climate

The coast has a Mediterranean climate, with average daily temperatures ranging from 29°C in summer to 10°C in winter. The steppe regions are warmer with less rain. In the mountains, there can be snow in winter. The south-east is arid desert with high temperatures (up to 46°C) and low rainfall.

Contacts

Syrian Embassy,
8 Belgrave Square,
London SW1X 8PH
020 7245 9012

TAHITI: see French Polynesia and South Pacific

TAIWAN

Climate

Tropical monsoon climate. Hot and humid in summer, with typhoons likely from July to September. In winter, the north-east coast gets almost continuous rain and there is snow on the mountains. The south-west is warmer and drier. Monsoon rains fall from June to August, especially in mountainous regions.

Contacts

Taipei Representative Office,
50 Grosvenor Gardens,
London SW1W 0EB
020 7396 9152
www.tro-taiwan.roc.org.uk

TAJIKISTAN

Climate

Continental to subtropical. Lower western areas have warm summers and cold winters. Very cold winters in the mountains. Low rainfall.

Contacts

Embassy of the Russian Federation,
5 Kensington Palace Gardens,
London W8 4QS
020 7229 8027
Russian Consular Information Service:
0900 1171 271

TANZANIA

Climate

Tropical. Especially hot and humid in the central lowlands, on the coast and in Zanzibar, though tempered by sea breezes. The central plateau is semi-arid. The highlands near the Kenyan border are semi-temperate. The rainy season runs from March to May. It can also be rainy in November and December to January. Inland temperatures average 25°C year-round.

Contacts

Tanzania Tourist Office,
80 Borough High Street,
London SE1 1LL
020 7407 0566
Tanzania High Commission,
43 Hertford Street,
London W1Y 8DB
020 7499 8951
www.tanzania-online.gov.uk

THAILAND

Climate

Hot and humid during the monsoon season, which, in most of the country, runs from May to October. The further south you go, the rainier it is. The dry season is from December to May. Best time to visit the north and west of the country is between November and February, after which temperatures rise in the run-up to the monsoon. Ko Samui, off the east coast, is best from May to September.

Contacts

Tourism Authority of Thailand,
49 Albemarle Street,
London W1X 3FE
020 7499 7679
Tourism Info: 0839 300 300
www.tourismthailand.org
The Royal Thai Embassy, Consular Section,
29 Queen's Gate,
London SW7 5JB
020 7589 2944
Visa Information Service:
0900 3 405456; 0900 1 600150

TOGO

Climate

Tropical, with average temperatures around 27°C. Temperatures are highest from mid-February to mid-April. Coastal regions are hot and humid; the interior is drier. The rainy season runs from May to October. The south has a dry season from July to September – a good time to visit.

Contacts

No embassy in the UK.
www.togo.gov

TONGA

Climate

Tropical oceanic climate – warm and hot year-round. High temperatures year-round, average around 26°C. Heavy rains, especially from February to March. The best time to visit is January or February, when humidity is low and temperatures are in the mid-20°sC to low 30°sC.

Contacts

Tonga High Commission,
36 Molyneux Street,
London W1H 6AB
020 7724 5828
South Pacific Tourism Organisation (SPTO),
203 Sheen Lane,
London SW14 8LE
020 8876 1938
www.tcsp.com

TRINIDAD & TOBAGO

Climate

Tropical and generally pleasant, with no real extremes of temperature. It is hot and humid much of the year, but trade winds relieve the humidity, especially from January to April. Rains throughout the year, especially between June and November, but the islands are far enough south to miss out on hurricanes.

Contacts

Trinidad & Tobago Tourist Office,
Mitre House,
66 Abbey Road,
Bush Hill Park,
Enfield,
Middlesex EN1 2RQ
020 8350 1000
Trinidad & Tobago High Commission,
42 Belgrave Square,
London SW1X 8NT
020 7245 9351

TUNISIA

Climate

Mediterranean: hot, dry summers and mild, warm winters (though winters in the north can be wet and windy). Not much rain; what there is falls mostly from October to March. Arid in the south.

Contacts

Tunisia National Tourist Office,
77a Wigmore Street,
London W1H 9LJ
020 7224 5561
www.tourismtunisia.co.uk
Tunisian Embassy,
29 Prince's Gate,
London SW7 1QG
020 7584 8117

TURKEY

Climate

Mediterranean on the coast; more extreme inland – cold, snowy winters and hot, dry summers. The wettest months are December to February. Istanbul has hot, sunny summers and mild, wet winters. Most rain falls between November and January.

Contacts

Turkish Tourism Office,
1st floor, Egyptian House,
170–173 Piccadilly,
London W1V 9DD
020 7629 7771
Brochure Line:
0900 1 887755
Turkish Consulate General,
Rutland Lodge,
Rutland Gardens,
London SW7 1BW
020 7589 0360
Visa Enquiries: 09068 347 348

TURKMENISTAN

Climate

Arid desert climate. Very hot in summer, below freezing in winter.

Contacts

No embassy or tourist information office in the UK.

TURKS & CAICOS ISLANDS
(UK Dependent Territory)

Climate

The best time to visit is February, when it's not too hot. There is no rainy season. Hurricane season is August to November, when it also gets uncomfortably hot. From December to July temperatures average 23°C.

Contacts

Turks & Caicos Tourist Office,
Mitre House,
66 Abbey Road,
Bush Hill Park,
Enfield,
Middlesex EN1 2QE
020 8350 1017
www.mki.ltd.uk

TUVALU

Climate

Hot and humid year-round, with plenty of rain. The wet season is November to February. Best time to visit is May to October when it is cooler and more pleasant.

Contacts

South Pacific Tourism Organisation (SPTO),
203 Sheen Lane,
London SW14 8LE
020 8876 1938
www.tcsp.com

UAE (United Arab Emirates)
(includes Abu Dhabi and Dubai)

Climate

Hot, humid summers (May to September), when temperatures can be in the low 40s°C but there is little rain. Winters are mild but night-time temperatures in the desert can be very low. Dusty winds blow in winter and spring. The best time to visit is November to February.

Contacts

UAE Embassy,
30 Prince's Gate,
London SW7 1PJ
020 7581 1281

Consular department:
020 7589 3434

UGANDA

Climate

Generally tropical – warm year-round but modified by altitude. Average temperature 26°C but cooler at night. December to February are the hottest months. In the south, the rains fall from April to May and October to November. In the north, the rainy season runs from April to October when it can be humid; the dry season is from November to March.

Contacts

Uganda High Commission and Tourist Office,
Uganda House,
58–59 Trafalgar Square,
London WC2N 5DX
020 7839 5783

UKRAINE

Climate

Continental. Temperatures in winter can go below freezing. The west is warmer than the east. On the coast, the climate is more Mediterranean, with warm summers and milder winters. June and July are the wettest months inland.

Contacts

Ukrainian Embassy,
60 Holland Park,
London W11 3SJ
020 7727 6312
Visa Information:
020 7243 8923

URUGUAY

Climate

Equable, mild, temperate, with warm, sunny summers and mild winters. Temperatures range from 15°C to 28°C (cooler at night) Coastal temperatures can be very hot in summer but cooler in higher inland regions. Moderate rainfall year-round.

Contacts

Uruguayan Embassy,
2nd Floor,
140 Brompton Road,
London SW3 1HY
020 7589 8835/8735

USA

Climate

Such a huge country has great variations in weather conditions. The south-east has hot, humid summers and mild winters (Florida and the Gulf States, like Hawaii, have a tropical climate). The south-west states have a desert climate, mostly hot and dry. The rest of the country is more temperate. Chicago has very cold winters and hot summers. Los Angeles has hot, dry summers and mild winters and can be affected by smog. San Francisco has mild summers with sea fogs and mild winters (November to March), which are also the wettest months. Miami has hot sunny summers and mild sunny winters, with May to October the wettest months, when there can also be lots of thunderstorms and the odd hurricane. Winter temperatures in the north can drop to -40°C (Alaska) and even in the south they can be very low. Long winters in the north. Sunny summers, often extremely hot. East coast seasons change gradually but the weather can be more extreme in the north – New York has humid heatwaves in summer and freezing winters (especially January and February). (New York can be hotter than San Francisco though far further north.) Cyclones can occur anywhere.

Contacts

US Embassy, Visa Branch,
5 Upper Grosvenor Street,
London W1A 2JB
020 7499 9000
Visa Information Line:
09068 200 290 (recorded)
General Information Line:
0991 500590 (manned, but costs £1.50 per minute)
The Visit USA Association, an umbrella organization for associated tourist offices in the USA: 09069 101020 (£1/min)
www.usembassy.org.uk – Ready Reference pages have answers to common queries.

US VIRGIN ISLANDS
(St Thomas, St Croix, St John)

Climate

Tropical and generally pleasant. Hot and humid much of the year but trade winds relieve the humidity, especially from January to April. It's wetter on the windward (north-east) sides of the islands and in the interior, with May to November seeing the highest rainfall. The hurricane season runs from June to November, with August and September the riskiest months.

Contacts

US Virgin Islands Tourist Office,
Molasses House,

Plantation Wharf,
London SW11 3TN
020 7978 5262
US Embassy: see USA
www.usvi.net

UZBEKISTAN

Climate

Dry and arid. Very hot summers; cold winters.

Contacts

Embassy of Uzbekistan,
41 Holland Park,
London W11 2RP
020 7229 7679

VANUATU

Climate

Tropical. The north is hotter and rainier than the south. The dry season, the best time to visit, runs from May to October. Between November and April it is wetter and hotter, and cyclones can occur.

Contacts

South Pacific Tourism Organisation (SPTO),
203 Sheen Lane,
London SW14 8LE
020 8876 1938
www.tcsp.com

VENEZUELA

Climate

Tropical, hot and humid but cooler in the highlands. Warm year-round, but hottest during the summer (May to August), which is also the wettest time of year.

Contacts

Embassy of Venezuela,
1 Cromwell Road,
London SW7 2HW
020 7584 4206
Visa Information:
0900 1171221
Consulate Section,
56 Grafton Way,
London W1 3SB
020 7387 6727

VIETNAM

Climate

In Saigon and the south, temperatures are fairly constant at around 25°C to 35°C year-round; the dry season runs from November to April, the wet season from May to October. In the centre of the country, the rainy season runs from May to December and is especially heavy in August and October. In Hanoi and the north, winter (November to March) is grey and cool but mostly dry, and the summer months (April to October) are hot, humid and wet; typhoons are possible at this time. The best time to visit is between January and April to May.

Contacts

Vietnam Embassy,
12 Victoria Road,
London W8 5RD
020 7937 1912
Vietnam Tourist Office, address as above;
020 7937 3174

VIRGIN ISLANDS: see British or US Virgin Islands

WESTERN SAMOA

Climate

Tropical and hot year-round, with high humidity, but tempered from April to October by trade winds. The hottest months are December to April, which is also cyclone season. The driest months are May to September, which is a good time to visit. Average temperatures are between 21°C and 32°C.

Contacts

South Pacific Tourism Organisation (SPTO),
203 Sheen Lane,
London SW14 8LE
020 8876 1938
www.tcsp.com

YEMEN

Climate

Hot desert climate but moderated by altitude. The southern coast gets little rain (most of it usually between July and September). This region is hot and humid year-round, with dusty winds. The central highlands are mild and dry; any rain falls in March to April and August. Winter nights can be frosty. In the western mountains rainfall is higher and falls steadily throughout the year, especially in July and August. The north and east are dry regions.

Contacts

Yemen Embassy,
57 Cromwell Road,
London SW7 2ED
020 7584 6607

YUGOSLAVIA
(Serbia and Montenegro)

Climate

Mediterranean on the coast, continental inland (hot summers; cold winters, with snow), but varies with altitude and from north to south. Rain is even throughout the year.

Contacts
Yugoslav Embassy,
5 Lexham Gardens,
London W8 5JJ
020 7370 6105

ZAIRE: see Congo

Democratic Republic of ZAMBIA

Climate

Tropical. Three seasons; cool and dry (May to August), hot and dry (September to October), wet (November to May). Droughts in the south-west.

Contacts
Zambia National Tourist Board,
2 Palace Gate,
London W8 5NG
020 7589 6343
Zambia High Commission: as above;

ZIMBABWE

Climate

Tropical but temperatures are moderated by altitude. Generally pleasant and warm. The winter months are May to October, when the weather is warm, dry and sunny during the day, with cool, clear nights (sometimes very cold). This is the best time to view wildlife as the animals cluster round the limited water holes. The wet season is November to March and April, which is also very humid.

Contacts
Zimbabwe High Commission &
Tourist Office,
Zimbabwe House,
429 Strand,
London WC2R 0QE
020 7836 7755

CHAPTER 18

THE FINAL COUNTDOWN

Six months to go

* Start reading up on your destinations. Find out what the climate's like in each country and work out your route accordingly, if possible.

* Call or visit several travel agents with your rough itinerary and dates. Ask them for estimates and compare prices.

Three months to go

* Book your ticket and pay a deposit. Take out travel insurance at the same time so you're covered if you have to cancel.

* If you're renting out your flat, you should be thinking about it now. (See Chapter 19 for details.) Visit a couple of estate agents and ask for a valuation for rental purposes. Ask your friends if anyone needs somewhere to stay, and put up notices at work.

* Make an appointment with your doctor to discuss vaccinations, malaria medication and contraceptive precautions.

* Start looking for someone to look after any pets or plants while you're away.

* Check your passport has enough time to run and plenty of blank pages for all your visas and stamps. If it has expired, apply now for a new one.

* Sort out what's going to happen with your finances while you're away. Have you arranged for bills to be paid by standing order? If not, set them up now.

* If you're going to be trekking or hiking, buy new boots now so

that they're well broken in by the time you leave. You can't go anywhere with blisters.

Two months to go

* Check if you need any visas and, if you do, apply now.

* Start recording tapes of your favourite music to take with you – it always takes longer than you think!

One month to go

* Go to the dentist/optician for a check-up.

* Check the dates on your credit cards. If they're due to expire during your trip, order new ones now.

* Check that things like camera/torch/Walkman are working properly. Do they need repairing/cleaning?

* Set aside a Saturday for shopping. Make a list (see page 147) and tick off everything as you go. Doing it now gives you time to buy anything you might forget.

* Organize any discount and communication cards (see Chapter 5).

Two weeks to go

* Order traveller's cheques and foreign currency.

* If parents/friends are paying bills for you while you're away, give them blank cheques and make sure there's enough money in the bank to cover them.

* If you've bought a new rucksack, make sure it's properly fitted to your frame.

* If you're taking Lariam, start it now so you have time to see if you experience any side-effects.

One week to go

* Deliver any pets and plants to whoever's looking after them. Leave enough money to cover food, cat litter, any injections, etc.

* Get your hair cut – who knows when you'll get the chance again!

* Get some passport photographs taken for visas *en route*.

* If necessary, arrange for the post office to redirect your mail.

* Prepare an itinerary with any forwarding addresses and copy it to your friends and family.

* Take two photocopies of your ticket/insurance details/passport and visas/credit cards. Leave one set with someone at home (in case of emergency).

* Arrange a *bon voyage* drinks with your mates. (Don't fix it up for the night before you leave – longhaul flights with a hangover are no fun!)

* Start taking your malaria tablets.

* Start making a pile of everything you're planning to take with you.

Three days to go

* Reconfirm your flight and check that any vegetarian or kosher meals have been requested.

* Go through the checklist in Chapter 13 to make absolutely sure you've got everything.

The day before

* Check which terminal your flight leaves from.

* Pre-book a cab to take you to the airport or ask a friend to give you a lift. Allow plenty of time – try to arrive two hours before your flight leaves.

* If your flight's an early one, and you're worried you'll sleep in, book an an alarm call through the operator, as well as setting your own alarm clock.

* Try not to stay too late in the pub (see *bon voyage* drink, above)...

The big day

Don't leave home without: passport with visas, tickets, money, insurance documents.

CHAPTER 19

ANY MORE QUESTIONS?

You've planned the route, bought the gear, read the books. So far, so good. But there are still a few more things you might want to think about...

I own a flat. What should I do with it if I go away for a year?

If you're planning to rent out your property, start thinking about this at least six months ahead. A company let is the safest (and probably most lucrative) option. Contact estate agents in your area and have two or three value your property for a letting.

Estate agents will find you a tenant, take up references, draw up a tenancy agreement and collect the first month's rent (for a fee, of course). For a larger fee, they'll collect the rent every month and take care of minor repairs, should any be required.

You can, of course, find tenants yourself. Ask among your friends if any of them need somewhere to stay, or if they know anyone who does. You can also put a notice on the e-mail or a bulletin board at work. You'll need to vet prospective tenants carefully and ask them for personal and employment references, bank statements, and a month's deposit plus a month's rent in advance.

Your solicitor should draw up a shorthold tenancy agreement which should be signed by you and the tenants. Make any obligations clear. Are the tenants responsible for maintaining the garden, for example? You should also draw up an inventory of contents, which both parties should sign. Anything of monetary or sentimental value should be locked away or given to friends to look after.

Always inform your building society and bank manager if you're letting out a property. Let your local council know, too.

You won't be responsible for community charge if you're abroad, but the tenants will be. Transfer all bills, including the telephone bill, into the tenants' name.

If you're leaving your home empty, or renting it out to tenants, check that your insurers are aware of the situation and that you're still covered. If you don't tell them, they could refuse to pay up if you're burgled in your absence. Tenants should make their own separate insurance arrangements.

If you have family or close friends, you could ask them to keep in touch with the tenants to make sure there are no problems. It also lets the tenants know there's someone keeping an eye on the place.

I'm going to travel round South America for a year, with a friend. My boyfriend can't come because he doesn't want to give up his job. Is there any chance we can keep our relationship going over that time and distance?

It can be difficult for someone whose partner is going off to travel, and they're being left behind, for whatever reason. Try to make him feel part of your plans. Get the atlas out and show him exactly where you're going to. Suggest that he flies out to join you for two or three weeks halfway through your trip or towards the end, so you both have something to look forward to.

The year will seem longer to him than to you – you'll be so busy having a good time, you'll probably find it flies by, though you're bound to miss him at first. Reassure him by writing on a regular basis. It doesn't have to be a 12-page letter every week – funny postcards and quirky cuttings from the local newspapers are a good way of keeping in touch. Ring him on special occasions, such as his birthday or your anniversary.

Sometimes a relationship can take it; sometimes it can't. We know plenty of people who've successfully sustained a long-distance romance – and plenty of others that didn't make it. It's not just your time away that can be difficult. The hardest bit can be coming home. He'll probably still be the man you left behind, but you may have changed more than you realize. You'll probably be more independent and self-reliant. Just bear it in mind...

I'm looking forward to my working holiday in Australia, but I'm very close to my family and worried that I'll miss them.

Of course you'll miss your family! When you're watching the

sun set behind Ayers Rock, you'll wish they could share it with you. As you pose in front of the Sydney Opera House, you'll think how much they'd love to be there. Homesickness hits most travellers at some point and nine months away from your family seems like a long time. But once you're on the road making new discoveries, meeting new people and enjoying new experiences every day, you won't believe how quickly the time will pass. Make sure you have contact addresses (see Chapter 11) where friends and family can write to you with all the family news, plus what's happening on *Brookside/Coronation Street* or whatever. If you feel the urge to talk to your mum/sister/dad, treat yourself to a phone call home occasionally. Don't worry about it too much. You'll be so busy having a great time, you'll be home again before you know it. Your family will probably miss you more, so don't forget to keep sending the postcards. Make them feel involved by buying them a map of the world and a set of map pins, so they can chart your progress around the world.

I don't speak any foreign languages. How am I going to manage?

If you're really lazy, you can get by on a mixture of English (it's very widely spoken) and sign language. But being able to communicate in the local lingo makes travelling so much easier and more fun. If you're visiting 15 different countries, you obviously can't hope (unless you're a raving genius) to be fluent in that many tongues but it's definitely worth making the effort to learn at least one other language. French, for example, can come in handy in places like Indo-China or West Africa, and it would be crazy to go to Latin America without learning some Spanish – plus it's so easy, there's no excuse not to.

Even with tonal languages such as Thai and Chinese, which are notoriously difficult to master, it's still worth trying to learn a little bit as people are always delighted you've made the effort. At the very least, you should know a few basic phrases (thank you, please, hello, numbers, etc.) for every country. If you're planning to spend a few months in one country, learning as much of the languages as you can before you go will ensure you get more out of your trip and make the whole experience of travelling around much easier.

Contact your Local Education Authority for details of language courses or check out the self-taught courses on CD Rom, tapes and books (you'll find them in bookshops and record stores), published by Berlitz, the BBC, Linguaphone,

Hugo and others. Lonely Planet and Rough Guides also publish a selection of phrase books.

Someone told me I should make a will before I go travelling. I'm only 27. Isn't this a bit morbid?

No one likes to think about it, but it is a good idea. You may not think you're worth much alive, but if you're insured, you could be worth quite a lot if you die. Also, you can stipulate in a will whether you wish to be buried or cremated, donate favourite items to favourite friends and generally relieve the burden on your family at a very emotional time. It's not difficult – WH Smith stock simply drawn-up wills you fill in yourself. All you have to do then is get a solicitor to sign it. You don't have to think about the subject again unless you marry/divorce/have a child.

Where will I stay while I'm away? How do you find places?

Don't worry about accommodation *en route*. You'll find a huge range of hotels, hostels, guesthouses, bungalows and dormitories on the travellers' trail, especially if you're following a well-worn route such as overland from Bangkok to Bali, or hostelling round Australia or New Zealand. The only time it might be wise to pre-book a room is for your first couple of nights away, especially if you'll be arriving late at night (which, of course, you should try to avoid). Most of the specialist agents mentioned in Chapter 2 will pre-book this for you at a discounted rate when you book your ticket. It's useful, too, if you're arriving in a country during a public holiday or festival and accommodation is hard to find.

Once on the road, never accept a room without seeing it first – it's perfectly acceptable to check it out before you commit yourself. Some places may have smart receptions but dreadful rooms. Check that the light switches/fan/air-con work and that the shower and toilet (if you have one) have water. Make sure that the doors and windows lock securely and that the mosquito screens over the windows are intact, or that there's a mosquito net. If you don't like the first room you're shown, ask if they have anything better. Otherwise, look for somewhere else. Remember that the first price you're quoted is often negotiable, especially if the hotel isn't busy. Try to arrive at places mid-morning to have the best choice of rooms.

Staying in shared dorms is a great way to meet people, but remember to take extra care of your valuables. Sadly, despite the travelling bond, a roommate is just as likely to nick things as any stranger on the street.

This may sound trivial, but I have lots of plants I've lavished tender, loving care on for years. What can I do with them – and with my cat?

Friends or family should be happy to look after your plants for you – after all, it doesn't take too much effort. Pets are another matter. You'll have to find someone who's a cat-lover and who wants to take on the responsibility of your pet. You should also leave them some money for cat food and possible vet bills. If someone volunteers, maybe you could take your cat there for a weekend to see how they get on. And don't forget to bring back some thank-you presents!

I'm going to South East Asia on my own. None of my friends share my desire to travel or seem interested in my plans. I'm worried we'll grow apart.

Perhaps you'll grow apart from some, but the rest will be proud that you're doing something you really want to do – and on your own, too! There's no law that says friends must do everything together. Some of our best friends are happily married mums who would no more want to travel round China than have all their teeth extracted. But they love hearing our stories and sharing our adventures second-hand. Your friends will, too, and just think of all the new friends you're about to make!

I have a job I enjoy, but can't resist the lure of taking a year off. Will future employers think I'm irresponsible?

Some people worry that employers will see the fact that they have taken time off as negative, but this is rarely the case. How can it be negative to have displayed qualities such as independence, self-reliance, confidence, initiative, organizational ability and success? You will be seen as a 'doer' and as having achieved something positive and worthwhile. Look around your friends who are working. Have their jobs changed dramatically in the last year? Have they been promoted to a brilliant new position? Increased their salary by £5,000? Probably not. Things don't usually change that much in a year. Remember, it's not the things you do that you regret, it's the things that you don't do. So what are you waiting for?

I've just returned from a round-the-world trip that I enjoyed hugely. So why do I feel so fed-up?

Coming home can be a huge anti-climax in the beginning. Friends and family are delighted to see you at first, but don't want to spend the next six weeks discussing every aspect of your trip. If you have any friends who have done something similar, get in touch with them. They'll understand your enthusiasm and will enjoy comparing notes and anecdotes. You have experienced so much while you've been away that it can be a surprise to find that nothing's changed at home – or that everything's changed. You've changed too – you'll probably find you're more independent, more confident, more adventurous. Family, friends or partners may even have trouble coming to terms with the new you.

Give yourself time to get back into some kind of routine and for people to get used to having you around again. If you find it hard being in one place all the time, after being used to being on the move constantly, perhaps you could go away for a few weekends. If all else fails, start planning your next trip!

'My 18 months away has probably knocked me back slightly on the professional ladder but I don't regret it at all. Other people who stayed behind may be ahead of me now but in a few years' time that will even out anyway. We'll be level again, but I'll have all that extra experience, knowledge and fun behind me!

When I went for job interviews after I came back, interviewers weren't concerned about the time off. In fact, both I and the friend I went with found that many employers were actually impressed by our travelling and saw it as a positive thing – they thought it showed courage, initiative and enthusiasm.'

'One of the things I enjoy most about travelling is meeting other travellers. When we were in Asia and Australia we met loads of Scandinavians and had a great laugh with them. So at the end of the trip, when we just didn't feel ready to go home, we went back via Denmark and Sweden to visit them. We would probably never have gone there otherwise, but it was brilliant. And I'm glad we did it then, while we were still fresh in their minds – we've lost touch now, so I would have missed out on the chance to see those countries with local friends.

'Friendships made travelling are incredibly intense. You become close to people much faster than you would at home, and for the time that you're together you're best friends – but they can also dissolve faster. Once people come home and settle back into their normal life, the differences become much greater and you can lose what you had in common, so I think you have to follow travelling friendships up quickly while you can still talk about your travels and what you did. I usually find they last a few years, then peter out – but there are some that I know will be friendships for life.'

'Coming home was difficult. I couldn't get a job for two months and I didn't settle down for at least six months. I found it difficult to be in one place because for the eighteen months we were travelling the longest we spent anywhere was a week. I found everyone at home quite dull – and I think I was a travel bore when we got back which horrifies me because I hate people like that!'

'Coming back was a big disappointment in many ways. It was such an anticlimax. Initially it was very nice to come back and see people and say where I'd been and what I'd done and bore everybody with the photos. And I looked quite healthy when I came back, after pleasing myself for all that time and not being under any immedate pressure, and having lots of sunshine and exercise. But then suddenly decisions had to be made about what was coming next. I went back and visited the place I'd worked before and they were very much still doing the same thing, sitting in the same chairs, still in the same routine, and it almost seemed – it sounds dreadful to say – that they were having the same conversations. And I felt as though I'd been away and seen so much and done so much and learned so much. I came back feeling really fresh but it took me a while to find something to channel all that energy into.

'There are lots of places still on my list to see. That first trip whetted my appetite for more and as soon as I get sufficient time I'll definitely be off again. It's a cliche but travel is a bug and once it gets you...'

'You should think carefully about what time of year you come back. If you come back for summer, you can go to festivals, meet other travellers there, and have a good time. You're used to living on a budget and it's a good time to travel round the UK. If you come back in winter, everyone looks tired and ill – and it can be a big shock having to be inside so much when you've got used to being outdoors a lot.

'I did find it hard to settle down when I came back. I thought of everything in terms of my trip – it was "this time a month ago", "this time a year ago", etc. When you're travelling you get used to travellers' camaraderie - then you're back here on the tube or bus and no one's speaking to each other. And the cost of going out to drink or eat is a shock – it's so much more affordable abroad.

'Luckily I managed to get a job that involved a lot of travelling and going to new places, so that helped. I couldn't have come back and gone straight back to a routine. And I liked having other travellers coming to stay because friends back home can't relate to how you're feeling unless they've done a similar trip. We were out of sync for a while.

'Lots of people said "so you've got it out of your system now then" – but it's not something to get out of your system. I came back thinking I wanted to plan my life so I could continue to do more of this, have more of this kind of experience – and I have. I've had no problem getting a job – a lot of employers saw it as a positive attribute. The time we had away made me think about life – I came back with a list of things I wanted to do – and I have done some of them. My friend and I both wished we had more practical skills – lots of people travelling could play guitar, cut hair, etc and we liked that idea of swapping skills, so when I came back I did an aromatherapy course. I also decided while I was away that I wanted to do voluntary work for Amnesty International and I have done. It's true to say that the trip completely changed my life – the ramifications have gone on and on.'

INDEX